The art of rendering; a condensed and comprehensive treatise on the culture of the three-fold nature and the mental method of reading and speaking, to be used in connection with Fenno.s science of speech

Frank Honywell Fenno

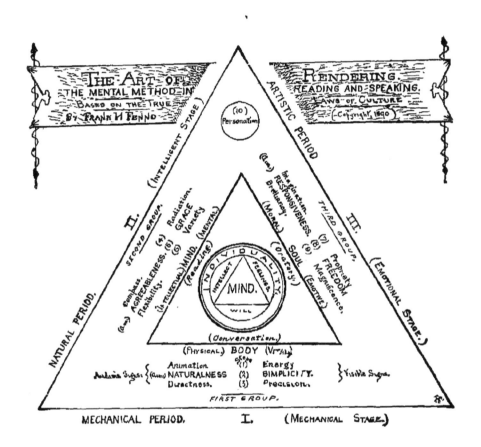

THE
ART OF RENDERING

A condensed and comprehensive treatise on the culture
of the Three-fold Nature and the Mental
Method of Reading and Speaking

To be used in connection with

FENNO'S SCIENCE OF SPEECH

Comprising

Chart of Delsartean Trinities, Aesthetic Physical Culture,
Physiology and Culture of Breath and Voice, Gesture,
Sixteen Steps in Rendering with Analyses and Classical Studies for Practice, Charts and Illustrations.
Designed to be used as a text-book in the
class-room, and for private study as well
as by readers and speakers generally

By

FRANK H. FENNO, A. M., F. S. Sc.
Teacher, Lecturer, and Author of 'Fenno's Elocution," "Lectures
on Elocution", etc., Compiler of "Fenno's Favorites

Revised and Enlarged by
MRS. FRANK H. FENNO, B. O.

———

CHICAGO
EMERSON W. FENNO, PUBLISHER
1912

DEDICATED TO THE MEMORY
OF

Emma Honywell Fenno

WHOSE

PURE, BEAUTIFUL SPIRIT OF DEVOTION

AND

WONDERFUL MOTHER-LOVE

HAS

MADE THIS AND OTHER WORKS POSSIBLE

———

THE GOODNESS OF HER QUIET LIFE SHINES
OUT WITH EVER-INCREASING
SPLENDOR

PREFACE.

An outline of study is presented in the triangular chart following. All culture whether of body, mind or voice, is a growth from the crude to the refined, and all drill must necessarily be in the order: 1. Mechanical; 2. Natural; 3. Artistic. Thus, all culture is based upon the Mechanical, passes through the Natural, and is completed in the Artistic.

This law applied to the rendering of thought gives :—1. Mechanical; 2. Intelligent; 3. Emotional. The basis of speech is Conversation, its higher form is Reading, and its highest form is Oratory. So culture in speech is based on Conversation, continues through Reading, and culminates in Oratory.

The character of all human expression is determined by the individuality of the speaker. The center of the individuality is the mind. Psychologically considered, the mind has three sides— the Will, the Intellect, and the Feelings :—the Will corresponding with the Body, Physical or Vital nature; the Intellect with the Mind, Intellectual or Mental nature; the Feelings with the Soul, Moral or Emotive nature. So the Audible (tones) and Visible (gestures) are either Vital, Mental or Emotive, according to which side of the mind prompts the action. Illustrations: Vital, the swagger and bluster of a bully; Mental, the careful utterance and gestures of a thinker; Emotive, the impassioned manner of the exhorter.

Our practical drill in Rendering trains successively the three sides of the mind. Beginning with the Will, we have our first group of exercises consisting of the three points, Animation, Naturalness, and Directness of voice, corresponding with Energy, Simplicity, and Precision of manner. The aim in this Mechanical period is Naturalness and Simplicity, which, when attained, carry the pupil into the second, the Natural Period.

In the second period we work for the three points, Compass, Agreeableness, and Flexibility of voice, and Radiation, Grace, and Variety of gesture; the aim being those artistic qualities; Agreeableness and Grace.

This aim being attained the student finds himself in the third, the Artistic Period. Here we work for Propriety, Freedom, and Magnificence of gesture, to cultivate Imagination secure Responsiveness of voice and body to mind, and add Brilliancy—that final polish and artist's touch—since " God himself signifies that his creation is complete by throwing over it the garb of beauty. "

TO THE STUDENT.

The student should approach this complex and many sided study—this fine art—as an architect who sets before himself the task of constructing some great work even a grand cathedral which shall endure through ages to bless and to ennoble the souls of men because of its beauty and its usefulness. The architect first must have within him. self his well-defined ideal, for his work cannot excel that, though as he works his ideal is constantly changing and ever beholding more complicated and loftier visions to be wrought out. He begins to gather about himself material for the work, much that is crude and commonplace and some that is rare and precious. He must chisel, refine and polish, toiling on long and faithfully, ever with positive hope, that he may bring out the ideals hidden in his soul. Out of a dream he constructs a real temple with walls and roof and buttresses, pinnacles, high-pointed arches of windows deeply recessed entrance way; within, the vaulted arches, the delicately fluted columns, the niches, carved panels, rose windows and delicate tracery work; a place worthy to echo back the grandest music of the masters, and the noblest and best thoughts and feelings of the world.

Or let the student begin his task as an organ builder. He gathers about him his material, shapes each part into suitable form, giving careful attention to measurements to suit the laws of sound. He is careful that all parts of his instrument are so nicely adjusted, with parts, each responsive to the other, that when finished, with each part in place, all *parts* are forgotten when it discourses wonderful harmony as it responds to the skillful touch.

In this commercial age, to many this will seem visionary and impracticable; but " he that hath ears to hear, let *him* hear. " Let him first have noble ideals for noble purposes then " undertake great things and expect great things. " The student of expression, like the student of music, painting, sculpture, or any other art, should take the needed time for development.

The student should go about his work with energy, with a willingness to work hard. Do not think because you are attracted to the study that you possess " talent. " The pianist or the artist along any other line will tell you that *talent* is largely the result of *hard work.* Genius is the result of an endurance and persistence in hard work. These mystic keys hold the treasure. In this study as in no other science or art " a *little* learning is a dangerous thing. "

Let us consider briefly the *material* needed by the student who would be the organ builder and the master musician, the artist and the work of art. (Material in large charts.)

Think of *self* to be used in this work not only as one but as three; three beings combined in one,— the Physical being, the Mental being, the Spiritual being. In the early part of the study, separate the three and think of them as distinct and wide apart; later in the study all may be considered as a unit, acting together.

The Vital or Physical side of life needs no definition as it is visible and easiest to know and think about.

The Mental, with its wonderful faculties of Reason and Memory and Imagination, lives within the body. We can think of the seat of all this power as located in the brain. We often judge of the mental faculties themselves by the shape of the head. We think of the brain and its faculties as something.

The Spiritual life dwelling within the Physical body should be thought of as something. It cannot be weighed, measured, and examined as is the brain with its gray matter. No dissecting knife has ever yet found a trace of its presence. It cannot be seen with the X ray. It ever eludes the keenest search. Though it is so mystic and fleeting, its influence is more real to us than anything else we know about. However mysterious all this may be and whatever may be our belief, let us, to gain the most helpful attitude toward the study in hand—which must be largely of things intangible and subjective— let us learn to think of this spiritual or emotive nature as something. Think of it as a perfect correspondence to the physical body, dwelling within it and fitted to it as though the body were its garment. Think too of this spiritual body as being so delicate and impressionable that the slightest wish of a friend will cause it to vibrate, as will all feelings, hopes, fears, aspirations. Because of the fact it is so easily moved it is called the Emotive nature. This Emotive or Spiritual has its faculties no less than the brain.

Physical body has its complicated Vital Organs, Nerves, Muscles, Blood and Breath.

Mental has its Perception, Memory, Imagination, Reason,

Generalization.

Emotive has its Affectional, Passional, Mystical, Spiritual, Ethical. In this is included a wide range of feelings of which faith, hope, love and their opposites are greatest. Sentiments and ignoble passions belong to the Emotive.

All three sides are capable of wonderful culture and development.

The principles and studies in " *The Art of Rendering* " in connection with " *The Science of Speech,* " which is an indispensable part of the study—though for convenience is published in a separate volume—give a true Mental Method which allows the child and the sage to study side by side, each working from his own standpoint, the progress of both being equally rapid because of a similar process going on in each—that of a natural, psychological growth.

Says Beecher.— " To make men patriots, to make men Christians, to make men the sons of God, let all the doors of heaven be opened, and let God drop down charmed gifts: winged imaginations, all-perceiving reason, and all-adjudging reason. Whatever there is that can make men wiser and better, let it descend upon the head of him who has consecrated himself to the work of mankind, and who has made himself an orator for man's sake and for God's sake. "

MRS. FRANK H. FENNO.

CHICAGO, ILL., MARCH 19TH, 1912.

CONTENTS

CONTENTS

SIXTEEN STEPS IN RENDERING

FORMING PICTURES 160

VITAL, ANIMATED PICTURES AND SCENES 181

FORMULA OF ANALYSIS FOR ANY ART.

I. Place in the arts.
    1. Architecture.
    2. Sculpture.
    3. Literature.
    4. Painting.
    5. Oratory.
    6. Music.

II. Purpose.
    1. The author himself.
    2. Character of the work.
    3. a. To entertain.
       b. To instruct.
       c. To ennoble.

III. Treatment.
    1. Unity.— The whole.
    2. Analysis.— The parts
    3. Symmetry.— Relation of part to whole.
    4. Harmony.— Relation of part to part.

IV. Essentials.
    1. Strong in conception.
    2. Interesting in subject.
    3. True in details.
    4. Good in influence.

V. Periods.
    1. Colossal.
    2. Effective.
    3. Realistic.
    4. Suggestive.

VI. Ultimate Aim. Beauty, Goodness, Truth.

THE FINE ARTS.

As Expression is a fine art, let us consider a few simple definitions of the word Art. Much of a complex and bewildering character has been written by its devotees, but with such technical terms as leave the uninitiated to wonder and admire. Delsarte has so simplified matters for us as to enable the earnest student of expression to understand and appreciate some of its profound secrets. Even the great art students of our times acknowledge that along certain lines the Delsarte Philosophy has thrown more light on all the arts than in such clearness and simplicity was never known before. We may profit by some of his definitions.

" Art is that which aims to touch the heart by the Good the Beautiful and the True.

> Beauty purifies the sense.
> Truth illumines the mind.
> Virtue (goodness) sanctifies the soul.

Art should interest by the True to illumire the intelligence, move by the Beautiful to regenerate the life, persuade by the Good to perfect the heart.

Art is not an imitation of nature. Art is better than nature, it is nature illuminated. "

Says Charles Dudley Warner: " Art is not nature, it is a suggestion, impregnated with the artist's personality. "

Says Walter Crane: " Art is the most subtle and expressive of language, taking all manner of varied forms in all sorts of materials under the paramount impulse of the selective search for beauty. "

" Art remains the one way possible of teaching truth. "
> Browning.
" Art is the telescope of a supernatural world. "
" The powers of art are the wings of the soul. "

"The artist — those whose calling is to point to the beautiful, the elevated, the refined, and by so doing to heighten the existence of mankind." Alama Tadema.

"Art is the manifestation of emotion, obtaining external interpretation, now by expressive arrangement of line, form or color, now by a series of gestures, sounds or words, governed by particular rhythmical cadence." Veron.

"Poetry, to speak generally, is the faculty of feeling internally the essence of life, and art is the faculty of expressing the same thing in external form. Artists, literateurs, painters, sculptors, musicians, really invent only the form to be taken by the poetic sentiment breathed into them by nature or by life." Thore.

"Art a search after the best."

"Artists aim: to represent the invisible in the visible, the Infinite in the finite, eternal truth in its priority by rendering it manifest in a sensible form and shape."

THE BEAUTIFUL.

"Beautiful purifies the emotions."

"Beauty — and what is beauty? A blind man's question." Aristotle.

"Beauty — the flower of virtue." Zeno.

"Beauty, the result of the good and useful." Socrates.

"My eyes turn toward the beautiful, Autolicus, as to a torch burning at midnight." Socrates.

Beauty is not prettiness, but the outward sign of Good.

"He alone is beautiful whose mental corresponds with his physical perfections." Plato.

"Beauty reigns supreme in art, nature, mankind and love."

" Beauty is the splendor of truth. "

Says Delsarte : " Beauty is the reason that presides at the creation of things; it is the invisible power that draws us and subjugates us in them.

The beautiful comprises three characters, which we distinguish under the following titles : ideal, moral, plastic beauty. "

THE TRUE.

" The True illumines the thought.   Truth is the gravitation principle of the universe by which it is supported, and in which it coheres. "   William M. Evarts.

" Truth is the planet that seeks the sun, yet grasps the soil. "   Robert Barclay Fox.

" Truth is everlasting, but our ideas of it are not. "
                    Beecher.

" To restore the commonplace truth to its first uncommon lustre, you need only to translate it into action. " Coleridge.

" The greatest homage we can pay to truth is to use it. "
                    Emerson.

" There is nothing so strong or safe in any emergency of life, as the simple truth. "   Charles Dickens.

" Truth is the apostle before whom every coward Felix trembles. "   Wendell Phillips.

"There are some faults slight in the sight of lore, some errors slight in the estimate of wisdom; but Truth forgives no insult and endures no stain. "   Ruskin.

" He who makes truth disagreeable, commits high treason against virtue. "   Woodruff.

" What is eloquence but truth in earnest." T. L. Cuyler.

" Truth is the concept of the Spirit in regard to the reality of things, and the laws which govern them. "   Rayner.

" Moral beauty is the brilliancy of the good. "

Says Delsarte: " The good is that which sanctifies the soul. "

The good seems to be that which can give to the greatest number of beings existing in the universe the greatest sum of happiness and perfection. We never tire of the good; it is a continual feast because we are lifted up and ennobled by it, while that form of art that simply entertains soon becomes stale and unprofitable. The good is the power that lifts the race into an ever widening and higher sphere.

The artist who has the power to awaken within us the Divine aspiration for Good becomes our hero. " He is the living light-fountain, which it is good and pleasant to be near. The light which enlightens : which has enlightened the darkness of the world; and this not as kindled by a lamp only, but rather as a natural luminary shining by the gift of heaven ; a flowing life fountain, as I say, of original insight, of manhood and heroic nobleness; in whose radiance all souls feel that it is well with them. "

THE ARTIST.

Beauty chased he everywhere,
   In flame, in storm, in clouds of air,
He smote the lake to feast his eye
   With the beryl beam of the broken wave;
He flung in pebbles, well to hear
   The moment's music which they gave.
Oft pealed for him a lofty tone,
   From nodding pole and belting zone.
He heard a voice none else could hear
   From centered and from errant sphere.
The quaking earth did quake in rhyme,
Seas ebbed and flowed in epic chime. *Emerson.*

Art and the Artist may here receive but a passing glance for these subjects are profound as is Philosophy and Religion. " The artist, no less than the preacher, is a proclaimer of the glory of God; no less than the philosopher, an expounder of the Absolute Idea. "   The aim here is only to drop a few seed thoughts, hoping they may fall into productive soil and set each student thinking for himself, that he may learn to use in an effective and artistic manner the material lying in abundance at hand ready for use.

Cicero tells us that " all arts that pertain to culture have a certain common bond. " Because of this the student may secure material aid by carefully studying principles in all the arts, especially paintings and artistic pictures.

The Reader or Public Speaker should be an artist along several lines.   He has far more to do than the artist with the brush if his impressions abide, for the expression the Reader gives is instantaneous, almost like writing in the water, or carving in the air, therefore, what he gives must be enforced with the ability to project mental pictures into the minds of his listeners.   This cannot be done with mere words.   He must have before he can give and can give only such as he has.

The Reader has more to do than he who acts a part in a play, for the reader must paint the scenery, portray the characters and suggest all action.   It would be impossible to do all this without a knowledge of the principles of art·

In the Drama the same principles are used as the Painter uses in the arrangement of his characters on the canvas. He uses superior and inferior — colors contrasts,— all is arranged with the most careful, studied effects that the central thought be placed in the best possible light.   In a Drama presented by a master we have living pictures with such perfect harmony of action and color and setting, should a painting be produced of a scene at any point, it would present all the essentials of a high class work of art. The reader must do that which will awaken all this, and more, if his impressions are lasting.

Because of a lack of carefully prepared and definite, artistic, mental background, we are obliged to listen to much that is utterly forgotten and lost, almost before the speaker has finished. If sermons, lectures and other forms of public speaking were something beside words, words, words; if the words had some force back of them to send them home and make them stay, the Stage and Dramatic Reader's platform could not be more fascinating than the Pulpit.

The speakers of the pulpit possess, as a class, the greatest intellectual and emotive wealth and have, by far, the broadest and most fertile subjects from which to draw material.

It does pay to see to it that what we give is so strong and alive with every possible advantage back of it that it may be received and accomplish that whereunto it was sent. This is the end that crowns all. There can be no giving without receiving. Attempting to give that which fails to be received is a monstrous waste of energy, even though it is practiced so largely and by wise and learned men.

It pays to study expression with a pencil, carefully outlining all details; then to throw mentally a bold sketch on a great canvas and lay upon it the suitable colors to make it a living, breathing reality, pulsating with a life so genuine that the listener may comprehend and participate in it; that he may gain an actual experience which will not easily be blurred and lost.

It pays to so identify yourself with the scene and situation as to be a part of it, presenting, beside the scene, the spirit and feeling it awakens, manifesting it earnestly, heartily and with fervor. It does not pay to undertake anything that is not worth doing well, or anything you cannot enter into with all your heart and art.

Too much can hardly be said of the importance of going thoroughly over the matter to be presented, making a clear *analysis* of all scenery, characters and feeling hidden under the lines. When this is once properly done, we have a key to gesture, voice, inflection and the elements of modulation. In this analysis may be found a way to avoid a common fault — unnatural expression. Analysis is often the most difficult part of the study. While some selections require careful study to bring out the subtle meaning, others are simple and easily disposed of.

FINDING THE UNITY.

Following are some homely illustrations so simplified as to assist the youngest to gain a clear and certain understanding of what we mean by *Unity*, for this is the starting point.

By Unity of a study we mean the Central Idea. It may be some object, a person, an emotion, a passion or some subjective feeling. A whole poem may have been written to bring out one sentence, or one idea.

As a selection of the Unity is the center of the study, and all harmony of arrangement of subordinate ideas depends upon it, let us use the simplest illustration possible to explain our meaning of this first step of analysis.

Here is a large pink rose we wish to place in a bouquet where it will be brought out to the best advantage. This rose is our unity. We easily decide that it should occupy the central position in our bouquet. Now follows that which is more difficult, for we have much liberty in our selection of something to place with this rose to bring it out best. Surely it will never do to place it surrounded by other roses, or even with lilies, for such rival beauties will obscure the favorite. We must select something inferior to be the background. We find too beside this contrast of superior with inferior, as to position, contrasts in color must next be thought about. The complimentary color of our pink rose is its own natural green leaves. There could be no mistake in using this background. Should we use flowers instead of leaves some inferior in size, white or cream may be used. A few pink rose buds may also be used as they will not assert themselves but lend themselves to the unity, the rose.

By *position*, by contrasting *superior* with *inferior*, by contrast in *color* we have brought out our rose. The artist may find much more than this to do, but let this simple analysis open the way for more complex work in the readings.

Let us next study a Selection with a single Character instead of a flower for our unity. " The Cheerful Locksmith " by Charles Dickens affords a simple, yet a useful study. Find the above study in " Studies in Rendering," under " Animation. " In this study we readily select the cheerful Locksmith himself as the central subject for our attention. The study divides into two scenes, (though it might be given in one, depending on the view point.) Scene I. is on the street, with workshop in sight. Scene II. is inside the workshop. We ourselves must be only an on-looker in both scenes. In the street we listen to the Lock-smith ; in the shop we see him. Picture the whole scene vividly, the locksmith and the interior of the shop. Bring out all the details, as the window, " the locks that hung around, " the cat ; see however that nothing eclipses the Locksmith himself. Take advantage of " a gleam of sun shining through the unsashed window and checkering the dark workshop with a broad patch of light, fell full upon him as though attracted by his sunny heart. " and make use of this high light and get the full artistic value.

Contrast the Locksmith's music with all the discordant

sounds, as the carts rumbling by, scolding, prison-door and jolting wagon, etc. Use all negative ideas as shade — all cheerful, musical ideas as light, bringing out the contrast, with light more pronounced than darkness This may be done by speaking of the " tink, tink, tink, " the music, and light as that of which we approve, while of the noise, the shade, the dark and disagreeable we disapprove. The light may be given on a touch of high pitch, the shade a slight degree of low pitch, a departure from the medium.

Make a careful study of the whole selection as if to illustrate it. See more than is mentioned in the selection, all details of the workshop, tools around, forge, anvil, the cat, most important of all, the man himself, his dress, and his facial expression. Do not be sparing of effort expended on this side of the study, all this gives to your expression a mental value of life and real interest. All this concentration of the mind on the scene and a participation in the spirit of it will give it such a value and an interest to the reader himself as will readily be imparted to the listener.

Paintings furnish excellent suggestions and helps for the reader or speaker. The student is asked to look over some helpful suggestions and to observe how the artist has made many things contribute to the central idea in one of the greatest of the world's paintings, " Christ Before Pilate. "

This painting is great, not alone from the fact that it is supposed to have cost $120,000.00, but because it leaves a never-to-be-forgotten impression on the mind of him who stands before it with a responsive heart and mind. This painting is costly and famous because of the thought and feeling the artist has put into it.

Let the student observe how the artist has brought out the chief and central theme, *Christ Before Pilate*. As to importance Christ stands first, Pilate second. Christ and Pilate are superior, all the other characters, inferior, lend-ing themselves to the unity. Great preeminence is given to the chief figure as it stands under the magnificent arch a little to the right of the center, with many long lines to add prominence. The second character, Pilate, has an exalted seat, the center of an inferior arch. Observe how the artist has made obscure the heads forming a background for the central head. Note the force of this. We can readily see in the painting how the artistic value would have been sacrificed had this background of inferior heads been made as large and clear cut as the central one. Other contrasts are marked. The robes of the central characters alone are white, in contrast with all the other robes. A great study is in the expression of the faces of the characters. The noble, kingly expression of the central character is sharply contrasted with much that is ignoble,— insolence, pride, hatred, scorn and mockrey. The hesitation and perplexity on the face of Pilate is contrasted with the confidence and assurance of the accusers. Another contrast is between the Roman soldier with his spear and the man with fettered wrists. We have noted a few simple suggestions for the student of expression hoping they may be useful in the analysis of the readings.

In Nebuchadnezzar's Dream, Daniel II , we find some points of similarity in the analysis to the painting we have above considered. We have two important characters, a few prominent characters, a crowd of people. The central theme however is neither the King nor Daniel, but the Dream.

We find the study divides into one important scene and several little scenes. Scene I. the King's bed chamber. The principal scene is in the throne room, where three acts take place : the astrologers, before the King, sending out a decree to destroy the wise men ; Daniel before the King; Daniel's second appearance before the King and the in-

terpretation of the dream.   Picture the whole scene vividly,
The King may be seated a little at the right of the center,
all ideas of the study are grouped about him.   Daniel may
stand on the left of the center, where he gives his speech
as an oration.   In telling the dream, near climax is reached
on — " a stone was cut out without hands, ... and the
stone that smote the image became a great mountain, and
filled the whole earth. "   The climax of the whole study
comes near the last of the interpretation — " In the days of
these Kings shall the God of heaven set up a kingdom which
shall never be destroyed : . . . and it shall stand forever."
The interpretation may be given as an explanation, with
mental inflections, rising to a climax of fervor on the part
about the kingdom, reaching highest point on — " *it shall
stand forever.* "

Bring out the side scenes, as the scene between Daniel
and Arioch, another at Daniel's house when he tells his
companions, then the night vision and Daniel's prayer and
thanksgiving, a second scene between Daniel and Arioch,
promotion of Daniel and companions at the close.

Work out a contrast between Daniel and the King,—
Daniel, always noble, while the King varies from perplexity in verse 3, angry threat in part of verse 5, angry accusa-
tion 5 and 9, furious command verse 12, awe and submission verse 47.

Contrast Daniel with magicians who boast then argue;
Daniel humble, for he says: " this secret is not revealed
to me for any wisdom I have more than any living. "

Subjective studies, lyrics, psalms etc. are more difficult
to analyze than the above numbers as the real heart of it
lies hidden beneath the surface.   It is often one mood, or
one feeling. For example the Psalm XXIII is a song of
trust.   The love and trust is told over and over again in
different ways, but never the occasion of sadness.

In Psalm VIII, the unity is contemplation. The poet is contemplating all God's works. He compares nature with man and decides man is greater than the other creatures because he has dominion over them. The poet seems to be talking to himself.

" Nightfall, " in the " Studies in Rendering, " has for the key thought " a melody of other days. " The nightfall meditations are all grouped about this thought. But there is little to indicate whether the memory is pleasant or sad so the student must add that important point.

Subjective lyrics are in the " Studies in Rendering. "

No study should be attempted without first making an analysis. The foregoing suggestions are far from complete, the aim being to set each pupil thinking for himself with a hope that individuality may be developed and natural expression result.

PHYSICAL CULTURE.

" Be ye therefore perfect. "

THE UPRIGHT MAN with his high Moral and Spiritual uprightness with elements of Truthfulness, Conscientiousness, Courage, and Duty Fulfilled should be Erect, Manly, Commanding.

We can do no better at this point than to quote from " The Place and Power of the Personality in Expression." by Dr. William R. Alger. Below the following principle he has given us two word pictures :—

A pure and free personality is a transparent medium for divine realities to shine through : but one preoccupied with individual peculiarities intercepts the divine realities it should reveal, and fixes attention on itself.

Suppose a person to advance in front of an audience with a club foot, a bent knee, a stiff hip, a crooked arm, a hunch back, a wry neck, a wabbling jaw, a lifeless lip, a sunken nose, a squint eye, a cadaverous skin and a wheezy voice. Suppose in addition, that in correspondence with this physical side of his being the spiritual side is made up of faculties narrow, mean, feeble and empty, destitute of knowledge or training and infested with all sorts of odious antipathies, envies, spites, so that he is as ignorant and bad as he is hideous. Suppose then that he should undertake to deliver an oration, or read a poem, or impersonate a dramatic character. The spectators, according to their several characters, would experience sensations of mirth, curiosity, amazement, pity, scorn, disgust, sorrow, distress or hatred. They could not experience emotions of approval, admiration, reverence or delight. They could not feel themselves pleased, enriched, edified, inspired. Why not? The reason is clear. It is because the ignoble, repulsive marks stamped into the unfortunate performer are the language of weakness, discord, vice, sin and misery: expressions of wrong and degradation, which inflict suffering and awaken instinctive abhorrence or pity. Beside they prove that he is so tied to himself, so confined to the revolting consciousness of his own wretched experience — such a symbolizer or reflecting mirror of the false, the bad, the ugly,— that he is utterly incapacitated to be a revelatory medium of the godlike freedom and glory of any noble forms of truth, goodness and beauty.

Every deformity or stricture of the body, every bias of the soul, enslaves the personality itself, and by this preoccupation of the medium with the individual, blocks the reception and transmission of what is universal.

But the business of the artist is to represent nature, justice, law, use, humanity, virtue, liberty, God — not to exhibit himself and his infirmities. Just so far as private peculiarities, either physical or spiritual, are protruded by him, his personality, instead of reflecting, intercepts those divine attributes, which alone have any claim to be loved and worshipped, and which alone, therefore, should ever be exhibited by any one for assimilation by others.

In contrast with this hideous and painful example, imagine now the opposite extreme. Conceive an orator whose physique is all symmetry and whose morale is all excellence. Let his form be perfect in proportions; his features vivacious, and glowing with health; his nerves surcharged with energy; his voice disciplined to every variety of tone, emphasis and inflection; his actions faultless in grace and dignity; his reason and imagination of the highest order; his knowledge covering all departments of history, science, art, and philosophy; his character everything that is pure and exalted; a devout patriot, philanthropist, seeker of perfection, and worshipper of God. Suppose him on an important occasion to address an assembly capable of appreciating the facts of the case. The effect must be overwhelming. The exemplification of all that can charm, instruct, move, convince and command — all that is clothed with divinest loveliness and authority,— would be such as to enthrall, and ravish his auditors, and carry them quite beyond themselves. Such would be the transcendent influence lent to his personality by the divine qualities dwelling in it and shining through it.

All the way between these two ideal extremes of repulsiveness and fascination, each example of personal expression will be charged with power to kindle loathing or longing in the measure of its climacteric type.

Dr. William R. Alger.

Publisher. E. S. Werner, 43 E. 19 th St. New York City.

PHYSICAL UPRIGHTNESS may be attained by a proper moral state, a proper mental state, a correct carriage of the body. Physical uprightness may be attained by **Physical Culture.**

The Physical Culture of the early Greeks has, so far as education is concerned, made them "the despair of all succeeding ages." "Greece has given us representative men in every department. We point to Greece for the greatest orator, for the greatest creative poet, for the greatest sculptor, for the first man in what we consider the highest mental philosophy. Plato intellectually stands at the head of all the philosophers of the world. We must remember, then, that that which made the Greeks what they were about four or five hundred years before Christ, was the natural evolution from physical culture."

The education of the ancient Greeks was more of a physical than of a mental culture. Young children till about their sixth year were trained at home, after this they were sent to a private instructor, music and gymnastics being the foremost subjects. In this way was attained a sound mind in a sound body.

Physical uprightness as related to the moral is illustrated by dwarfs and deformed characters, as Shakespeare's Richard III, Dickens's Fagain. There are however some exceptions. The moral shows its relation to the physical by the beauty the spirit imparts to it, moulding even ugly features into beauty of expression. Real beauty emanates from the soul, chiseling the features into harmony and grace by the character that permeates the entire being and leaves its imprint on the countenance from the life back of it.

Of the various Systems of Physical Culture may be mentioned that of the ancient Greeks with severe muscular exercise with games and races; the Romans, wrestling, gladia-

torial sports. In mediæval history were the tilts, tourna-
ments, horsemanship and archery; more modern, German
Calisthenics and military training. To-day we have Leside
what is known as athletics, physical exercise found in our
gymnasiums and what is known as German, Swedish, the
French or Delsarte, Americanized Delsarte or Æsthetic
Physical Culture. The Emerson System may be called a
modified Delsarte, with such changes as secure strength as
well as grace. The results secured in the last named are
sufficient proof of the merits of this system of exercises.

UNIQUE FEATURES OF EMERSON SYSTEM.

1. Repetition —(Understood by the Greeks).
2. Movements authorized and required by the laws
of our being.

Objects Sought.

1. Vital supply of the entire body.
2. Proper position of the vital organs.
3. Develop vital organs by exercising the muscles
that surround them.
4. Deep breathing.
5. Preserve the due balance between the energy that
supplies and the energy that wastes.
6. Strengthen the centers while freeing the surfaces.

Dominant Centers {
Chest center of body.
Lips center of articulation.
Nerve centers. Spinal Column

Control of Centers {
Conservation of energy at centers.
Freeing of Articulations.
Sympathetic action of parts.

7. To develop due relationship between different
groups of muscles.

8. Develop opposing muscles or opposition of agents.

    a. Muscular sense and equilibrium.
    b. Relation of muscles to nerves.
    c. Education of nerve centers.
    d. Reflex action.
    e. Overworked muscles and nerves relieved.

9. Preserve true balance between the life sustaining forces and the brain.

    a. Healthy attitudes of mind.
    b. Hygienic and Æsthetic value.
    c. Hygienic: strength, symmetry, health.
    d. Æsthetic: grace, harmony, beauty.

Manner of Taking Exercises.

    a. Slowness.
    b. Evenness.
    c. Perfect time.
    d. Animation.

Summary of Advantages.

Health.
    Strength.
        Grace.
            Expression.
                Improved address.

Improved Manners { In Social Life.
                    In Business Life.
                    In Public Life.

The Ideal System:— For home use. No apparatus. Adapted to the strength of all. Grace not ugliness. Movements psychological, not acrobatic; not an over-development of large muscles at expense of delicate or heart.

Aim to cultivate the blood-making power.

Vital organs are diminished in size by carelessness.

Vital organs often abnormally low from the cramped position of the chest pressing them down.

Exercise assists the arteries, so the blood may flow without pressure.

Muscles of vital organs never rest but alternate. Physical Culture strengthens them.

We may compare the culture of the body to the thoughtful construction and adjustment of parts of a system with all connections ready to turn on the power, when the unobstructed message may carry with unerring force.

That nature gives body, mind and voice, and that the highest results may be secured only through culture, none can deny. It is to be regretted that the training the average person receives in school is largely of the mind with a disregard to the other sides of the individual.

The physical body is capable of culture as well as the mind. The body may be made strong, flexible, and so expressive, one may almost say " his body thought. " The body may be so trained that instead of being as an instrument, all in one piece, like an axe, for example, it may be trained to act in parts, independent as well as dependent upon each other, complex yet each self-centered.

The body may be trained to move without friction, in this way securing economy of energy.

When the body is properly adjusted to the soul, and an all-round harmony of being is secured, with the physical body at its best, it is found that the influence of reflex action is most elevating and refining on the inner life. By placing the body in noble attitudes we cultivate noble feeling. So as we physically assume a virtue, repeatedly we unconsciously grow along that line. James's Psychology under " Consciousness and Movement " says:—

Using sweeping terms and ignoring exceptions, we might say that every possible feeling produces a movement, and that the movement is of the entire organism, and of each and all its parts. . . . . We have now experimental proof that the heart beats, the arterial pressure, the respiration, the sweat glands, the pupil, some of the vital organs, as well as the voluntary muscles, may have their tone and degree of contraction altered by the most insignificant sensorial stimuli. In short, a process set up anywhere in the centers reverberates everywhere, and in some way or other affects the organism throughout, making its activities greater or less. The whole neural organism is, physiologically considered, but a machine for converting stimuli into reactions.

Under the chapter on " Emotion " Prof. James says:—

The feeling in the coarser emotions, results from bodily expression. Our natural way of thinking about these coarser emotions is that the mental perception of some fact excites the mental affection called the emotion, and that this latter state of mind gives rise to bodily expression. My theory, on the contrary, is that the bodily changes follow directly the perception of the exciting fact, and that our feelings of the same changes as they occur is *the emotion.*

Common sense says, we lose our fortune, are sorry and weep; meet a bear, are frightened and we run; we are insulted by a rival, are angry and strike.

The hypothesis here to be defended says, that this order of sequence is incorrect, that one mental state is not immediately induced by the other, that the *bodily* manifestations must first be interposed between, and that the more rational statement is that we feel sorry because we cry, angry because we strike, afraid because we tremble, and not that we cry, strike or tremble because we are sorry, angry or fearful as the case may be. Without the bodily states following on the perception, the latter would be purely cognitive in form, pale, colorless, destitute of emotional warmth.

Particular perceptions certainly do produce wide-spread bodily effects by a sort of immediate physical influence, antecedent to the arousal of an emotional idea.

From the foregoing from such a recognized authority we may gather most important scientific facts: that there is a reflex relation between action and feeling as well as between feeling and action. Much may be gained by assuming a noble feeling though we possess it not. Continued repetition of noble attitudes will cultivate noble feelings. The mental impression causes action of the body. The action of the body causes emotion in harmony with the expression. This is a fact of importance in character building with the physical culture as an aid and in training the body for gesture. The coarser feelings and passions may be tamed, cultivated, refined and mastered as the body acquires skill in noble, graceful movement. No thoughtful person who is interested in the betterment of the race can ignore facts of such value.

We find an astonishing amount of ignorance and indifference along these lines, even among the learned who do not stop to think the matter through. Little distinction is made between Physical Culture and physical exercise while the difference may be as great as between the pugilist and the pianist; both exercise — but the pianist may send out his very soul into his finger tips, causing them to vibrate with emotion second only to the vocal cords of the human voice. Such skill comes not by nature or by exercise alone, but by careful, thoughtful culture. Other parts of the body beside the fingers may be so cultivated as to quiver and pulsate with the thought and feeling from the inner life. Even as the pianist is benefited by the expressions sent out of exalted emotions, so the other parts of the body may respond to noble thoughts and feeling and find satisfaction through the reaction back to the source.

Men and women will tell you they get all the physical culture needed in their daily work and so believe it to be, making no distinction between physical exercise and physical culture, ignoring the fact that the way in which they are taking their exercise is cramping and deforming their bodies and souls too, day after day. Such thoughtlessness as is exhibited in looking after the bands and sockets and levers of the human body bestowed on any ordinary piece of machinery would soon work its ruin. Too much strain on any one part or on all parts causes friction and waste of energy and inability to perform its proper functions. All ready to repair the loss stands the grand army of physicians, it would seem outnumbering the grand army of the world.

The Creator of us all is the author of order and harmony, in all nature. Man must be taught " be ye perfect. " In order to be so we must give some attention to the joints and pulleys and see to it that some of the wheels are not clogged or overworked, instead of tugging along just any way till there comes a general breakdown. It sometimes is true the flaw at first might have been covered with the point of a pin, some point in a nerve where the energy failed to pass. There is sometimes an unconscious stiffening of some part of the spine, causing a jar and discord. There may be, for some cause, a frown on the face or some anxiety within disturbing the breath and circulation. Numberless things might happen to interfere with the perfect, harmonious, balanced, rhythmic action of the physical body.

" In times of peace prepare for war. " No person should think himself too strong or too busy or too wise to give not only exercise but culture to the body. With proper attention to these matters one may not only add life to one's years but years to one's life. Surely here if anywhere is discovered the long sought " Fountain of Perpetual Youth."

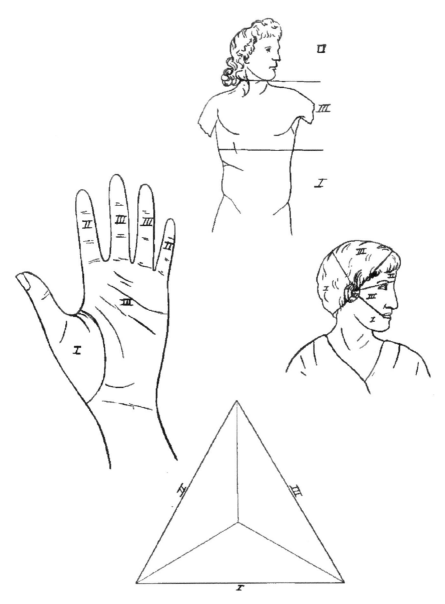

THE THREEFOLD NATURE

The Threefold Nature manifests through chosen tracts as indicated by divisions and subdivisions.

I. Physical   II. Mental   III. Emotive

The following physical exercises are based on Psychological principles and the Delsarte Philosophy.

Let us consider briefly Delsarte's threefold division of the body in harmony with the threefold nature as illustrated by the chart. We find the three forms of nature are manifested through the three tracts — from the waist line down the physical,—the head, mental,— the chest is a center of the emotive. As an illustration of an expression of the physical is the man who stands with his hands in his pockets and gesticulates with his thumb. An example of the mental, a teacher would be conscious of her head and mark nice mental points with the first and little fingers. An illustration of the emotive, the chest as the leading agent of expression — courage, the chest high and square to the front. Pity seems to come from the chest. We turn the chest away from what we dislike, " give the cold shoulder, " and " get the back up. "

The following exercises aim to give a harmonious action of the parts of the body acting together; for example, in a salutation the expression comes from all the emotive divisions and subdivisions, the chest, the top of the head and the palm of the hand.

Says Henry Ward Beecher whose oratory is still ringing and will continue to ring down through the ages:— " One of the very first steps in Oratory is that which trains the body to be the welcome and glad servant of the soul — which it is not always, for many and many a one who has acres of thought has little of bodily culture, and as little grace of manners; and many and many a one who has sweetening inside has cacophony when he speaks. Harsh, rude, hard, bruising, are his words. The first work therefore is to teach a man's body to serve his soul. "

" Not stark and stiffened persons, but the new-born poetry of God — Apollo and the muses chanting still. "

PHYSICAL EXERCISES.

POISE.   Our first step will be to poise the body properly.

As a reason governing what follows we take the chest as the center because it is the seat of manifestation of the highest life.   The immortal soul, whose servant is the mind, stands first; not the physical body, for it is not immortal, it soon dies.   The highest nature manifests its emotions through the chest, the great emotive center of the whole. So we should aim to train the chest as the center of the *body*; the center of *strength*; the center of *expression*.

Let us now use a Rule to govern the poising of the body.

In that the emotive nature is superior to the physical nature and on this account we say, should be carried with greatest prominence, we find a reason for Da Vinci's Law for Posing Statues,—   *A vertical line from the chest should fall through the ball of the foot.*   An other poise: stand with the toes about three inches from the wall the chest touching the wall should leave the abdomen free.

This poise with the chest over the balls of the feet should be observed in walking and standing.   With the chest in the lead instead of the abdomen, one not only presents a better appearance and feels nobler, but it is found in walking gravity works for one instead of against, which is a point of economy of energy.   In walking let the chest lead.   It is quite impossible to put the weight on the ball of the foot first, but let the chest go first so walking is a series of falling down.   Do not strike out and overdo on this way of carrying the body when the idea is new, as the carriage may at first be far from graceful; but practice the poising exercises.   Think the idea of proper poise till it naturally takes possession of you, so it may be as natural to carry yourself with ease and grace as it was to do otherwise before.   Do not " put on " any unnatural manner.

We need not only to give attention to the position of the chest with relation to the feet but to the positions of the feet themselves.

Principle,— *Weakness takes a strong attitude and strength a weak attitude.* Weakness would stand on a broad base with the feet wide apart, while strength would take a narrow base, feet near together or weight on one foot.

Weakness taking a strong attitude is illustrated in the child learning to walk, or in a drunken person, or the old and feeble who stand with the feet wide apart or braced.

The narrow base is not only an expression of strength but grace as well. The narrow base makes most prominent the longest line of beauty in the body. An active chest bears us up as on wings. Let us rather than plod with the whole flat foot, touch the earth lightly with the ball of the foot.

Poise. Exercise I

With a sense of strength in the chest, with weight on both feet, poise the body forward while counting one measure— then back to position— back— position. (Let the ankles serve as hinges for the sway forward and backward as far as is possible either way without loosing poise.)
Now rise on tips of toes— down— rise again— hold— down to position.

Right foot. Repeat with weight on right foot same as both feet.

Left foot. Repeat the same as right.

In poising feel you are drawn in each movement by an influence leading or drawing out from the chest.

Hips. Exercise II.

With tips of fingers on shoulders, first count, sway onto right foot; second, push the hip out; third count, still hold push down; forth count, glide weight over onto the left foot and repeat same as right. Repeat right. Repeat left.

Waist.   Exercise III. .

Exercise the muscles of the waist, as carefully directed in chapter on Breathing, before attempting this exercise. Practice carefully the panting exercise there described and see that the waist exercises here are taken with the same action as in the panting.   Contracting and expanding is simply long pants.   The training of the waist muscles is so important in correct breathing and voice culture, wrong practice will do more harm than good.   The assistance of a competent teacher is almost indispensable.

Place the hands lightly at sides of the waist, contract through two counts; expand through two counts; repeat expanding; repeat contracting.   Position.

Chest.   Exercise IV.

With tips of fingers lightly touching the chest, lower it slowly, at the same time pushing the chin out; that is to say, take a mean attitude, slowly through two counts; now lift the chest high as possible, chin in; that is take a noble attitude.   Repeat both down and up, giving two measures for each movement.   Position.

Bending.   Exercise V.

The Bending exercise at any time and apart from the other movements is most restful and may act in the place of the doctor for some ailments.   The spine with its " silver cord " demands careful attention.   The Physician tells us that the nerves supply life and motion to every organ and muscle of the body.   The nerves come down from the brain through the spinal column and pass inside through holes between the vertebræ.   The openings for the nerves may be injured giving us " pinched nerves. "   " Respectability" stiffens the spine; pride stiffens the neck; uncomfortable clothing imposes a burden with derangement of the vital organs.   The spinal column has a responsible part to play as the backbone of life. From the pressure upon it, it is shorter at night than in the morning.

Now let us relax, with arms hanging lifeless at the sides, begin to bend. Relax as if going to sleep. Feel as if the head is tied on with a string. Think to bend at the topmost joint, following along down, one vertebra at a time, continue to bend till the head hangs limp in front, through two measures. Still relaxed, head hanging, sway with one measure to each position following   Left— front— right— front— left— front— right— back — left— front— left— back— right— front— Position.

Head. Exercise VI.

With head easily erect, facing front, rest of the body dead still, turn face till it looks straight over the right shoulder ; up— (Look directly overhead.) twist back— down— front. Repeat the same as to the left side. Count one measure of four beats for each position.

Inhaling. Exercise VII.

All arm exercises are to be taken with the weight of the body on the right foot when the right arm is active, on the left foot when the left arm is active, on both feet when both arms are active. The student will be saved from confusion in working out the following by observing the above which is true of gesture.

Suggestions for inhaling will be found in the chapter on Breathing.

In practicing the Inhaling, take the breath in through the nostrils while raising the arm and exhale while lowering it. Reach the arm well out, making large circles with a vigorous backward reach. Right foot— right arm— (Inhale through two measures and exhale through two) up— down— again. Repeat same left. Repeat both.

Reaching. Exercise VIII.

In practicing this exercise and all following in the series the important principles " *Opposition of Agents,* " found in chapter on " Gesture, " and what is given at the close of this treatment of the Physical Exercises about *Flexibility* and *Strength at the center and freedom at the extremities* should be continually borne in mind as the foremost aim in view. This of course must come after the mechanical order of learning the movements.

Prepare to learn the Reaching Exercise by imagining yourself inside a cage about 12 ft. high by 8 ft. wide.

The reaches are in six directions. In each reach the foot is opposed to the hand : for illustration, when the right hand pushes toward the right side of the cage the left foot pushes toward the left side, and so in all the directions the hand and foot are opposed. This makes a sort of a diagonal stretch of the body equal to a vigorous yawn.

The reaches are Lateral Right ; Lateral Left ; Backward Right ; Backward Left ; Forward Right ; Forward Left.

Preceding each arm action the free limb is given a full swing around the one bearing the weight. Position of the foot or both feet is always taken first as in all the other movements and in gesture.

Give particular attention to the progressive order of the energy of each movement. Begin with the body lifeless, sway the weight over on to the right foot, swing the left one count, gradually begin to raise the arm, with the wrist leading ; as the arm rises increase the tension till the whole energy is exerted ; push with the palm near the wrist, the opposite foot near the heel. Take two measures to reach the highest tension, hold one measure, relax slowly as the arm falls through two measures, limp at the side ready for the next reach. Alternate relaxation and tension. This is as much an exercise for the foot as for the hand; make the stroke of foot and hand together. Stretch and grow. Stretching makes straight. Stretching makes flexible.

Weight on right foot— swing left— right arm— up— reach— hold— rest— down— Same as to Lateral Left, Back Right, Back Left, Front Right, Front Left.

In all but the lateral reaches the hand reaches toward the different upper corners of the cage and the foot toward the lower corners.

Hands and Wrists. Exercise IX.

The aim in this exercise should be for flexibility of wrist.

A stiff wrist is as great a detriment to ease and grace of expression as a stiff neck, and far more common. We say the hand is a second face. In many cases it seems to be a tool only. How often people tell us, if not always in words, " I do not know what to do with my hands. " Really our hands should be no more in the way than our faces, and will not be when they have been made expressive.

Let us first work out the stiffness out of the wrist. Let the wrist bend a bit, it is not the handle of a shovel which will be ruined if you let go. A bend of the wrist will give more grace. In all the arm movements let the wrist lead rather than the tips of the fingers. . In lifting the arm feel the hand is being drawn through the water, the fingers trailing. Move the arms in all directions, up, down, out and in, fingers floating in the water. Train the palm to come well open, let it touch the imaginary water too Cultivate " openhandedness " rather than " tightfistedness. " The hand not only reveals but trained to express thought helps to cultivate correct thinking. Train the hand to manifest thought and feeling ; do not allow it to wear the face of an idiot, without any thought. When it is made responsive the public speaker will have something in it to give and will not need to hide it behind him, or put it in his pocket or what is worse, use it in meaningless gesticulation; this being a way of showing how empty it is. This series of exercises for the flexibility of the wrist is especially helpful to the pianist.

For further study of the hand see chapter on "Gesture," and Laws of the Hands in "Science of Speech."

Take the Wrist exercise with active chest, free, limp arms, shake the forearm vigorously, up and down— out— (Make large circles outward.) in— (Making large circles inward, rotating the wrist in both outward and inward movements.) —up and down— Rest.

Arms. Exercise X.

The arm moves in opposition to the head. When the arm is raised the head is lowered, when the arm is lowered the head is raised, when the arm sweeps out to the right the face turns as far to the left, etc. This is as much an exercise for the head as for the arm.

Weight on right foot— right arm— up— down— push back— up again— down.

Same as to left foot and arm.

Same as to both feet and both arms.

Both arms overhead, fingers of both hands nearly touching— out, back of hands leading to arm's length out— up overhead, palms leading up— out again, palms leading out— up, backs of hands leading up — front of chest, push— out, arms length at the sides— down to position.

In all arm movements let the wrist lead. Observe in all the movements the points of action and the points of rest.

Sweeps of arms. Exercise XI.

Sweeps of arm out from the chest to the lateral are to be made with the hand in three different positions. First the back of hand leads out, palm leads back; second, the palm of the hand leads out and the back of the hand leads back; third, the side of the hand leads out, palm down and the side of the hand leads back. Observe the oppositions of hand and head. Work for an active chest, making climax of the stroke with chest and arm reach together, relax on arm's return.

Weight on the right foot— right arm— out— back— out— back— out— back— Position.

Repeat the same as to left side.

Arms, Salutation. Exercise XII.

Weight on right foot reacting back on left as the body inclines slightly as head is lowered to meet the hand.

Weight on right foot, raise the right arm, with the palm facing outward, as the hand rises the head is bowed to meet the palm as if to be placed on the head, two measures, next the hand falls to the side as the head is raised and the weight of the body returns to the right foot, two measures; repeat the same with the same time; the third time the same save the hand rises only on a level with the chest; fourth, the same as the first only a sweep of arm overhead with the fingers nearly touching left side of head; fifth same as the third; the sixth the same as the fourth; the seventh the same as the third. Position. Repeat the same, left foot and arm.

Repulsion. Attraction. Exercise XIII.

In this exercise, as well as in all the others be particular to let the chest lead. Feel conscious of the action in the chest first. In repulsion, let the chest slightly react before the hand attempts to push outward. Try to respond with the whole body.

Weight on the right foot, bring hand to the ear as if listening, hold one count; body reacts and hand pushes outward as if repulsing something offensive, hold one count; repeat the same; listen, the third time something attractive, the arm is raised, hand held as expecting to receive, the

whole body, chest, face, ear, eye and hand is attracted.
The measures for attraction are: right arm— up—
hand— hold— back— repeat the same then rest.

Weight on left foot repeat both " repulsion, " and " attraction. " Position.

Hands Finish.   Exercise XIV.

Weight on both feet; wrists leading, backs of both hands
uppermost, lifted above waist line, one count; down, backs
leading down. Repeat, palms leading up; over, palms
leading down. Position.

Bow.   Exercise XV.

In order to acquire this useful accomplishment so it is
a genuine expression of our feelings without affectation
let us find the reason back of the bow. Review the chart
given concerning the threefold divisions of the body.
The bow should be an expression of respect, admiration,
love or reverence. Of whatever degree, it is an expression
from the emotive nature. In this all the emotive divisions
of the body respond together: eye first, chest, top of head,
palm of hand. The free foot is inclined to swing behind
the strong foot, crossing behind it as the knees are crooked
and the chest lowered. Bend at the hips.

The hearty bow moves the body with a long diagonal
sweep toward the strong foot. The formal bow, without
heart, with the weight on both feet, bow more directly in
front. The heathen bows or prostrates himself directly
before his lifeless, loveless idol; true warmth and hearty
love and reverence give more sway and grace to the bow.

With the meaning of the bow in mind overdo in practice.
Bow slowly and profoundly. In one form : stand with the
weight on the right foot, as the body is bowing, the chest
lowered, sway the body toward the active right foot; on
return to position, let the weight fall back onto the left foot.

The eyes should not be allowed to drop while making a bow, save in humility or timidity, but should rest upon the person or persons to whom the respect is shown.

Sitting and kneeling are simply forms of bowing, though sitting has not a similar significance in meaning.

Practice with the weight on the right foot, bow, 2, 3, 4, 1, 2, 3, 4; rise, 2, 3, 4, 1, 2, 3, 4.

After overdone practice, greet the friends with but a slight suggestion of that overdone, yet feel it pass like a wave passing over the entire body even as in the deep bow, with movements of ease, grace and expression instead of a bob or jerk of the head, so common, expressing an attack of recognition merely, but of little respect. Let us manifest all noble feeling in a noble manner. To associate exalted thought and feeling with all the Physical Exercises adds much to their value giving fervor and earnestness.

STRENGTH AT THE CENTER.

Law.— *Strength at the center gives freedom at the extremities.* No law of Expression can be of greater value than this if fully appreciated and mastered.

As we have said before, the chest is the center of the body, the center of physical strength, the center of feeling. Think of the chest as the great powerhouse and dynamo that demands attention that it may be supplied with all needed to maintain it and to prevent waste and leakage of valuable power. The nerve energy being wasted is quite as valuable as electricity and it is time to learn to save it for we need it in the serious business of life.

We can readily understand it is a waste of electricity to turn on the lights in the day time, or to send out power when it is not needed. We may not be aware of the fact we are daily doing this very wasteful thing when we send out to the hands or feet or head or any part of the body nerve force when it is not needed, or too much when it is needed, or what is still worse, leave it all turned on all the time. To illustrate what we mean by wasting the nerve energy, observe the child just learning to write. The little hand uses enough energy to drive a plane instead of a pen. Look at women out shopping grasping a hand bag with sufficient energy to hold the reins in driving a high-spirited horse. They return home wondering why they are so tired. To multiply illustrations is quite useless for you are apt to find a living illustration of this unconscious slavery in the first person you meet, even should it chance to be in the mirror. In fact very few have learned this priceless secret of economy of human energy.

No attempt can be made in this limited space to treat fully this important matter. A few hints on the practical side of it may help the student to find out for himself the value of saving and wisely spending his life energy.

We go to sleep and rest. We relax and the energy goes to vital centers of life and we are renewed in strength. We may not sleep while we are awake but we may train ourselves to rest while we are awake. Not to rest from our labors but rest *in* our labors. Those who gain this rare ability must be willing to pay the price for it. It cannot be taken like patent medicine from a spoon, leaving you only to just wait for a charm to be wrought upon you. It may not be attained by hearing about it though hearing may be needful.

The race is to the swift.

Get the idea of carrying the chest high — a noble attitude firmly fixed. Feel that in the chest is the center of life, the hub of the wheel. Learn to relax the extremities when not necessary to use them. Let the hands and feet relax and go to sleep when not employed. This is really easier said than done. We may tell a wire to relax, it may try but cannot. We may tell a bow-string as stiff as a wire to relax. It is nearly as helpless as the wire, but as it is made of yielding material by working it and stretching it, it may be limbered up so it can be made tense or slack at will. So there may need to be considerable working and stretching of muscles and tense cords before they can relax even when they will to do so. Stretching exercises make plastic and responsive.

In exerting great energy send it out from the chest. In lifting think to put the strain on the chest instead of on the biceps. It often happens, the man with the great biceps has a weak chest for the great arm muscles have been quietly robbing the vital organs and the weaker and more delicate muscles. The great athlete often suddenly breaks down, because the balance has been taken from the natural vital center and the harmony broken.

In working for strength at the center, we may find an unerring guide in nature's own gymnastic: the yawn with a stretch. Observe how this homely exercise is performed. We first fill the lungs with a good full breath that seems to be drawn from the tips of the toes, then with the breath begin to lift the chest, raise one shoulder and the opposite limb a bit at the same time, send out the energy to all the extremities, hold tense an instant then relax— but not suddenly— slowly the energy returns to the center, and we come out of it with a sense of being awakened and invigorated or if not we try again. When we practice the Physical Culture as yawn culture we come near to nature's way and need not fear the results. So let the yawn be a guide for the stretching in the physical exercises. There is a rhythm in this alternate, even contraction and relaxation of the muscles, quieting the nerves and stimulating as a nerve tonic. In taking the stretching, feel that the muscles are rubber — stretch slowly and evenly to their limit— let the tension out evenly so the cords will not kink. In this way we may gain flexibility of body capable of responding to the most delicate thought and feeling, even as the violin strings may be attuned to finest expression because of the flexibility. So make the whole physical body flexible that there may be a responsive element for the divine soul within to play upon.

PHYSICAL CULTURE NOTES.

"THE SPINAL COLUMN contains all of the motive power of man; upon the spinal column depends all the symmetry of the body. Nearly every malformation results from wrong positions of the spinal column. Preach the gospel of the spinal column everywhere, as our physical culture is based upon it. The spinal column cannot be overstraightened. Elevating it produces instantaneous effect upon the stomach nerve, with very beneficial effect upon digestion.

GOING UP STAIRS is hurtful or not, according to how it is done. The mind has much to do with it. If you feel hurried, you do not do it easily or gracefully. Think only of keeping the chest high, then the head seems to float up. Various ways of ascending stairs,— pounding up because a feeble will makes any one feeble; bustling up out of breath. Don't put the foot up and climb up after it. Learn from the Greeks to poise the Mental Kingdom on the physical, with the mind shining from the candlestick of the body. Keep the crown of the head firm. Never surrender your manhood or womanhood to your activity— your individuality is greater than anything you can do; maintain it ever.

LEADERSHIP of the spinal column is the crown of the head, leadership of torso, the chest; of arm, between hand and elbow; limb, in walking, half between the knee and ankle."

Dr. Charles W. Emerson.

THE BREATH OF LIFE.

The blood and breath are the vital forces of life; neither can exist without the other. It has come to be of greater importance that we have *red blood* in our veins than that we have *blue blood* even. It is the breath that keeps the flame of life glowing and gives the red blood.

It makes a difference *what* you breathe, *how* you breathe, and *how much* you breathe.

If all virtues of medicine, all kinds of physical exercises, all kinds of voice culture could be summed up in one thing, it would come nearer to being a concentrated whole in this one act: correct breathing. It is through this more than through any one thing you may gain nerve to master your circumstances; and in this way, if any may you "add years to your life and life to your years." No person can any more afford to be careless about breathing than about other nourishment for his body.

The advantages gained by cultivating the breath are very numerous; among them may be mentioned, health and strength; a cure for nervousness and embarrassment; increase of bodily warmth; control of rhythmic circulation of the blood; a basis for improved voice production and means of speech.

" Calenus and Galen and other Greek and Roman physicians recommended deep breathing and retention of air as a daily exercise and as a remedy. They believed thereby to increase the heat of the inner organism, to enlarge the chest, to strengthen the respiratory organs, to remove the impurities from the breast, to open the pores of the skin, to thin the skin itself, to drive the fluids through it."

Says Gladstone — " All time and money spent in training the voice and body is an investment that pays a larger interest than any other."

BREATH ORGANS.

The Organs of Breath are the Diaphragm, Lungs, Trachea and Bronchial tubes with all their Muscles and assisting Motive Organs.

Think of the lungs themselves in a general way as a big rubber bag without power of its own to act. It possesses great elasticity and can be expanded. The pressure of the outside air comes in the lungs when opened and fills them as a bottle is filled with air when the cork is taken out. Of course certain muscles assist in pumping in the air besides. The air may be expelled from the lungs by the pressure of certain muscles. There are several ways of doing this, some of which are far from right, yet we pass without discussion; but will endeavor to present that which experience and careful investigation have shown to be the right way.

However large and ample the lung capacity may be, naturally with a cramped chest there can be but little room for the expansion of the lungs, as the case of bone and flesh covering them is heavy, and easily crushes the very delicate lung tissue out of its rightful place and gives too little room for vigorous and healthy working.

In expanding the lungs, first stand erect, lift the bony corselet with the ribs at the sides, lifting up and out like two bucket handles, that there may be room for the air of heaven to come in. Do not be satisfied with little sips of air, the whole heaven is full of it free at your disposal; so as you value your life and want to nourish it partake freely of all of this life giving sustenance, and cultivate a camel's capacity for holding it. Feel as if the limbs are hollow tubes through which you draw the air into your body. In this way seem to breathe from the tips of the toes. Try to inflate the whole lung tract. And it is wonderful how accommodating the lungs are, how elastic, how quickly a little effort will cause them to expand.   The progress may be noted with the aid of a Spirometer.

As in blowing up a rubber bag you aim directly at the bottom of it first, in the same way aim to fill the lower part of the lungs first.

People afflicted with some forms of lung difficulties often receive benefit by going to a climate of rarer atmosphere.   This kind of a change of climate makes it necessary for the patient to breathe deeply in order to satisfy, thus making it needful to exert the breathing organs with more vigor.   From this increased activity of the breath organs comes much of the benefit derived from the change.
One may gain the same advantage at home by exerting the will and learning to expand the lungs and to take in the breath of life.

When we consider how few people breathe correctly we must admit nature is very generous with her children, and compromises in every way possible to help out in some other way, even making it more difficult for us to do wrong than to do right.

Most people are unwilling to be convinced that they are breathing incorrectly, thus allowing themselves to be deluded and cheated. While being able to breathe naturally is an advantage, yet the trained cultivated breathing organs far surpass the natural.   We find examples of natural breathing in animals and little children.   The natural breathing in children begins to change when selfconsciousness begins; still greater changes come with embarrassment, which is little fear and disturbs the breath.

THE DIAPHRAGM is the great motor muscle concerned in breathing.   This muscle may be trained even as a hand to work the bellows that supplies the wind for a great organ. The exercises for training this most important muscle will be found at close of the chapter under Breathing Exercises.

LUNG CAPACITY.   Recognized authorities tell us that the lung capacity of a man of average height is 335 cubic inches. 225 cubic inches of air can be expelled, while 109 cubic inches remain in the lungs.   The lung capacity bears a uniform relation to the height of the person — increasing 8 cubic inches for every inch above 5 feet.   When sitting or lying down the lung capacity is diminished.   After a hearty meal the lung capacity is lessened from 10 to 20 cubic inches.

SKILL MORE THAN STRENGTH.   Inspiration is the opening and enlarging of the chest cavity.   Expiration is the diminishing of the size of the chest cavity.   Inhalation is the passive part of breathing.   Exhalation is the active part of breathing.

INHALE ONLY THROUGH THE NOSTRILS. "Shut the mouth and stretch the nostrils wide." The reasons for doing so are plain.   The nose is so made as to filter out the dust from the air.   The crooked passage through the nostrils to the lungs affords an opportunity to warm the air, that it may be of the same temperature of the body before it comes into the lungs, that it may not chill the delicate membrane.

Taking the breath through the nose prevents dryness in the throat of the speaker.   The breath taken through the mouth, even in speaking or singing absorbs the saliva and causes dryness making it necessary to exert greater energy, causing unnecessary fatigue.

The tongue pressed against the hard palate at the moment of taking the breath serves as a barrier to prevent the passage of the air beyond through the mouth.

MOUTH BREATHING cannot be too strongly condemned. Aside from the bad effects on the organs of respiration, lungs, bronchial tubes, throat etc., it has a harmful influence on the nervous system.   Careful tests show that mouth breathing weakens the intellect.   The habitual mouth

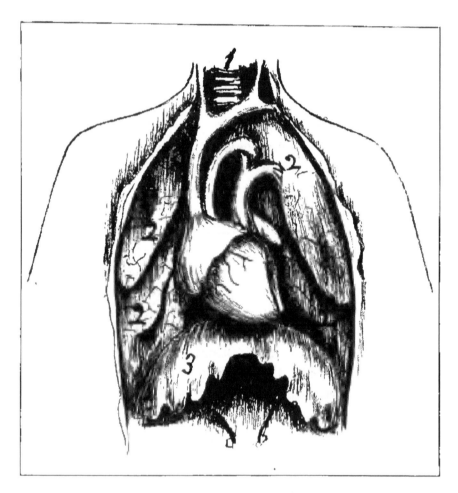

BREATH ORGANS

1. Windpipe   2. Lungs   3. Diaphragm

breathers of the public schools are, almost without exception, dull and stupid and from no other cause than this vicious habit of breathing through the mouth.

Athletes keep the mouth closed while under great physical exertion. The mouth is closed in any feat requiring great physical power.

"Upton's Tactics" which has been adopted as the official drill book of the United States Army contains the following — "In marching double time and at the run, the men breathe as much as possible through the nose, keeping the mouth closed. Experience has proved that by conforming to this principle men can go much further with less fatigue."

The face of the mouth breather is branded with an expression that grows more and more repulsive the longer it is practiced. Dr Clinton Wagner gives a picture of this face. "The habitual mouth breathers can at once be recognized, there is no mistaking them as the practice stamps itself indelibly on the physiognomy. The retracted lips, open mouth, receding gums, protruding teeth — especially the upper ones—shrunken alæ, diminished size of the orifices of the nostrils, wrinkles at the outer angles of the eyes, giving the wearer an idiotic and silly expression, which is by no means agreeable to look upon." The student will not need to search long among the wretched, who are not to be found entirely among the poor and ignorant for such faces as described above. When once the attention is called to the cause of such ugly faces and conditions, we should find here a warning in the impression of mouth breathing on the countenance, if it had no other, to prevent any sane person breathing through the mouth either asleep or awake.

It has been proven beyond a doubt that a long list of lung, throat, nose and ear disorders, difficulties in other parts of the body, are traced directly to mouth breathing as a cause.

We are told that insanity and diseases of the mind are unknown among tribes of Indians who breathe through the nose only.

EXPRESSIONS OF THE BREATH.

Says Delsarte — " Logical respiration constitutes respiration itself.   Suspension expresses reticence, disquietude. Inspiration is an element of dissimulation, concentration, pain.   Hence, we have normal, oppressive, spasmodic, superior, sibilant, rattling, intermittent, crackling, and hiccoughing, respiration.   Expiration is an element of trust, expansion, confidence and tenderness.   If the expression contains both pain and love, the inspiration and expiration will both be noisy; but the one or the other will predominate according as pain predominates over love, or vice versa.

The source of passional respiration lies in the heart. The effect of respiration is most powerful, for the slighter and more imperceptible the phenomena are, the more effect they have upon the auditors. "

Respiration and silence are a means of falling exactly upon the suitable tone and inflection.

As the breath has a powerful influence over the pulse to quicken or quiet its action the breath plays an important part in pause and pitch in expression.   There seems to be a rhythmic relation between the pulse and breath and the pulsations of attention.   Some verse we find is so arranged as to breathe out a single idea with each expiration.

The action of the breath may have some influence over the average length of sentences used by some writers.   The " long winded " sentences are tedious and tiresome, while the sentences just suited to a gentle respiration with its proper pulse or accent charms the ear and holds the attention.

BREATHING EXERCISES.

In breathing, nearly all of the muscles of the trunk of the body, both front and back, should be brought into action. The DIAPHRAGM is the great motor muscle in breath. ing and to the training of this muscle as the center of the breath we now turn our attention. A study of the physiology of this muscle would be helpful at this point. The active part of this muscle is in the middle of the organ. It has the power to contract and relax like a puckering string; or it is a round muscle like the muscle around the mouth and can, like the mouth, pucker up at will, gently or forcibly. It is also an involuntary muscle and does its work so quietly many are never aware they own such a muscle; but there it is waiting like a willing servant all ready to be trained for our service. Let us come into our possessions and train this dormant muscle and make of it a voluntary muscle, strong and active ready to help the breath, the circulation and the digestion.

As we begin to train this muscle let us remember that " it is hard to teach an old dog new tricks. " With some the wrong way of taking the breath has become so settled and established through long practice, it is difficult to draw a breath save in the same old way. The involuntary is so much easier than the voluntary, besides the old servants cannot be turned out of business so easily. We also find that even when the new way is supposed to be settled and the new habit fixed, unconsciously the muscles fall back to the old way. There are a number of wrong ways with only one right way. The farther you travel on the wrong road, remember at this point, the farther you are from the destination — even farther away than before you ever started. The old adage " Well begun is half done, " is particularly applicable in learning the Breathing Exercises.

To gain a consciousness of the Diaphragm and to secure a sense of relaxation of the muscles of the waist, practice the following panting exercise.

Exercise I.   Panting.

Place the hands lightly at the waist line, with muscles relaxed, pant like a dog when he is tired. This is to be done with the breath. Think to draw in the breath as if astonished or frightened, puff it out as if blowing out a candle. This may be practiced slowly at first then make the action rapidly when it becomes panting. Some find difficulty in the very simplicity of this exercise and fail because of too great effort. Any such may practice the following to help in awakening the muscles used in the breathing exercises. Lie on the back with the clothing loose; place the hand on the waist in front; raise and lower the hand by the inhaling and exhaling of the breath or panting as directed above. In beginning to train the diaphragm take some time, perhaps a week practicing daily the preliminary panting, and make sure of action of proper muscles before attempting other breathing exercises.

Caution — Do not let the chest rise and fall in panting, keep it perfectly quiet with the action at the waist. The aim should be for a quiet chest in breathing. Aim also to gain more and more ability to relax the waist muscles and the diaphragm. Practice the panting a little in contrasting ways — the first named, with muscles of waist stiff, is wrong. First hold up the chest as high as possible, stiffen the waist, pant forcibly. Second, relax all possible, dropping the chest, pant easily and gently. " Shake the diaphragm down to a jelly. " Note the difference between the two ways; beware the first, cultivate the second. *Work for a quiet chest, relaxed muscles at the waist, shaking like " jelly " the diaphragm. Breathing is an outgrowth of panting.*

Exercise II.   Contracting and Expanding.

Place the hands at the waist near the floating ribs, with
the chest perfectly quiet. Contract slowly through two
measures — 1, 2, 3, 4, 5, 6, 7, 8.   Expand through two
measures — 1, 2, 3, 4, 5, 6, 7, 8.   Repeat both Contracting
and Expanding.   Count silently so the action of the muscles may move slowly and evenly. Aim to bring into action
the same muscles and in the same way as in the Panting
Exercises, save with slower movements.   See page 26.

Exercise III.   Hygienic Exercise.

Lie flat on the back — the floor is a suitable place —
with the body relaxed and dead still, save the breathing
muscles, arms thrown over the head, or if too difficult, the
hands may be placed at the waist as in the panting.   Now
slowly inhale, packing the lungs to their fullest capacity,
hold au instant, exhale slowly whispering " one, " prolong
the breath as long as possible, at the last, contract the muscles tightly as if to squeeze out the last bit of air.   Relax
slowly and evenly.   Repeat the same whispering " two, "
and so continue to repeat up to " fifty " when you will be
conscious of the fact you have exercised.   If too vigorous
for one in feeble health, the number of counts may be less
but not the energy.   Each should exert his full strength.

Practice the same exercise for the voice by substituting
the vowels for the counts which may be given in different
ways, either whispering, spoken aloud or shouted, as may
also the counting.   Blowing also may be substituted.

This exercise is positive and immediate aid for indigestion.
It immediately quickens the circulation, for it is exercise.
The dyspeptic will find it better than medicine, for it brings
the blood where it is needed to invigorate and give strength.
For voice production train the breathing muscles till like
bands of steel; the diaphragm a muscle of resisting power.

Exercise IV.   With Breathing Pipe.

Beside the work to *develop the breathing muscles* and strengthen them there must be practice to gain *breath capacity* and *breath control*.   These three points are almost concentrated in the following exercise with the Breathing Pipe.

Let us remember that the voice is produced with the outgoing breath; the active part of breathing is this exhaling. Too much breath sent out in making a tone destroys its purity.   So work for breath control must advance with the increase in lung capacity.   We may cultivate a muscle by training it to move slowly, evenly, with energy through the alternating extremes of relaxation and tension.   A quick, jerky movement requires less strength than a slow, even movement.   Applying this to the breathing muscles we find in order to control them and to secure slow even action while inhaling and exhaling we may gain much of the desired control by practice with a breathing pipe.   A short piece of hollow reed or piece of a clay pipe stem may serve for a breathing pipe.   Place this between the lips through which you may inhale and exhale.   While this practice is through the mouth it is not to encourage mouth breathing but, more particularly, to train the diaphragm and other breathing muscles to send out a small, even, vigorous flow of breath.   When inhaling through the nostrils it is quite impossible for one to take in a small stream of air.   When one exhales through the mouth the breath is not easily controlled, before the muscles are trained, but comes with a puff over the vocal cords.   In this, aim to inhale and to exhale a small, even, concentrated stream of breath and to train the breath organs that they may attain skill in performing all their work.

To practice this exercise : after panting, place the breathing pipe between the lips; inhale slowly at the same time raise both arms as in Inhaling, Exercise VII. Page 27.

When the arms are lifted as high as possible and the lungs filled, hold an instant,— exhale slowly through the pipe as the arms are lowered. Pant,— Inhale,— Hold,— Exhale. Repeat five or six times at a practice time. Practice daily, you may do so to advantage several times a day, in open air.

One should be able to inhale from 30 to 45 seconds and to exhale the same length of time. The first efforts will be less than this. The beginner need not be discouraged if his best is only 10 seconds. Should it be so, here is an opportunity to test what persistent effort will accomplish in a short space of time. In whatever stage of practice never try to do more than can be done without straining, lest there be injury instead of growth.

It is more important to prolong the outgoing a little longer than the ingoing breath, for it is on the outgoing breath we send out the speech and song. As the prolonged exhalation is more difficult for some than the inhalation, the exhalation may be prolonged somewhat longer if the inhalation is not prolonged to the full limit of the capacity. Do all gently. Do not force the breath. There should be no sound.

This exercise may be varied giving vigorous exercise for all the breathing muscles, especially the diaphragm, giving it sustaining power. Practice the same as that given above lifting a chair or some weight above the head while inhaling, lowering it while exhaling. The panting should be taken while bending over the back of the chair before the inhaling and lifting it at arm's length overhead. To this drill with the chair may be substituted voice exercises in the place of exhaling through the pipe as the arms are lowered. Remember. in voice production it is not so much how full you are able to fill the lungs with air as how to manage and control it when you come to spend it. Skill comes through repetition, repetition, repetition.

THE VOICE.

" The voice is like an orchestra.   It ranges high up, and can shriek like the scream of an eagle; or it is low as a lion's tone; and at every intermediate point is some peculiar quality.   It has in it the mother's whisper and the father's command.   It has in it warning and alarm.   It has in it sweetness.   It is full of mirth and full of gaiety.   It glitters, though it is not seen with all its sparkling fancies.   It ranges high, intermediate or low, in obedience to the will, unconscious to him who uses it ; and men listen through the long hour, wondering that it is so short, and quite unaware that they have been bewitched out of their weariness by the charm of a voice, not artifical, not prearranged in man's thought, but by assiduous training made to be his second nature.   Such a voice answers the soul, and is its beating. "

Henry Ward Beecher.

" There is no power of love so hard to get and keep as a kind voice.   A kind hand is deaf and dumb.   It may be rough in flesh and blood, yet do the work of a soft heart, and do it with a soft touch.   But there is no one thing that love so much needs as a sweet voice to tell what it means and feels ; and it is hard to get and keep it in the right tone. One must start in youth, and be on the watch night and day, at work and play, to get and keep a voice that shall speak at all times the thoughts of a kind heart.   It is often in youth that one gets a voice or a tone that is sharp, and it sticks to him through life, and stirs up ill will and grief, and falls like a drop of gall on the sweet of home.   Watch it day by day as a pearl of great price, for it will be worth more to you in days to come than the best pearl hid in the seas.   A kind voice is to the heart as light is to the eye. It is a light that sings as well as shines. "   *Elihu Burritt.*

There is nothing in the nature of man more intimately connected with his happiness than the human voice. By it we may manifest our desires and feelings, hold communication with our friends and convey to them words of cheer hope and encouragement. By the aid of the voice we obtain instruction, and by its aid we may impart it to others. In business life, in public life, in the home circle the voice is daily employed ; should we bestow on it a passing thought we would find it is of tenfold the importance we had ever once given it.

" There is no one thing in man that he has in perfection till he has it by culture. "

" The Voice in rudimentary state, is like an image leaving the mould ; a canvas with the design, without the embroidery ; the mere outline of an instrument ; a body without a soul. "

FIRST STEPS IN VOICE CULTURE.

The first steps in Voice Culture are quite the same as the first steps toward purchasing a grand piano. Do not misunderstand — *purchasing a piano*. Not having it given, but having to personally earn the means for it. Having no instrument, no money, no capital save a desire to own so great a treasure. If the desire be genuine and strong the other difficulties soon vanish. So the first steps in voice culture must be a high ideal to awaken a DESIRE. This must be more than a burst of schoolgirl enthusiasm, but a deep, settled longing after an inborn ideal, strong enough to cost sacrifice and make one willing to do genuine hard work. Voice Culture cannot be given only as the learner is able to take. Begin this study then with lofty ideals, for we must ever remember : water never rises higher than its source. As the study advances, it charms and grows ideals Second in our study comes a knowledge of the instrument.

ORGANS OF VOICE.

While the human voice has been compared to an orchestra, yet when we consider the instrument, it is like an organ with its bellows, its vibrating tongues, its body to modify the tone.

Briefly stated : voice is produced by the air from the lungs passing over the vocal cords, being modified by the cavities of the mouth and nose.

THE VOCAL CORDS are in structure, a bundle of elastic tissues, covered with mucus membrane, in color a pearly white. They are capable of wonderful rapidity of motion. Average length in man a little more than $\frac{1}{2}$ inch, in woman some less. As in the violin, the more the cords are tightened the higher the tone ; the more the cords are slackened the lower the tone.

THE GLOTTIS is the opening between the vocal cords. The high tones with tense cords make the chink of the glottis narrow. The low tones with the cords relaxed give wide opening of the glottis. The medium tones make the medium opening of the chink of the glottis.

THE LARYNX is the expanded upper end of the trachea or windpipe. The Larynx may be depressed to produce a low tone — for the deepest tone it may be depressed $\frac{1}{2}$ inch. For the highest tones the larynx may rise $\frac{1}{2}$ inch.

RESONANCE of the voice depends on the cavities of the mouth, nose and chest, making a secondary vibration with the vocal cords. The vibration of the vocal cords is modified and mellowed by these resonators as the violin body is made to vibrate with the strings, or the box of the piano with its strings. The resonance modifying the first tone may also be illustrated by a tuning fork. Ring it, listen; hold it against the table. Ring it again, hold it against a glass; again, now against a silver bell; against different objects and note how the same tone from this tuning fork is changed in quality by the article it touches. Note also how hard substance gives a clearer ring than soft substance. Ring the tuning fork once more, place it against a silver bell; again, now against a rubber ball. Let us remember for our profit this simple fact: hard substance modifies the tone giving a clear ringing sound while soft substance gives a muffled, deadened sound. In taking advantage of this self evident, simple fact and right use of the breath lie the secrets of voice development. Think again how the voice is formed: the breath passing over the vocal cords giving a sound like the tuning fork but what we hear in the voice is modified by the mouth cavity, nose and chest. Let us examine some of these modifiers and find out what kind of substance they are made of. We find in the front of the roof of the mouth a hard, firm bone, in the back of the mouth quite the opposite, soft yielding substance. We may naturally decide that it makes quite a difference which of the two vibrates with the vocal cords, the front or the back of the mouth, for the difference in substance is as the silver bell compared with the rubber ball. Let us learn to use this bone in the front of the mouth, called the nares, as the resonator instead of the back of the mouth, for it is the hardest, firmest bone in the body. Let us think of the nares as the center of the voice. The voice being allowed to fall back into the throat for resonance accounts for the cause of so many poor voices and for the cause of many forms of throat disorders. Throat diseases of a chronic character are relieved and cured by training the resonance of the voice to focus in the hard bone in the front of the mouth.

This fact concerning the resonance in the front of the mouth is no longer kept a guarded secret, being bequeathed as a legacy and sold for fabulous prices, but its value is still unchanged and here it is revealed, free for your profit.

Rule,— Front tones are human ; back tones are animal. Tone made to vibrate in the front of the mouth may be made " clear as a silver bell, " with wonderful carrying power, because it is musical. The tones formed in the throat are dull and rasping, harsh noises, requiring far greater exertion and, consequently, soon cause fatigue. The front tones are produced with perfect ease and like the rare old violin, grow sweeter with age. We can well afford to give careful study to this point of resonance.

There are three essentials in producing tone, either with a musical instrument or the human voice,— a motive element,— a vibratory element,— a resonant element. In the organ the power that operates the bellows is the motor element. The reeds or little tongues are the vibrant element. The body of the organ, with certain parts, specially arranged for that purpose is the resonant element.

In the violin the hand that wields the bow is the motor, the strings the vibrant, the body of the violin the resonant.

In the piano the motor element is in the fingers that strike the keys causing little hammers to strike the strings, which are the vibratory element. The vibrations of the strings are modified by the body of the piano and the space within it, making it mellow and resonant. The quality of the tone may be changed by lifting the top of the piano.

The human voice is much like the organ. The Motor element is the diaphragm,— the Vibrant element, the vocal cords; the mouth and nasal cavities, the chest and other parts of the body are the Resonant element.

The organ builder gives careful and patient attention to adjusting all parts, that the bellows may be ample in size and just strong enough for the work it is to do — that the power that furnishes the air works evenly and vigorously — that the vibrating tongues or reeds have free play — that nothing obstructs the sound after it is once produced.

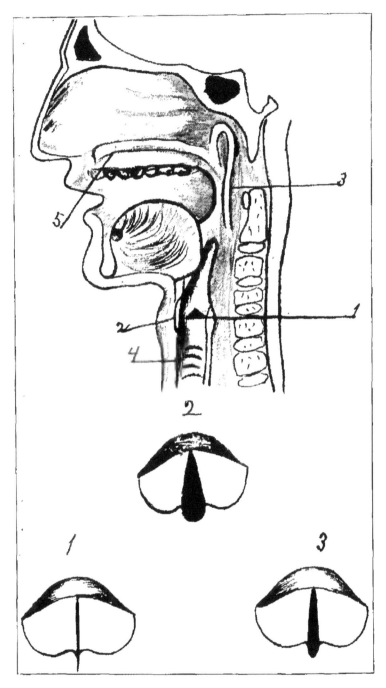

VIBRATORY ORGANS OF VOICE

1. Vocal Cords   3. Pharynx   5. Hard Palate
2. Larynx   4. Trachea

TENSION OF VOCAL CORDS

1. High Pitch   2. Low Pitch   3. Medium Pitch

Then beside all this, much care and thoughtful attention must be given to the resonant body : the pipes, the stops; how to reinforce and modify all into a harmony pleasing and musical.

We can hardly say too much of the importance of developing the lungs to their fullest capacity. It is surprising how readily the lungs may be expanded, sometimes to double their undeveloped capacity. A great lung capacity without corresponding breath control, especially the outgoing breath, is of no advantage to the voice. Too much wind forced against the reeds of the organ makes the tone wheezy and impure. Too much air from the lungs gives a breathy, labored tone in either speech or song.

VIBRATORY AGENTS OF THE VOICE.

The culture of the Vibratory agents of the voice, the vocal cords, is left largely to the soul that must play upon these mystic strings with thought and feeling, yet teachers of voice attempt to give exercises for tensioning the vocal cords — for the stroke of the glottis etc. This particular, delicate work best be taken under the direction of a careful, experienced teacher.

The Larynx may be exercised by use of the following —
E- (as in eve)   A- (as in father.)   oo- (as in boon.)

Larynx may be lowered on   E, A, OO.
Larynx may be raised on   OO, A, E.

The drill to develop resonance in the nares, and the drill for dynamic, proper breathing, reward the student's efforts with immediate results indicating a start and growth most encouraging, when the exercises have been faithfully taken. In the efforts to focus the voice in the front of the mouth the student may know and feel the vibrations distinctly. To illustrate and leave no room for blunder, the student is asked to hold lightly the bridge of the nose, closing the nostrils, pronounce " knee, knee, knee, " observe the little vibration or buzz in the nose against the fingers. This kind of tingle, buzz, or ring or vibration of the hard bone just back of the upper, front teeth is what we should aim to secure. The vowel formed farthest front is long E. Repeat " E, E, E, " many times rapidly and note the vibrations in the front of the mouth.

Caution. In working for this quality in the voice, while practicing the following exercises, there are two important points to observe — *Do not practice any of this series of voice building exercises forcibly. Gently, gently. Loudness overshoots the mark. Noise is not music. Force tensions the muscles of the throat and pinches off the vibrations and defeats the whole effort.*

The second point is more difficult than the first,—

Start the tone with the breath, snuff it through the nose as if gently blowing thistle down or some airy substance through the nose. Whisper the exercise first then make the tone, always as gently as possible.

VOICE EXERCISES.

Exercise I.

Hold the nose, practice up and down the scale, letting go the nose on the seventh note coming down the scale when the tone should ring clear. Practice " knee, "

```
                    knee   knee
               knee           knee
            knee                 knee
         kn ee                     knee
       knee                          knee
      knee                             knee
    knee                                 knee
 knee                                       knee
```

Exercise II.

Practice " hng " up and down the scale, letting it ring in the roof of the mouth and the nasal cavity. Let the mouth come well open, wide enough to insert between the teeth the width of the first and second fingers.Let the lower jaw hang lifeless, the throat open as if to yawn. Inhale through the nose, making one breath last as long as possible.

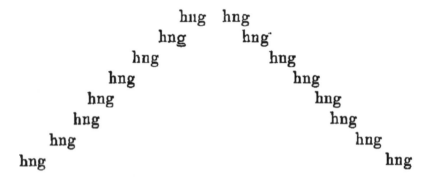

Exercise III.

Practice the same as Exercise II " hng-ah-nah " up and down the scale.

Exercise IV.

Practice up and down the scale with much lip action. " Mnome. "

Exercise V.

Practice with much lip action on three pitches, the voice medium, high and low— " Most men want poise and more royal margin. "

Exercise VI.

Say lightly on different scales and pitches, prolonging at the close " ah. " " 1, 2, 3, 4, 5, 6, ah. "

Exercise VII.

Practice saying and singing on different pitches, prolonging " o " and " EN " in " golden, golden, golden, golden."

OPEN THE MOUTH that the tone may come out. You may as well place the hand over the mouth in producing tone as to keep the mouth closed or the jaws near together. The tone so is muffled and shorn of carrying power.

A device for opening the mouth used by some teachers gives an idea of the position of the jaws for the leading vowels The ivory wedge to place between the teeth while making a tone is $2\frac{1}{4}$ inches long at the base, $1\frac{7}{8}$ inches at the long end and $\frac{1}{4}$ inch on the short end with 18 notches on the upper edge. With this wedge we may test ourselves and find what we are able to do, though we should not use it in voice drill as it would cause unnatural action of the muscles.

A pronounced as in the word father opens the jaws the widest, as measured by the ivory wedge, 10 to 14 notches.

o as in rose from 8 to 12 notches.

A as in pale from 4 to 6 notches.

oo as in coo, from 6 to 8 notches.

E as in see the least open

Order of exercise — A, O, A, OO, E   Sounds as above

A as in father is the vowel on which the voice should be most frequently exercised.

Practice also lists of words with the following vowels —

1. { o as in moan.
A as in ah.
oo as in moon.

2. { E as in breeze.
A as in day.
A as in that.

3. { U as in use.
I as in night.
U as in up.

4. { E as in end.
I as in it.
OY as in joy.

5. { OU & OW as in loud.
A as in and.
AR as in air.

The speech organs are passive in the vowels and active in the consonants.

THE TONGUE must be trained to lie flat in the mouth and not be allowed to take a whale-back shape in the back or middle of the mouth; rather the reverse shape. This is the unruly member, but it must not be allowed to rise up and obstruct the tone. While it is unruly, exercise with a mirror shows it too can be trained.

THE THROAT must be open and free. A stiff jaw puts a strain on the throat and closes it, giving hard tones and makes voice production tiresome and injurious to the throat, mangles the words, making them indistinct.

A complete list of exercises for each set of muscles separately might be given for opening the mouth, for lowering the tongue, for opening the throat, for relaxing the jaw, but all may be condensed into one simple exercise, thus saving time and producing better results.

Yawning relaxes all the muscles of the throat and jaw, relaxes and flattens the tongue and opens the mouth.

In practicing — draw in the breath, yawn, making the throat pear shaped. Now the muscles are in readiness for voice exercises.

Still another idea to secure relaxation, open throat and open mouth : try to think the lower jaw is useless in making tone. It is physical, so drop the jaw and tongue as if not needed, especially in song, the voice being produced above the larynx then resounding in the roof of the mouth.

THE LIPS must not be allowed to be drawn tightly over the teeth as they slightly prevent the unobstructed tone. Practice with a smile to lift the lip from the teeth. Let it be a smile from within and from the eyes; not altogether a " grin. " With a clear passage from the vocal cords, tone has the right of way and will grow in strength and beauty.

After once securing a clear understanding of the reasons of the foregoing Voice Exercises, all may be summed up in short gymnastics of the voice to be used in daily voice drill, requiring only a few minutes at each practice time.   Daily, systematic work, even though little time is given to it, will yield better results than irregular exercise. Repetition, repetition, repetition with thoughtful practice will transform the natural into the cultured, beautiful, responsive voice. Remember " the constant dropping wears the rock. "

In this brief space we have not exhausted the subject of voice exercise, but have given the fewest possible of the best and the most essential exercises for voice building.

ORDER OF DAILY VOICE DRILL.

I.   Panting.
II.   Breathing Exercise. (Exercise IV. with pipe.)
III.   Voice Exercise I — " knee. "
IV.   Voice Exercise II — " hng."
V.   Voice Exercise III — " hng-ah-nah. "
VI.   Voice Exercise IV — " mnome. "
VII.   Voice Exercise V — " most men want poise."
VIII.   Voice Exercise VI — " 1, 2, 3, 4, 5, 6, ah. "
IX.   Voice Exercise VII — " golden. "

Practice the above voice exercises with the relaxed, pear shaped throat as if ready to yawn.   Take the panting before each breathing and before each voice exercise.   Keep up the breathing exercises, the work for resonance, for the proper action of the jaw, tongue, lips, and throat.   Do not be discouraged because of the many things to be done. Take plenty of time to do this work well, giving the voice time enough to grow and become established.   It is to be your own for life.   It necessarily requires time to train these delicate, wonderful muscles of the voice to respond in a new way, naturally. We may be surprised to find how readily the muscles go back to the old way of producing tone, especially is this true when one is not in the best humor. The old muscles are so used to responding they spring into action before one is aware.

Much may be gained by silent practice, by thought, and by gently whispering and humming the voice exercises, using care to bring into play the proper muscles as when practicing aloud. The whispering and humming have the advantage of no strain on the throat. In the early part of this work do not use the voice in singing or speaking carelessly or loudly, but treat the voice organs while learning. to yield themselves to be awakened and trained as delicate creatures, newly born requiring gentle nurture in their infancy. It is best to leave the heavier exercises of the voice— especially the impure qualities found in some readings, till the voice has become well established. But should it be found necessary to do some of this heavy work, the voice may be saved much strain by putting the expression on to the body instead of the voice. To illustrate— In the quarrel scene between Cassius and Brutus in Shakespeare's " Julius Cæsar, " Cassius says,— " Urge me no more, I shall forget myself : have mind upon your health, tempt me no further. " In this threat the muscles of the body should be tense, the fists clenched in anger. This bodily action relieves the voice and is as if the expression were from life and natural ; but if in making this angry threat the muscles are relaxed and the strain of this assumed feeling comes on the voice this agent of expression would be overloaded and thereby injured. Should it be necessary to overload any part, let it be the large muscles of the body as in gesture rather than the most delicate muscles of all, the muscles of the voice. Let the action of the body lead. This helps to give natural expression to the voice.

We may wonder why we are hedged in with such caution as to the use of the voice but a child can kick and scream all day and come out with a voice uninjured for the next day. Let an adult try to imitate the child's cry and he has rasped the throat and made himself hoarse in five minutes. It would seem in this the child has superior skill to the man. But the child obeys natures laws and kicks and screams all over. The man screams only with his throat which is unnatural to put on the voice alone. The child's scream comes from his innermost, from the man it is a cry " put on, " so it instantly makes him hoarse.

Great care should be exercised in expressing the baser passions and emotions. No person should undertake to render selections of this character who has a throat trouble, only as the body is able to lead in the expression. •

The mechanical drill and gymnastics of the voice are of great value which may be increased by associating noble thought and feeling with the practice for voice building, but all artistic, magnetic effects come from the thought and feeling, expressions of the mind and soul. Let us think of the vibrations and resonance of the voice as the physical medium — the telegraph wire, if you please, over which travel the magnetic messages from the mind and soul.

Though the voice be the medium, important as it is, yet the messages to be sent out are far greater. The voice is the mystic hand with which we reach out from our minds and souls and touch the very minds and souls of those around us. If the spirit within be gentle and filled with the love of human welfare, then will the touch of this hand be most gracious and charming, blessing whatever it touches, and attracting by its magnetic sweetness. If, on the other hand, the life within be a den of wild beasts, then the touch of the voice will be as the sting of the serpent, the growl, the snarl that cause anxiety and fear.

Voice culture should begin with soul and mind culture and should end with mind and soul culture. The voice is like the perfume of a flower, subtle and mysterious in its influence, yet ever certain in effectiveness. A beautiful voice is more to be coveted than costly jewels, yet is within the reach of nearly every person who will appreciate its worth and cultivate the voice organs and develop the latent possibilities within. A good voice is often thought to be a gift. In reality, vocal cords, diaphragm and voice organs are gifts common to all. All own a musical instrument far superior to any mechanical instrument ever produced by mechanical skill, in the human voice. No one has a right to own a disagreeable voice, when a little study and drill will result in improvement to any one.

The student will note as he progresses that the more resonant the voice grows the less breath is used in making tone. Breath control helps to make the voice resonant. It will be found that breathing exercises aid the voice and voice exercises aid the breath. The progress of both may be tested by inhaling and counting aloud as far as possible.

Volume of voice: deep, rich tones should be cultivated. Chest resonance should be cultivated with resonance of the nares. Chest resonance may be felt by placing the hand on the chest and in lowest pitch repeat " awe, awe, awe. " Volume of voice comes from the mind side. Drill for this element of voice is found under Volume of Voice in the " Studies in Rendering. "

Scientific experiments reveal the fact that there are flowers of speech not only in a literary but in a real sense made by vibrations of the voice. The cultured voice vibrates in waves producing varied flowers and geometric shapes. The following illustrations are of the voice vibrations on a delicate film, given in the famous lecture " Harp of the Senses, " by John B. DeMotte, A. M. Ph. D.

GESTURE.

Gesture may be defined as muscular expression, also as visible expression. Gesture is the interpreter of the emotions; it is the language of the soul. Gesture appeals to the innermost soul of the beholder. Gesture is an elliptical language given to man to express what speech is powerless to say. There is something marvelous in the language of gesture. " A gesture, like a ray of light, can reflect all there is in the soul. " It has relations with another sphere. It is the world of grace. " Gesture is carving in the air. " Gesture is magnetic. Gesture is soul communicating with soul. It is even more than music, or any other form of expression, a universal language. Gesture is the ancestor of the word and goes before it to foretell its coming.

Of the three modes of manifesting thought.— word, voice, gesture — gesture stands the highest. It is the language of our highest nature. It makes appeal to the highest by way of the finest of the senses, the eye. Some may not at first see the way clear to accept the statement concerning the rank of gesture as compared with voice and the spoken word but study will convince one of the importance of this subtle language. Culture of the muscles and how to speak through them require special study and exercise, for skill can no more be attained, without effort, than skill of a pianist can be acquired through the study of mere theory. In this, one becomes by doing. The gesture language is not so much with many a " dead language " as a dormant language.

" The body needs educating as well as the mind. " A person without this physical education, even though he may have the mental, should not presume to set himself up as an authority being guided by his own blind fancy, a case of

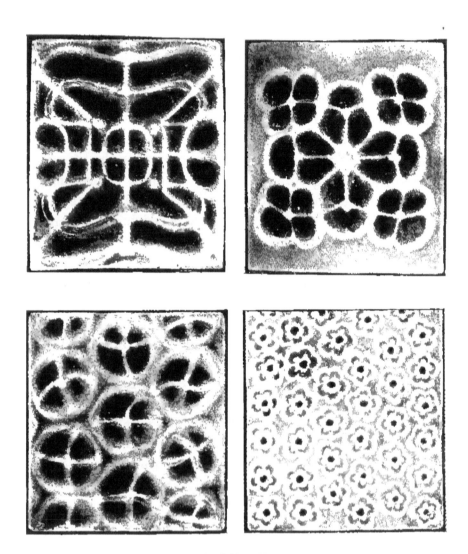

Impressions made by VIBRATIONS OF VOICE on a
delicate film

Photographed from experiments with the voice in the laboratory of
of Prof. John B. DeMotte, A. M., M. D., Ph. D. and reproduced here by
his permission.

the blind leading the blind, an invasion not to be tolerated in any other department of study. A thorough knowledge of this muscular language requires careful investigation as that of anatomy by the student of medicine before he can secure his M. D. The medical student must dissect and examine the muscles themselves, while the student of expression must study the action of the muscles under the influence of endless emotions playing upon them. He also must study this subject in a twofold manner — as self expression and as the impression the gesture makes on the listener or beholder.

Gesture is important in that it reveals the noble emotions of the soul. As we manifest our noble emotions through the muscles we also cultivate and refine the feelings while we cultivate the muscles. Gesture makes its appeal to the highest of the five senses, the eye. That which offends the eye cannot be tolerated. But what charms the eye will allow other defects to pass. " If the gesture is good, the most wretched speaker is tolerated. "

By gesture we do not mean gesticulating with some part of the body — the hand and arm, for instance, with the rest of the body dead still. Such action is a spasm rather than gesture.

One definition of the word muscle is " a little mouse." The ancients compared the action of the muscles to mice under the skin. We may use this ancient idea to illustrate a principle of value in gesture. Suppose one mouse became frightened and bristled with fear; we can readily see what the result would be should there be more than two hundred of them instead of one expressing the same thing. Should there be a single one in the number that kept itself inactive while all the others were wild with action, we could but think it stupid or asleep or dead. With the person whose muscles have not been awakened it happens that the two hundred or more are asleep with one awake and active to respond to the feeling. This is an imperfect expression. We may sum up the whole matter into a Law —

The highest expression results when the greatest number of muscles unite in harmonious action.

There would be a decided lack of harmony, if some of the muscles were inactive, others stiffened with chronic pride or anxiety. Any effort to secure a harmony of action has its reward in feelings of poise and self possession.

We may simplify this complicated study of gesture by dividing it up under headings — *the culture of the muscles — a knowledge of Expression.* A knowledge of expression would include self expression and the ability to interpret in others. We should also be able to know something of the kind of impression an expression is likely to make or does make on the listener or beholder. The first named, the culture of the muscles is treated under the chapter on Physical Culture. The second, the study of Expression has an almost limitless field. We may say, wherever we find life we find some kind of expression worthy of our attention; and all the Arts, especially music, painting and sculpture. Of great importance is the study of human expression from life on the streets, in public or private, anywhere. Children, animals and even birds offer a rich field. It is well to keep a note book for this purpose also a scrap book for reproductions of paintings and artistic pictures and photographs from life. Studies of statuary and works of the masters help one to form correct ideals; then with a free body, natural expression should result, after the laws of expression and the ideals are established in the subjective mind. A careful study of laws of expression can not be over estimated. We should so prize the truth as to be willing to accept it though it may not be of some favorite system. Delsarte's Nine Laws of Gesture contain much from a Philosophy of great value in all the fine arts. In substance they are as follows.

LAW OF MOTION.

Motion is force expending itself. Gesture is the muscular action by which the soul expresses itself.

There are three kinds of motion:—

 Eccentric or from the center.

 Concentric or toward the center.

 Poised or balanced.

All thought or feeling is either of self or something outside of self or a blending together of the two.

Thought about any thing outside of self requires eccentric motion.

Thought about self requires concentric motion.

Thought about self and something outside of self at the same time requires poised motion.

Eccentric motion is in harmony with the physical side of the being. It has to do with objective thought.

Concentric motion is subjective and has to do with concentric, mental states.

Poised motion is expressive of exalted moods and noble emotions.

 Examples of Eccentric Motion,—

Ye eagles, playmates of the mountain storm !
Ye lightnings, the dread arrows of the clouds !
Ye signs and wonders of the elements !
Utter forth God and fill the hills with praise.

        Coleridge.

" The battle, the battle !   How goes the battle ? "

" Be it said in letters both bold and bright :
        Here is the steed that saved the day
By carrying Sheridan into the fight
        From Winchester — twenty miles away. "

Examples of Concentric Motion.

" The tender tune, faint floating, plays,
In moonlit lays, a melody of other days. "

            " O Hamlet speak no more :
Thou turn'st mine eyes into my very soul :
And there I see such black and grained spots
As will not leave their tinct. "

Examples of Poised Motion.

" My heart is awed within me, when I think
Of the great miracle that still goes on
In silence round me,— the perpetual work
Of thy creation, finished yet renewed forever. "

" My lord, if you ask me, if in my life-time
I thought any treason, or did any crime
That should call to my cheek, as I stand alone here,
The hot blush of shame or the coldness of fear,
Though I stood by the grave to receive my death-blow,
Before God and the world I would answer you, no ! "

    " My bounty is as boundless as the sea,
My love as deep ; the more I give to thee,
The more I have, for both are infinite. "

Passion tends to expansion.   Thought tends to contraction.   Love or affection moderates gesture.

LAW OF VELOCITY.

Velocity is in proportion to the mass moved and the force moving it. Sublime sentiment with profound appreciation moves slowly. Light feeling moves rapidly.

Examples of Slow Movement,—

And slowly, slowly, more and more,
The moony vapor rolling around the king,
Who seem'd the phantom of a giant in it,
Enwound him fold by fold, and made him grey
And greyer, till himself became as mist
Before her, moving ghost-like to his doom.

Tennyson.

" It must be by his death and for my part,
I know no personal cause to spurn at him,
But for the general. He would be crown'd.
. . . . What he is, augmented,
Would run to these and these extremities:
And therefore, think him as a serpent's egg which,
Hatched, would, as his kind, grow mischievous,
And kill him in the shell. "

" The heavens declare the glory of God; and the firmament showeth his handywork. Day unto day uttereth speech, and night unto night showeth knowledge. There is no speech nor language where their voice is not heard. "

The above lines read by a careless schoolboy would move more rapidly than if rendered by one who could comprehend and appreciate the full value of the thought. Whatever the sentiment the above law holds good. In speech large bodies move slowly. Superficial sentiment moves lightly as in the following examples.

Examples of Rapid Movement.

" Fill again to the brim! again to the brim!
For water strengtheneth life and limb!
To the days of the aged it addeth length,
To the might of the strong it addeth strength;
It freshens the heart, it brightens the sight,
' Tis like quaffing a goblet of morning light! "

" Oh, the buxom girls that help the boys,
    The nobler Helens of the humbler Troys
As they strip the husk with rustling fold
    From eight rowed corn as yellow as gold,
By the candle-light, in pumpkin bowls,
    And the gleams that showed fantastic holes
In the quaint old lantern's tattooed tin,
    From the hermit glim set up within;
By the rarer light in girlish eyes
    As dark as wells, or as blue as skies. "

LAW OF DIRECTION.

The lengths are vital. The heights and depths are mental. The breadths are emotive. Concentration tends toward our selfish states, while giving out and going out of self corresponds to our benevolent states.

Example of Vital Action in Lengths.

    Lie still, lie still! till I lean o'er
And clutch your red blade to the shore.
Ha, ha! Take that, and that, and that!
Ha! ha! So through your coward throat
The full day shines!   *Jaquin Miller.*

Down Eros! Up Mars! *Chariot Race.* " Ben-Hur. " *Wallace.*

In meditation and other thoughtful moods the eyes seek the blue — either the height of the blue sky or the depth of the blue water.

Examples of Mental Action in Heights and Depths,—

When I consider Thy heavens, the work of Thy fingers, the moon and the stars, which thou hast ordained; what is man that Thou art mindful of him? and the son of man that Thou visitest him?
Contemplation.   *Psalms VIII.*

> " Ah, once more, " I cried, " ye stars, ye waters,
> On my heart your mighty charm renew;
> Still, still let me as I gaze upon you,
> Feel my soul becoming vast like you! "

" *Self-Dependence.* "   *Matthew Arnold.*

Examples of Benevolent Action in Breadths,—

" These glorious truths shall be diffused throughout the whole earth. "

" The Lord doth build up Jerusalem: He gathereth together the outcasts of Israel. He healeth the broken in heart, and bindeth up their wounds. "

LAW OF REACTION.

Action and reaction are equal. Extreme emotion tends to react to its opposite. Elasticity, spring and a tendency to rebound are marks of life.

Examples of reaction are found in expressions of admiration: a painter admiring his work would react away from it. In anger there is a recoil before the blow. In milder emotions action and reaction are equal.

LAW OF FORM.

Forms bounded by straight lines are vital in their significance.

Forms bounded by curved lines are mental and reflective.

This subject will be found treated further under the heading—"Significance of Lines," in "Science of Speech," page 42.

Examples of Vital Action in Straight Lines,—

" Charge for the golden lilies, upon them with the lance. "

" Then clasp me round the neck once more, and give
me one more kiss;
And now, my own dear little girl, there is no way but
this. "
With that, he lifted high the steel, and smote her in
the side,
And in her blood she sank to earth, and with one groan
she died.

" *The Fate of Virginia.* "   *T. B. Macaulay.*

Mental gestures may trace out all the lines of geometry,— circles, illustrate shapes, measure, indicate lines. The mystic is suggested in the motion of smoke.

" And my prayer like a perfume from censers
Ascendeth to God night and day. "

" And the glory of the Lord abode upon mount Sinai, and the cloud covered it six days. . . . And the sight of the glory of the Lord was like a devouring fire on the top of the mount in the eyes of the children of Israel. "

" And Aaron shall burn thereon sweet incense every morning when he dresseth the lamps. "   *Exodus*, 24, 30.

LAW OF OPPOSITION.

" *In opposition of the agents of expression is the harmony of gesture. Harmony is born of contrasts. From opposition, equilibrium is born in turn. Equilibrium is the great law of gesture and condemns parallelism.* " *In so far as we observe this law may we have grace of motion. Opposition is the balance of parts around the center of gravity. In gesture the chest should be the center of balance. The greater the number of agents of expression acting in harmonious opposition the higher the form of expression.*

Study poise in ideal figures in paintings and statuary, observing oppositions of head and hand,— of all parts of of the body.

LAW OF SEQUENCE.

Impression precedes expression. We must have before we can give, and give in the order of having. The eye is the central agent of expression. The eye leads in expression, next the face, head, hands, then the rest of the body, the word last.

If the expression be vital it is expressed in shorter time than if emotive.

Vital springs into action quickly.

Mental takes time to consider.

The emotive is influenced by both mental and vital. It is second to the vital in point of time.

The gestures of the face should make those of the arm forgotten.

NUMBER OF GESTURES.

Gestures should not be too numerous. We are moved by only one sentiment at a time ; it is useless to multiply gestures. But one gesture is needed for the expression of an entire thought. The gesture is not to express the word, but the thought. As much expression as is possible should be given to the face.

LAW OF FORCE.

Weakness takes a strong attitude and strength takes a weak attitude. This law applies to the mental and to the moral life as well as to the physical life.

RHYTHM.

Rhythm is the measure of time or motion in regularly recurring impulses or accents, as in poetry and music. In gesture it is the inflection with the unfolding of the parts of the body as the action passes over it from joint to joint. Rhythm of gesture is subjective and objetive.

Objective rhythm is expressive of the vital nature.

Examples of Objective Rhythm may be found in various expressions,— it delights in beating time with a sharp accent, as in ragtime music. As to gesture, the accent is eccentric, outward.   The stroke is as in the old calisthenics, and as in certain gestures known as "sledge hammer " and " pump handle " gestures and gestures often used to "pound " the Word, rather than to expound it.   Children and savages and natures where the vital is in the ascendency delight in this outward stroke or Objective Rhythm.

Subjective Rhythm is a manifestation of the mental and emotive natures. It expresses itself in subtle pulsations from the center with a return to the center. Pulsations of motion correspond to pulsations of emotion. Subjective Rhythm delights in the artistic — literature, music, heavy and light, making rhythmic inflections.

Subjective Rhythm may be likened to a person who when expressing a thought is mindful of its impression on the listener. The thought sent out returns to its source but is colored in the mind of the speaker with the impression it has made. Objective Rhythm is like the person who speaks hit or miss, unmoved as to the impression it makes. One thing is sent out, nothing returns. It is like the child who delights himself pounding with a stick, even to the distraction of sensitive nerves, is unmoved and satisfied so long as he may give vent to his animal spirits.

Applied to gesture, Subjective Rhythm starts from the center with impulses in turn from each of the bodily agents of expression in natural sequence. For example : the bow begins with a look from the eye. The start in giving the feeling of respect is sent out from the lower chest as a center, passes to the head, the hands, the feet ; then the body returns to position with the chest lifting or leading back to the erect position.

DIRECTION OF GESTURE.

It has been said that man stands on one globe and bears another on his shoulders. We may say he lives within a globe limited by his reach from the soles of his feet to the arm's reach overhead and to the tips of the fingers with the arms reaching horizontally. Our gestures are made to correspond with this globe in which we live.

This globe of which we are the center may be divided into three general divisions,— the Zone of the Superior, the Zone of the Inferior, the Zone of Equality.

The Zone of the Superior is the region of the Beautiful, the Good, the True, Faith, Hope, Love, Heaven, the dwelling place of God, the Positive Pole.

The Zone of the Inferior is the region of the Bad, the False, the Ugly, the Uncertain, the Occult, the Evil, Fear, Unbelief, Hate, the abode of the Evil One, the Negative Pole.

The Zone of Equality is the region of Here, Now, the Real, Zone of the Senses, Material Things, Our Fellows on our own plane.

Zone of Superior corresponds to Ascending,— Zone of the Inferior to Descending,— Zone of Equality to the Horizontal in Law XCIII, page 144 " Science of Speech."

FINESSE OF GESTURE.

Suggestions of a subtle and delicate character often make a strong appeal, especially is this true of that which appeals to any of the five senses.

The fingers may indicate different kinds of surface as hard like marble, delicate as velvet, the feel of granulated or powdered substance, temperature, hot and cold. Each of the five senses may play an important part in gesture.

Touch can suggest heat, cold, hardness, softness, roughness, smoothness, figure, solidity, motion, extension, agreeable, gentle heat, stroke of a soft body — fur, a zephyr.

Smell may suggest the odor of flowers, perfumes, etc. In offensive odors an effort is made to close the nostrils, to hold the nose, to snuff the offensive odor out of the nostrils. The unpleasant odor is rejected, scorned. In the impolite " turning up the nose " is an effort to close the nose.

Taste has a part to play in expression. Bitter taste affects the back part of the tongue; sour affects the front or near the middle; sweet the tip of the tongue ; salt the extreme tip of the tongue. Figurative language that refers to the taste is expressed as tasting of the literal things themselves. We speak of " bitter experiences, " " sour words," " sweet child. " We " smack the lips " and the " mouth waters, " some things " set the teeth on edge. " We puff out of the mouth that which is distasteful. Pooh ! Pshaw !

Hearing is an exalted sense. Various sounds in life, in nature may be suggested, pleasant and unpleasant. The impression of the imaginary sounds demands a response as well as what the eye sees. The eye and the ear are the leading avenues of impression, and enter largely into all gesture. The eye is the central agent of expression.

BEARINGS, ATTITUDES, INFLECTIONS.

The bearing is the air, the mien, behavior, deportment, the habitual carriage of the body.

Attitude is an arrest of motion. A gesture held for a moment is an attitude.

Inflections are little gestures, movements of the head, the brows, the mouth, expressions of the hands, and fingers.

The public speaker, the singer the musician may awaken his own feelings and cultivate the emotions by throwing the body strongly into the attitude necessary to portray the desired emotion which is not always ready to respond. Repeat over and over. You may overdo in practice and work up a background of fervor, then the public performance may be with few gestures. Acquire a broad knowledge of Laws of Expression and well trained responsive body.

DUAL FORM OF STUDY OF EXPRESSION.

Scientific. Artistic.   Theory. Practice.

We may avoid confusion in the study of this many sided subject, and bring harmony out of what would otherwise be confusion by dividing the whole subject into the Scientific and the Artistic.

By the Scientific we mean a knowledge of the Laws of Expression,— Voice, Gesture, Articulation, Analysis etc., training of the body through Physical Culture, the Voice by means of the Breathing exercises and Vocal Gymnastics.

By the Artistic side we mean a free, spontaneous, unconscious use of all this culture of body mind and voice, so that without apparent effort the material acquired in the Scientific part of the study may be used easily and naturally, under the direction of the thought and feeling.

We may illustrate the process by comparing it with the construction of a work of architecture. There must be a time of planning,— designing, shaping, selecting the great variety of material to be used in its construction. Then comes a time when this material is fitted to the place it is to occupy. After much labor of varied kinds, patient thinking and doing, with helps from many sources, part is fitted to part and we have a completed whole, yet a work that may be made more and more attractive during a lifetime.

Another illustration of the twofold form of the study,— thought and plans for a gown to be worn on some grand occasion. There must be a time to think about the material of which it is to be made, selecting that best suited in texture and color to the wearer, the style, the making and a number of perplexing things must be thought and done in the private side before it is completed. When the time comes for the gown to be worn is quite a different thing. If the gown is worn gracefully, it must be forgotten, lest, it be even like Dickens' Squeers who " appeared ill at ease in his clothes. " We must divide our work into two distinct parts lest we appear to be fitting the gown while we are wearing it and seem self-conscious and affected, a common fault.

There must be one time for getting and another time for giving.

In Rendering or Speaking in Public, aim to reach the voice and all the bodily agents of expression wholly through the mind and feelings. The body and voice should be so trained that the whole being will naturally and agreeably respond to thought and feeling. This is a reliable method because it is founded on Psychological Laws. To educate is to draw out,— when Rendering is so studied as to draw out the powers of the mind and soul, natural expression will result. First find out how, then do. In doing one may become. You can never learn to swim without getting into the water. Be content with your best. Your best to-morrow will be better than your best yesterday because you lived yesterday and were content to do your best, however poor the best may be, for herein is growth. So may you ever be content to say " my best is good enough for me. "

Too much emphasis can hardly be given to the Mental Method which has for its foundation principle,— *strength at the center gives freedom at the surface.*

As so much of value is bound up in the above brief principle, lest we miss some of its deeper meaning, let us consider just what is meant by the " center. "

Without using any confusing terms we would say simply,— the center is all that lives in the body of mind and spirit, in our triangular outline called Mental and Emotive.

MENTAL TRAINING.

The mind should be so trained as to comprehend the thought and to concentrate upon it as to appropriate it to self and make it as an actual experience, a living reality. Read thoughts, not words, for " the letter killeth, but the spirit maketh alive. "

TRAINING OF THE FIVE SENSES.

The five senses should receive special culture, as they are but poorly developed in the best of us.

THE SENSE OF TOUCH may be trained,— the pupil blind-folded, train the sense of touch to distinguish fifty or more different kinds of objects, different kinds of cloth, leaves, flowers, etc.

TASTE. The pupil blindfolded, experiment with different objects, with the shape of the article destroyed. One test should not follow too quickly after another.

SMELL. The pupil blindfolded,— fifty or more objects, many common objects,— oils, perfumes, flowers.

HEARING. Listen for sounds in nature. Distinguish between the different kinds of birds, fowls, animals; different kinds of musical instruments as organ, violin, flute, etc.; various noises made by the wind, various keys of song or of instrumental selections.

SIGHT. Observe carefully as to size, shape, color,— recall objects as vividly as when before the eyes, then note whether or not it is a true image of the object.

Above are given but hints for training the five senses. From them the pupil should be able to devise many tests to practice to awaken and quicken the neglected senses.

" Our senses as our reason are divine. " The power of
the fine arts over the human sensibilities can never be estimated. The manifestations through the senses make a
deep appeal, and in an artistic sense. Pleasant odors minister to social luxury and refinement. They arouse religious
feelings and devotion and serve as tributes of affection.

" I thought of the dress she wore last time,
   When we stood 'neath the cypress-trees together,
In that lost land, in that soft clime,
   In the crimson evening weather.

Of that muslin dress (for the eve was hot),
   And her warm white neck in its golden chain,
And her full, soft hair, just tied in a knot,
   And falling loose again ;

And the jasmine flower in her fair young breast ;
   (Oh the faint, sweet smell of that jasmine flower l)
And the one bird singing alone in his nest ;
   And the one star over the tower. "

    " Bring flowers, flowers for the joyous,
      And flowers for the sad,
   Flowers for the bridal wreath
      And flowers for the early dead. "

The office of taste is utility, so real taste comes only after hunger is satisfied. The ends sought by appeal to this
sense are individual gratification, social culture, and religious refinement.

By touch we perceive heat, cold, hard, soft, roughness,
smoothness, figure, solidity, motion and extension.

Sight and hearing are too large and important subjects
to consider here. Touch, taste and smell are subjects over-
looked in the study of expression.

TRAINING THE EMOTIVE.

Shakespeare tells us that " it is the mind that makes the body rich. " While this is true, our greatest wealth lies deeper than the mind. It is more precious than the mind.

Let us, because of the lack of any all-inclusive term, call this the Emotive Nature. In a multitude of bewildering ideas, without regard to creed or sect, let us meet upon a common ground and call that which wills and feels by a name in order to simplify our study all possible. Let us think of this emotive nature as something just as we think of the brain as something— only this nature is more plastic and impressionable. Think of this pulsating being within our bodies impressed and moved by all that is taking place around us, subject to fear, hate, love and hundreds of emotions. We find some of these emotions are helpful, others are injurious. We have it within our power to choose, to a certain extent, which of these two shall dominate us, even as we may select studies to train the mind.

The greatest feelings— the most powerful and the farthest reaching are love and hate. We find many feelings are subordinate to or modifications of these two leading feelings. Love is life. It quickens the circulation and places the whole being : physical, mental and emotive in the most favorable condition, like a healthy plant growing in the sunlight. Hate is death — it not only retards the circulation, but throws poison into the blood, stunts and deforms, chills the very sap of life ; a poisonous weed growing rank, in the dark.

Let us consider the effect of these two leading feelings on expression. Love and its modifications known as magnanimity, sympathy, reverence, respect and appreciation and kindred emotions cause a relaxation of the muscles, ease and grace of movement, beautiful tones in the voice, all that is delightful and fascinating, more effective and charming than anything money can buy or study can attain. But hate tensions the muscles, makes the movements abrupt and angular, imparts harsh and disagreeable tones and ugly inflections. The whole expression is so repellent that the much coveted graces of expression are utterly out of reach. Some of us may be unwilling to believe that this negative element colors and clouds our emotive nature but as we value our success, let us take some fair and honest test examinations of ourselves. Though we may not be afflicted with the most hideous form of this malady yet some germs or mild forms of it may exist and prevent the true, normal action of the emotive even as the mental is not able to calculate correctly with the multiplication table incorrectly learned. " Orient thyself, "that your shadow may not fall before you.

How we feel — the condition of the affectional nature is of greater importance than what we eat or what we think, though the three are intimately related. How we feel modifies the whole being.

The highest and most desirable condition for any person where he may receive the best and be the best is when he places himself in the most perfect submission to the Infinite. There is self-aggrandizement in obedience to the greatest commandment,— "Thou shalt love the Lord thy God with all thy soul, with all thy mind and with all thy strength, and thy neighbor as thyself."
When we do even a little of this we may lay up treasures on earth in our own body, mind and spirit and " treasures in heaven " as well. When we have mastered this central lesson, we are ready to respond in body, mind and spirit.

"From abundance of life comes sweetness. " The most abundant life in the Physical comes by the breath and red blood ; the Mental, concentration of thought; the Emotive or spiritual, obedience to the Infinite.

STUDIES FOR PRACTICE

FIRST STEP IN RENDERING.
ANIMATION.

As we enter upon this first step in Rendering we begin to climb stairs. Such should be our whole life's activity physically, mentally, morally, spiritually. We must start climbing from the bottom of the stairs, in nature's own appointed way as at the base of our triangle, with physical, vital life. Animation may be defined as physical life, red blood, energy, spring, bound, hearty. No amount of study can atone for a lack of soul fervor and natural, living spontaneity. You may overdo in animation : swing the pendulum too far and it will return to its center of gravity. Feel a necessity for utterance of deep, intense thought. Do not think how HE would say it but think IT intensely and YOU will say it. Use bold outlines. Do bold sketching. Do not be bound in.

Aim to awaken and animate the three sides of the being,— Physical, Mental, Emotive.

Physical animation comes from dynamic breathing and red blood.

Mental animation comes from imagination and concentration of thought.

Emotive animation comes from obedience.

It is a well-known fact that many who have never giv_en any study to Elocution or Oratory have sometimes taken the laurels from students who have given most careful study to these subjects. On this account it would seem to those who fail to look deep enough that only those who have natural talent may hope to succeed. In reality, this natural ability that wins such favor in the market place is largely from a free, fearless, spontaneous expression from a soul alive and animated, responding directly and simply to that which impresses it. On the other hand the student of Expression may be so burdened with rules he has hardly mastered and a vain attempt to put them into practice that the avenues of expression are overloaded with no room for the matter to be rendered, so we have artificial, unnatural expression as a result. As Animation clothes the amateur performer in garments of praise it can do even more for the student of Expression who works long enough on this first step in rendering — Animation.

The starting point in the study of a selection should be made with a pencil. Make a careful analysis, finding the unity as directed in a previous chapter. After a careful analysis has been made strike out free from all restraint. Dare to speak up and speak out. Be true to your own convictions and interpretations. Render it heartily and as if it is the most important thing in the world.

Much freedom may be gained by impersonating some vital character where one need not be particular save to give it with animation. Acting a part in a simple school play has loosened the fetters on many a tongue.

A child learning to walk must be content to use the ability he already has. Should he observe his elders moving with ease and refuse to go only in the same way, he would limit himself for life, but he moves any way, impelled from the life within and so grows. Study the following selections.

THE CHEERFUL LOCKSMITH.

From the workshop of the Golden Key there issued forth a tinkling sound, so merry and good-humored that it suggested the idea of some one working blithely, and made quite pleasant music. Tink, tink, tink — clear as a silver bell, and audible at every pause of the street's harsher noises, as though it said, " I don't care; nothing puts me out; I am resolved to be happy. "

Women scolded, children squalled, heavy carts went rumbling by, horrible cries proceeded from the lungs of hawkers; still it struck in again, no higher, no lower, no louder, no softer; not thrusting itself on the people's notice a bit the more for having been outdone by louder sounds,— tink, tink, tink, tink, tink.

It was a perfect embodiment of the still, small voice, free from all cold, hoarseness, huskiness, or unhealthiness of any kind. Foot-passengers slackened their pace, and were disposed to linger near it; neighbors who had got up splenetic that morning felt good-humor stealing on them as they heard it, and by degrees became quite sprightly; mothers danced their babies to its ringing ;— still the same magical tink, tink, tink, came gayly from the workshop of the Golden Key.

Who but the locksmith could have made such music? A gleam of sun shining through the unsashed window and checkering the dark workshop with a broad patch of light, fell full upon him, as though attracted by his sunny heart. There he stood working at his anvil, his face radiant with exercise and gladness, his sleeves turned up, his wig pushed off his shining forehead— the easiest, freest, happiest man in all the world.

Beside him sat a sleek cat, purring and winking in the light, and falling every now and then into an idle doze, as

from excess of comfort. The very locks that hung around
had something jovial in their rust, and seemed like gouty
gentlemen of hearty natures, disposed to joke on their infirmities.

There was nothing surly or severe in the whole scene.
It seemed impossible that any of the innumerable keys
could fit a churlish strong-box, or a prison-door. Store-
houses of good things, rooms where there were fires, books,
gossip, and cheering laughter— these were their proper
sphere of action. Places of distrust, and cruelty and restraint, they would have quadruple-locked forever.

Tink, tink, tink. No man who hammered on at a dull,
monotonous duty could have brought such cheerful notes
from steel and iron: none but a chirping, healthy, honest-
hearted fellow, who made the best of everything and felt
kindly towards everybody, could have done it for an instant. He might have been a coppersmith and still been
musical. If he had sat in a jolting wagon, full of rods of
iron, it seemed as if he would have brought some harmony out of it.

CHARLES DICKENS.

NEBUCHADNEZZAR'S DREAM.

In the second year of the reign of Nebuchadnezzar, Nebuchadnezzar dreamed dreams, wherewith his spirit was troubled, and his sleep brake from him. Then the king commanded to call the magicians, and the astrologers and the
sorcerers, and the Chaldeans, for to show the king his
dreams. So they came and stood before the king. And
the king said unto them, " I have dreamed a dream, and
my spirit was troubled to know the dream. " Then spake
the Chaldeans to the king in Syriack, " O king, live forever! tell thy servants the dream, and we will shew the

interpretation." The king answered and said to the Chaldeans, " The thing is gone from me : if ye will not make
known unto me the dream, with the interpretation thereof, ye shall be cut in pieces, and your houses shall be made
a dunghill. But if ye show the dream, and the interpretation thereof, ye shall receive of me gifts and rewards and
great honor : therefore show me the dream, and the interpretation thereof. "

They answered again and said, " Let the king tell his servants the dream, and we will show the interpretation of it. "

The king answered and said, " I know of a certainty
that ye would gain the time, because ye see the thing is gone
from me. But if ye will not make known unto me the
dream, there is but one decree for you : for ye have prepared
lying and corrupt words to speak before me, till the time
be changed : therefore tell me the dream, and I shall know
that ye can show me the interpretation thereof. "

The Chaldeans answered before the king and said, " There
is not a man upon the earth that can show the king's matter :
therefore there is no king, lord, nor ruler, that asked such
things at any magician, or astrologer, or Chaldean. And
it is a rare thing that the king requireth, and there is none
other that can show it before the king, except the gods,
whose dwelling is not with flesh. "

For this cause the king was angry and very furious, and
commanded to destroy all the wise men of Babylon. And
the decree went forth that the wise men should be slain ;
and they sought Daniel and his fellows to be slain.
Then Daniel answered with counsel and wisdom to Arioch
the captain of the king's guard, which was gone forth to
slay the wise men of Babylon : he answered and said to
Arioch the king's captain, " Why is the decree so hasty
from the king ? " Then Arioch made the thing known
to Daniel. Then Daniel went in, and desired of the king

that he would give him time, and that he would show the king the interpretation.

Then Daniel went to his house, and made the thing known to Hananiah, Mishael, and Azariah, his companions; that they would desire mercies of the God of heaven concerning this secret; that Daniel and his fellows should not perish with the rest of the wise men of Babylon.

Then was the secret revealed unto Daniel in a night vision. Then Daniel blessed the God of heaven. Daniel answered and said, " Blessed be the name of God forever and ever; for wisdom and might are his, and he changeth the times and seasons; he removeth kings, and setteth up kings; he giveth wisdom unto the wise, and knowledge to them that know understanding; he revealeth the deep and secret things; he knoweth what is in the darkness, and the light dwelleth with him. I thank thee, and praise thee, O thou God of my fathers, who hast given me wisdom and might, and hast made known unto me now what we desired of thee; for thou hast now made known unto us the king's matter. "

Therefore Daniel went in unto Arioch, whom the king had ordained to destroy the wise men of Babylon: he went and said thus unto him. "Destroy not the wise men of Babylon; bring me in before the king, and I will show unto the king the interpretation. "

Then Arioch brought in Daniel before the king in haste, and said thus unto him, " I have found a man of the captives of Judah, that will make known unto the king the interpretation."

The king answered and said to Daniel, whose name was Belteshazzar, " Art thou able to make known unto me the dream which I have seen, and the interpretation thereof? '

Daniel answered in the presence of the king, and said, "The secret which the king hath demanded cannot the wise men, the astrologers, the magicians, the soothsayers, show unto the king; but there is a God in heaven that revealeth secrets, and maketh known to the king Nebuchadnezzar what shall be in the latter days. Thy dream and the visions of thy head upon thy bed, are these;— As for thee, O king, thy thoughts came into thy mind upon thy bed, what should come to pass hereafter: and he that revealeth secrets maketh known to thee what shall come to pass. But as for me, this secret is not revealed to me for any wisdom that I have more than any living, but for their sakes that shall make known the interpretation to the king and that thou mightest know the thoughts of thy heart.

Thou, O king, sawest, and behold a great image. This great image whose brightness was excellent, stood before thee; and the form thereof was terrible.

This image's head was of fine gold, his breast and his arms of silver, his belly and his thighs of brass, his legs of iron, his feet part of iron and part of clay.

Thou sawest till that *a stone* was cut out without hands which smote the image upon his feet that were of iron and of clay, and brake them to pieces. Then was the iron, the clay, the brass, the silver, the gold, broken to pieces together, and became like the chaff of the summer threshing floors; and the wind carried them away, that no place was found for them: and *the stone that smote the image became a great mountain and filled the whole earth.* This is the dream; and we will tell the interpretation thereof before the king.

Thou, O king, art a king of kings; for the God of heaven hath given thee a kingdom, power, and strength, and glory. And wheresoever the children of men dwell, the beasts of the field and the fowls of the heaven hath he given into thine hand, and hath made thee ruler over them all. Thou art this head of gold. And after thee shall arise another kingdom inferior to thee; and another third kingdom of brass, which shall bear rule over all the earth. And the fourth kingdom shall be as strong as iron : forasmuch as iron breaketh in pieces and subdueth all things : and as iron that breaketh all these, shall it break in pieces and bruise. And whereas thou sawest the feet and toes, part of potters' clay, and part of iron, the kingdom shall be divided ; but there shall be in it of the strength of the iron, forasmuch as thou sawest the iron mixed with miry clay. And as the toes of the feet were part of iron, and part of clay, so the kingdom shall be partly strong, and partly broken. And whereas thou sawest iron mixed with miry clay, they shall mingle themselves with the seed of men : but they shall not cleave one to another, even as iron is not mixed with clay.

And in the days of these kings shall the God of heaven set up a kingdom, which shall never be destroyed : and the kingdom shall not be left to other people, but it shall break in pieces and consume all these kingdoms, and it shall stand forever.

Forasmuch as thou sawest that the stone was cut out of the mountain without hands, and that it brake in pieces the iron, the brass, the clay, the silver, and the gold ; the great God hath made known to the king what shall come to pass hereafter : and the dream is certain, and the interpretation thereof sure. "

Then the king Nebuchadnezzar fell upon his face, and worshipped Daniel, and commanded that they should offer an oblation and sweet odors unto him. The king answered unto Daniel and said, " Of a truth it is, that your God is a God of gods, and a Lord of kings, and a revealer of secrets, seeing thou couldest reveal this secret. " Theu the king made Daniel a great man, and gave him many great gifts, and made him ruler over the whole province of Babylon.   *Daniel 11.*

A RILL FROM THE TOWN-PUMP.

I hold high office in the town, being guardian of the best treasure it has; and I exhibit, moreover, an admirable example to the other officials, by the cool and downright discharge of my business, and the constancy with which I stand to my post. Summer or winter, nobody seeks me in vain; for all day long I am seen at the busiest corner, just above the market, stretching out my arms to rich and poor.

At this sultry noontide, I am cupbearer to the parched populace, for whose benefit an iron goblet is chained to my waist. To all and sundry I cry aloud, at the very top of my voice: "Here it is, gentlemen! here is the good liquor! here is the unadulterated ale of Father Adam! better than brandy, wine or beer; here it is, and not a cent to pay. Walk up, walk up gentlemen, and help yourselves!"

It were a pity if all this outcry should draw no customers. Here they come. "A hot day, gentlemen! Quaff and away again, so as to keep yourselves in a nice cool sweat. You, my friend! will need another cupful to wash the dust out of your throat, if it be as thick there as it is on your cowhide shoes. I see that you have trudged half a score of miles to-day, and, like a wise man have passed by the taverns and stopped at the running brooks and bubbling springs. Drink, and make room for that other fellow who seeks my aid to quench the fever of last night's potations, which he drained from no cup of mine.

Welcome, most rubicund sir! You and I have been great strangers hitherto! But mercy on you, man! The water absolutely hisses down your red-hot gullet. Fill again, and tell me, on the word of an honest toper, did you ever, in tavern or dramshop, spend the price of your children's food for a swig half so delicious!

Who next? O my little friend! you are just let loose from school, and are come here to scrub your blooming face, and drown the memory of certain taps of the rod, by a draught from the Town-Pump. Take it, pure as the current of your young life ; take it, and may your heart and tongue never be scorched with a fiercer thirst than now.

There, my dear child, put down the cup, and yield your place to this elderly gentleman who treads so gingerly over the paving-stones. What! he limps by, without so much as thanking me, as if my hospitable offices were meant only for people who have no wine-cellars.

Well, well, sir! no harm done, I hope? Go! draw the cork, tip the decanter ; but when your great toe shall set you a roaring, it will be no affair of mine.

This thirsty dog with his red tongue lolling out, does not scorn my hospitality, but stands on his hind legs, and laps eagerly out of the trough. See how lightly he capers away again ! Jowler ! did your worship ever have the gout ? "

NATHANIEL HAWTHORNE.

LAW.

Law is law — law is law; and as in such and so forth and hereby, and aforesaid, provided always, nevertheless, notwithstanding. Law is like a country dance, people are led up and down in it till they are tired. Law is like a book of surgery, there are a great many desperate cases in it. It is also like medicine, they that take least of it are best off. Law is like a homely gentlewoman, very well to follow. Law is also like a scolding wife, very bad when it follows us. Law is like a new fashion, people are bewitched to get into it : it is also like bad weather, most people are glad when they get out of it.

We shall now mention a cause, called " Bullum versus Boatum : " it was a cause that came before me. The cause was as follows.

There were two farmers: farmer A. and farmer B. Farmer A. was seized or possessed of a bull : farmer B. was seized or possessed of a ferry-boat. Now, the owner of the ferry-boat, having made his boat fast to a post on the shore, with a piece of hay, twisted rope-fashion, or, as we say, *vulgo vocato*, a hay-band. After he had made his boat fast to a post on shore ; as it was very natural for a hungry man to do, he went up town to dinner : farmer A.'s bull, as it was very natural for a hungry bull to do, came down town to look for a dinner ; and, observing, discovering, see-ing, and spying out some turnips in the bottom of the ferry-boat, the bull scrambled into the ferry-boat ; he ate up the turnips, and, to make an end of his meal, fell to work upon the hay-band : the boat being eaten from its moorings, floated down the river, with the bull in it : it struck a-gainst a rock ; beat a hole in the bottom of the boat, and tossed the bull overboard ; whereupon the owner of the bull brought his action against the boat, for running away with the bull, the owner of the boat brought his action against the bull, for running away with the boat. And thus notice of trial was given, Bullum versus Boatum, Boatum versus Bullum.

Now the counsel for the bull began with saying : " My lord, and you gentlemen of the jury, we are counsel in this cause for the bull. We are indicted for running away with the boat. Now my lord, we have heard of running horses, but never of running bulls, before. Now, my lord the bull could no more run away with the bcat, than a man in a coach can be said to run away with the horses ; therefore, my lord, how can we punish that which is not punishable ? How can we eat what is not eatable ? Or, as the law says, how can we think on that which is not thinkable? Therefore, my lord, as we are counsel in this cause for the bull; if the jury should bring the bull in guilty, the jury would be guilty of a bull. "

The counsel for the boat observed, that the bull should be nonsuited; because, in his declaration, he had not spec. ified what color he was of; for thus wisely, and thus learnedly, spoke the counsel!—" My lord, if the bull was of no color, he must be of some color; and, if he was not of any color, what color could the bull be of?" I overruled this motion myself, by observing, the bull was a white bull, and that white is no color besides the law can color anything.

This cause being left afterwards to a reference, upon the award, both bull and boat were acquitted; it being proved, that the tide of the river carried them both away: upon which I gave it as my opinion, that, as the tide of the river carried both bull and boat away, both bull and boat had a good action against the water-bailiff.

My opinion being taken, an action was issued; and upon the traverse, this point of law arose— How, wherefore and whether, why, when, and what, whatsoever, whereas, and whereby, as the boat was not a *compos-mentis* evidence, how could an oath be administered? That point was soon set tled, by Boatum's attorney declaring, that, for his client, he would swear any thing.

The water-bailiff's charter was then read, taken out of the original record, in true law Latin, which set forth, in their declaration, that they were carried away either by the tide of flood or the tide of ebb. The charter of the water-bailiff was as follows— *Aquæ bailiffi est magistratus in choisi super omnibus fishibus qui habuerunt finnos et scalos, claws, shells, et talos, qui swimmare in fresh-ibus, vel saltibus riveris, lakis, pondis, canalibus, et well boats ; sive oysteri, prawni, shrimpi, turbutus solus :*

that is, not turbots alone, but turbots and soles both together.
But now comes the nicety of the law; the law is as nice as
a new-laid egg, and not to be understood by addle-headed
people. Bullum and Boatum mentioned both ebb and
flood, to avoid quibbling; but it being proved, that they
were carried away neither by the tide of flood, nor by the
tide of ebb, but exactly upon the top of high water, they
were nonsuited; but such was the lenity of the court, upon
their paying all costs, they were allowed to begin again, *de
novo.*

STEVENS.

APPLEDORE.

How looks Appledore in a storm?
　I have seen it when its crags seemed frantic,
　Butting against the maddened Atlantic,
When surge after surge would leap enorme
　Cliffs of Emerald topped with snow,
　That lifted and lifted and then let go
A great white avalanche of thunder,
　A grinding, blinding, deafening ire
Monadnock might have trembled under;
　And the island, whose rock-roots pierce below
　To where they are warmed with the central fire,
You could feel its granite fibres racked,
　As it seemed to plunge with a shudder and thrill
　Right at the breast of the swooping hill,
And to rise again, snorting a cataract
Of rage-froth from every cranny and ledge,
　While the sea drew its breath in hoarse and deep,
And the next vast breaker curled its edge,
　Gathering itself for a mighty leap.

North, east, and south there are reefs and breakers,
   You would never dream of in smooth weather,
That toss and gore the sea for acres,
   Bellowing and gnashing and snarling together;
Look northward, where Duck Island lies,
And over its crown you will see arise,
Against a background of slaty skies,
   A row of pillars still and white
   That glimmer and then are out of sight,
As if the moon should suddenly kiss,
   While you crossed the gusty desert by night,
The long colonnades of Persepolis,
And then as sudden a darkness should follow
To gulp the whole scene at a single swallow,
The city's ghost, the drear, brown waste,
And the string of camels, clumsy-paced :—
Look southward for White Island light,
   The lantern stands ninety feet o'er the tide ;
There is first a half-mile of tumult and fight,
Of dash and roar and tumble and fright,
   And surging bewilderment wild and wide,
Where the breakers struggle left and right,
   Then a mile or more of rushing sea,
And then the light-house slim and lone ;
And whenever the whole weight of ocean is thrown
Full and fair on White Island head,
   A great mist-jotun you will see
   Lifting himself up silently
High and huge o'er the light-house top,
With hands of wavering spray outspread,
   Groping after the little tower,
   That seems to shrink, and shorten and cower,
Till the monster's arms of a sudden drop,
And silently and fruitlessly he sinks again into the sea.

You, meanwhile, where drenched you stand,
  Awaken once more to the rush and roar
And on the rock-point tighten your hand,
As you turn and see a valley deep,
  That was not there a moment before,
Suck rattling down between you and a heap
  Of toppling billow, whose instant fall
  Must sink the whole island once for all —
Or watch the silenter, stealthier seas
  Feeling their way to you more and more;
If they once should clutch you high as the knees
They would whirl you down like a sprig of kelp,
Beyond all reach of hope or help ;—
  And such in a storm is Appledore.

JAMES RUSSELL LOWELL.

Gratiano,—   Let me play the Fool :
  With mirth and laughter let old wrinkles come ;
  Why should a man, whose blood is warm within,
  Sit like his grandsire cut in alabaster ?
  Sleep when he wakes ? and creep into the jaundice
  By being peevish ?   I tell thee what, Antonio,
  I love thee, and it is my love that speaks ;
  There are a sort of men, whose visages
  Do cream and mantle like a standing pond ;
  And do a willful stillness entertain,
  With purpose to be dress'd in an opinion
  Of wisdom, gravity, profound conceit ;
  As who shall say, *I am Sir Oracle,*
  And when I ope my lips let no dog bark '
  I'll tell thee more of this another time ;
  But fish not with this melancholy bait.

" *Merchant of Venice.* "   *Shakespeare.*

THE SECOND STEP IN RENDERING.
CONVERSATIONAL STYLE.

Conversation is a talking with ; familiar intercourse ; intimate association ; colloquial discourse ; informal dialogue. Conversation implies not only one or more listeners but the speaker himself must be a listener. In song we " sing to " ; in Oratory we " speak to " the listeners. In the Dramatic style the speaker talks " for " the listener. In Conversation the speaker " talks with." In the Conversational style we must not only express our own thoughts but ever be mindful of the listener and aim to bring him out. In reading this style suggest the comments from the listener wherever an opportunity presents itself.

Elements belonging particularly to the conversational style :—

I. Directness.

II. Pauses varied in length.

III. Weight of words, light and heavy.

IV. Speaker shows how he feels about it.

V. Suggest a response from the listener.

VI. Conversation includes good listening.

The Conversational style is the simplest and the most common. Much of our literature comes under this class. Talk of all kinds is largely conversational, yet this style is not always the easiest to render. Because of its simplicity, it is too often rendered in an affected, stiff, artificial, unnatural manner. Let us profit by attention to the following.

An important and effective element in the conversational style is Directness of utterance. This action of the speak_er's mind toward his listener keeps the listener alert and wide awake, and following closely that he may be ready to reply. Thought given out in a diffuse, general way leaves the listener passive, while directness makes him active. Even an animal knows when spoken to directly, by whatever name it may be called. When the mental action is direct the response rebounds like a ball.

A common fault in rendering the Conversational style a fault that often defeats and stamps as unnatural and without the true ring that which has points of excellence, is a continuous flow of words and a uniform length of pauses.

It would really seem that the antique rule for pauses — to count ten and let the voice fall — is being observed to the letter. In conversation the stream of words does not flow evenly, but in pulses, regulated by the depth and intensity of the thought. Observing what the listener thinks about it and considering what to reply will vary the length of pauses. There can be no more tiresome monotony than pauses of the same length.

Another peculiarity of the Conversational style is a tendency to pass lightly over groups of words, barely touching some, yet giving as much weight to some one word as is given to a whole phrase. Illustrated in the following.

> " Hast thou named all the birds without a gun ?
> Loved the wild rose, and left it on its stalk ?
> At rich men's tables eaten bread and pulse ?
> Unarmed, faced danger with a heart of trust ?
> And loved so well a high behavior,
> In man or maid, that thou from speech refrained,
> Nobility more nobly to repay ?
> Oh, be my *friend*, and teach me to be thine. "

" Well, " said the judge, " I won't detain you any longer. The case is dismissed. "

The family group had reached the door, the court and audience were laughing and talking within when Granny suddenly turned back, and rattling on the door to attract attention, said : " Ax yo' pardon, Jedge, but who *won* de case, please, Sir ? "

In all the world of borrowed things I don't believe anything can be so completely lost, however, as a borrowed book. Now, if I should drop a book overboard far out at sea ; or if I should let it fall into the crater of Vesuvius, or if some sudden tornado should come along and blow it off the earth before my astonished eyes, I am not sure that I would be in too great haste to replace it. I think I would wait, in the faint hope that maybe, some how or other, some way or other, some time or other, it might come back from the realms of space ; it might return from the drifting smoke, the sea might yield it up. But when a man comes along and *borrows* a book. then I go down town and buy another copy for myself, if I want to read it again. That book is gone. Isn't it? (Cries of " Yes ! Yes ! " and " That's so ! ") "

" *Chimes From A Jester's Bells.* "   *Robert J. Burdette.*

Perhaps the greatest fault in rendering the Conversational style, making it unnatural, is the tendency to give only words, words, words in a colorless manner. But in animated conversation, it will be observed, the speaker shows how he feels about it. He is giving away himself in all he says, if he merely mentions a person's name, the careful listener can detect what he thinks — much or little, well or otherwise. The words themselves carry comparatively little significance — the running comment of feeling adds life and naturalness. Without this comment of feeling or self-expression the choicest selection will be stupid and un-interesting. The more of personal responsiveness— pro-vided the personality is noble and worthy — the truer and richer will be the expression. Get the thought and let the whole being respond to it. As responsiveness is one of the highest aims to be attained in the study of expression the student need not be discouraged if all skill is not attained at the start. Honest effort will bring success.

It is found there is a wide difference in the ability of pupils to render successfully this simplest of all styles. To some it comes easily as conversation itself, but most pupils are not so fortunate. However difficult or easy this style may be to render successfully there is no doubt about it being the most effective style. The Great Teacher used it and we are told, " never man spake as He spake. "
We find his sermons, parables and illustrations afford the most excellent studies for this step. In such studies we should take into account the dramatic situation,— as to the scene, the characters and the theme and its aim and motive.

Mark Anthony's Oration in Shakespeare's " Julius Cæsar" though called an Oration is Conversational for he wins his point through responses from his listeners. Note how skill-fully he draws out from his auditors their opinions, lead-ing them most cautiously only as they are ready to go from one point to another till he has completely captivated their hearts and minds, and uses them at his will to work his purpose. For some time he is unable to gain a single re-sponse from them, without which his efforts would have been fruitless. " My heart is in the coffin there with Cæsar, and I must pause till it come back to me. "
While he pauses he listens to their comments, which give him a starting point. He soon wins responses directly from them, he agrees with them, after this he wins them all

over on his side and before they are aware they agree with him.   Practice the Mark Anthony Oration in the conversational style.

A good speaker must also be a good listener.   We find in conversation some draw us out while others freeze us up. On account of this we may gain freedom and ease of expression by reading to the most sympathetic listeners, those who bring out of us our best.   Read stories to children in a way to suggest you are talking with them.   Adapt your expression to their comprehension.   Respond to their real or imaginary questions and comments.   Should there be greater freedom reading to some friend, practice the readings with the friend to bring out the thought of the matter as if it is original.   It is desirable to be able to respond easily and naturally as this forms a foundation for all other forms of expression.   When we gain ease in the presence of one or more we may gradually widen our circle.

This style may be practiced sitting as if in conversation, then give the reading standing with the same ease as when sitting.

THE BACHELOR'S DREAM.

My pipe is lit, my grog is mixed,
    My curtains drawn, and all is snug ;
Old Puss is in her elbow-chair,
    And Tray is sitting on the rug.
Last night I had a curious dream,
    Miss Susan Bates was Mistress Mogg —
What d'ye think of that, my Cat ?
    What d'ye think of that, my Dog ?

She looked so fair, she sang so well,
    I could but woo and she was won ;

Myself in blue, the bride in white,
    The ring was placed, the deed was done!
Away we went in chaise and four,
    As fast as grinning boys could flog —
What d'ye think of that my Cat?
    What d'ye think of that my Dog?

What loving tete-a-tetes to come!
    But tete-a-tetes must still defer;
When Susan came to live with me,
    Her mother came to live with her!
With Sister Bell she could n't part,
    But all *my* ties had leave to jog —
What d'ye think of that, my Cat?
    What d'ye think of that, my Dog?

The mother brought a pretty Poll,
    A monkey, too— what work he made!
The sister introduced a beau;
    My Susan brought a favorite maid.
She had a tabby of her own,
    A snappish mongrel christened Gog—
What d'ye think of that, my Cat?
    What d'ye think of that, my Dog?

The monkey bit, the parrot screamed,
    All day the sister strummed and sung;
The petted maid was such a scold,
    My Susan learned to use her tongue;
Her mother had such wretched health,
    She sat and croaked like any frog—
What d'ye think of that, my Cat?
    What d'ye think of that, my Dog?

No longer deary, duck and love,
    I soon come down to simple " M! "

The very servants crossed my wish.
    My Susan let me down to them.
The poker hardly seemed my own,
    I might as well have been a log—
What d'ye think of that, my Cat?
    What d'ye think of that, my Dog?

My clothes they were the queerest shape,
    Such coats and hats she never met!
My ways they were the oddest ways!
    My friends were such a vulgar set!
Poor Tompkinson was snubbed and huffed,
    She could not bear that Mr. Blogg—
What d'ye think of that, my Cat?
    What d'ye think of that, my Dog?

At times we had a spar, and then
    Mamma must mingle in the song,
The sister took a sister's part,
    The maid declared her master wrong,
The parrot learned to call me " Fool! "
    My life was like a London fog—
What d'ye think of that, my Cat?
    What d'ye think of that, my Dog?

My Susan's taste was superfine,
    As proved by bills that had no end;
I never had a decent coat,
    I never had a coin to spend!
She forced me to resign my club,
    Lay down my pipe, retrench my grog—
What d'ye think of that, my Cat?
    What d'ye think of that my Dog?

Each Sunday night we gave a rout
    To fops and flirts a pretty list;

And when I tried to steal away
　　I found my study full of whist !
Then, first to come and last to go,
　　There always was a Captain Hogg—
What d'ye think of that, my Cat?
　　What d'ye think of that, my Dog ?

Now was not that an awful dream
　　For one who single is and snug,
With Pussy in the elbow-chair
　　And Tray reposing on the rug?
If I must totter down the hill,
　　'Tis safest done without a clog—
What d'ye think of that, my Cat?
　　What d'ye think of that, my Dog?

　　　　　　　　　　　　THOMAS HOOD.

AUNT NANCY'S ACCOUNT OF A FASHIONABLE PARLOR RECITAL.

Well now, I hadn't the faintest *kind* of an idee of sayin'
anything myself to-night.　I'd a be'n settin' down there
with you folks if it hadn't a be'n that my niece, by marriage, Mrs. Hiram C. Bodge, has to stay down in the dressin'
room there to fix her daughter's hair and get her ready to
sing.

I suppose you're all acquainted with my nephew I'm visitin'— Mr. Hiram C. Bodge.　You'd ort to be, sence
I judge he passes the most of his time where I found him
when I came, day before yesterday.　He wasn't to the train
to meet me, but I laid it to sickness and set out to find the
house; and *who* should I see a standin' on the corner but
him— a talkin' politics, on his way to meet me.　I knowed
him the minute I saw him— you ain't goin' to forget a boy

you've spanked as often as I have him— and he knowed *me*
and a *worse* beat man you never saw.

"Aunt Nancy! s'he; can't be I'm behind time for your
train!" He was so completely beat that I says, to ease
his feelin's, that likely the train was *before* time.

But what I started out to say was that, of them that
comes next on the program ain't ready, they asked me to
come out and talk to you a spell, so's you wouldn't feel neglected and get mad and go home. And my niece, by marriage, Mrs. Hiram C. Bodge— nice a woman's ever lived—
she wanted me to tell you about a new-fangled "recital"
I attended whilst to my nephew, Martin Bodge's— brother
to Hiram — that I was visitin' before I come here.

Hiram as you know, is jest ordinary well-to-do, but Martin, his brother in the city, is *extraordinary* well-to-do.
Some folks would go ahead and tell you what he was wu'th,
but I ain't the braggy kind.

But Martin is jest as plain and sensible a man as you
ever saw; if there is any high falutin' foolishness in the
house, it's because of his wife— Henrietta. (I dont s'p-
ose my niece, by marriage, Mrs. Hiram C. Bodge 'lowed I
was going to tell all this, but I tell'm whilst I ain't a talker,
when they get me started I am going to have my say.)

Well, whilst to Martin's I chanced to hear Martin say to
his wife that he had not forgot my goodness and he pro-
posed to entertain me to the best of his ability, but Henrietta
put in that she simply *would not* give a dinner for me; said
nothing showed deficiencies like a dinner; and I did not
blame Henrietta for that, a mite; for there's no use pre-
tendin' that the cookin' done in that house can compare
with *my* cookin', and it would be dreadful humiliatin' for
her to have such a deficiency showed up to me before company. So they finally settled on what she said was a "Parlor Recital;" and it seems that a "Parlor Recital" is

where you set down and listen to folks play and speak and sing, and so forth.

Howsumever, except for a frowsy headed young feller a playin' the piany, 'twas all did by one girl, and after the piany playin' was over — and what a relief it was! — in she come.

I won't say she wa'nt pretty, for when she smiled and bowed to the folks she certainly did look so, but 'stead of bein' dressed suitable for the occasion, she had on as simple a made, white dress as you ever saw. Every one says, " How exquisite! " I 'spose they thought like me, that we ortn't to judge— not knowin' other folks' circumstances.

Well, then she begun. I jest said we ortn't to judge, but I've heard *speakin'* in my day, and no one on earth could call what she done anything but plain talkin'. 'Twas plain she'd lived in the country and if I hadn't known contrarywise I'd declared 'twas our old place she was describin'.
I declare it made me home-sick! And I spoke out and s'I : " That's our old lane and barn and cows to a T. " And every one around smiled and said, " That is praise indeed. "

Yes, 'twas evident she had lived in the country and 'twas to her credit she wa'nt ashamed to tell it, but as for callin' it *speakin'*!

Then she began on something else and thinks I, " maybe she'll do better. " But landy! she talked for half a dozen people at onct. What her idee was in tryin' to give a *dialogue* by *herself* I don't know, unless 'twas them that expected to take part didn't come, and she, bein' quick minded, had remembered their parts and went ahead and done the best she could — and if so she deserved credit, and I spoke out and said so.

Then the frowsy young feller played and then I expected something fine, for she was goin' to sing, and some woman whisperin' behind me (not knowin' I was related) had

said that the Bodges would never have paid her her price
if it hadn't be'n they wanted to show off; so I was expectin'
some fine singin'; but— I declare I'm ashamed to tell it
for if I'd a had my eyes shut, I'd a declared up and down
that 'twas my darky wash-woman; and more'n that, she'd
stop and talk, jest like Polly does to her baby. I let
her bring her baby ain't a mite o' trouble; plays with the,
clothes pins on the floor. Aunt Polly's a real good singer!
for darky singin', of course, I mean. Pa always sets
around wash-days jest to hear her; but the idee of her singin' identical with my old darky wash-woman before them
city people! I was completely *beat*, and I said right out:
" Well, that's my darky wash-woman to a T. " And
every one around smiled and said something about " complimentary. "

Then come the last of her doin's, and if I couldn't make
head or tail out of her dialogue, I was worse put out at this.
I jest can't describe it! First, she seemed to be strewin'
leaves on the ground — the young feller meanwhile was
playin' mournful soundin' music,— and her face looked sad
and weary and finally down she sinks and I saw she was
goin' into a faint, and I called out for some one to hurry
up and ketch her; but they all set still; so I rose up and
handed my fan and campfire to a man on the front row o'
seats and told him they'd revive her, but a woman sittin'
beside me pulled me back and said I didn't understand—
that it was a pantymime of " The Seasons; " that when
she seemed to be strewin' leaves, she was portrayin' Autumn;
that now whilst she appeared to be in a faint, she was depic-
tin' the deep repose of Winter, and that then would come
Spring. And sure enough, up she waked as sweet as you
please, smilin' and seemin' to listen to the birds and lookin' at herself in the water; and then she began runnin' and
dancin' and gatherin' her lapful of flowers— it was Sum-

mer she was now portrayin',— and the young feller's music got jest as lively as could be, and, altogether, it was real gay. I found myself *more'n* a laughin'. I always do laugh when I hear any one laugh like her; and then she finally danced out of the room and the people got up and said how much they enjoyed it; and I do believe every one in that room said they was glad to see I'd enjoyed it so much. I don't know what in the wide world give them the idee *I'd* enjoyed it, for you know my opinion of every last thing she done. But I don't pretend to understand city ways— and I must be a goin'; the girls is surely through with their primpin' by this time and ready for their speak-in' and singin'.

I jest come back to say whatever you do don't let on to the girls about what I've been a tellin' you— might dis-courage them from tryin'.

MARY M. BOYNTON.

Reprinted by the courtesy of the Eldridge Entertainment House, Franklin, Ohio, from whom additional readings by Mary M. Boynton may be secured.

TILDY SAID.

I know some things I bet you don't,
 About what bad boys gits
When dey does wrong, and don't do right;
 And how dey ketches fits
When dey goes off on Sundays
 A fishin' in de creek;
And how de bad man fixes 'em
 So dey can't move or speak.

Ole Tildy told me all about
 A heap of things she knows;

'Cause she sees goblins in de dark,
　　And when de roosters crows,
She goes out on de portico,
　　And sees a heap of things
That's big as folks, and black as her,
　　An' 's got some horns and wings.

An' dey tells Tildy all about
　　What folks does when dey's dead;
An' sometimes dey takes chillen off,
　　An' hides 'em, Tildy said;
An' makes 'em sleep in puddle-holes,
　　An' drink ole mud an' stuff;
An' sometimes when dey's been right bad,
　　Dey kills 'em sure enough.

One Sunday, Tildy said, two boys
　　Went fishin' in de creek,
An' when de fish commenced to bite,
　　Dey couldn't move or speak;
An' nobody couldn't move 'em,
　　Nor lift 'em from de spot;
An' dey staid dere a hundred years,
　　Until dey died and rot.

An' Tildy said, one Sunday night
　　A boy come from de lawn,
Where he'd been a playin' marvels,
　　An' found his *home* was gone.
An' two great big, black, ugly things
　　Was standin by de fence
An' run him till he couldn't move,
　　An' didn't have no sense.

Tildy said, once a man was dead,
 An' when some boys come in
What had been a stealin' apples,
 De man commenced to grin,
An' all de boys run out of doors,
 An' fell down on dere knees,
An' limbs growed out, an' dey stayed dere,
 An' turned to apple trees.

I'm skeered to go about Tom Prince,
 'Cause once he stole some cake:
An' I bet some time he'll wake up,
 An' find he ain't awake,
An' find some big, ole, wooly things
 A standin' round his bed,
To take him off to some dark place,
 An' make him wish he 'as dead.

BOOTH LOWREY.

Man was saying: " How can we,
In our little boats at sea,
Pass the guarda-costas by ? "
" Row ! " said Woman in reply.

Man was saying: " How forget
Perils that our lives beset,
Strife and poverty's low cry ? "
" Sleep ! " said Woman in reply.

Man was saying : " How be sure
Beauty's favor to secure,
Nor the subtle philter try ? "
" Love ! " said Woman in reply.

VICTOR HUGO.

THE KATYDID IN OPERA.

In the season, we have music every night. The silence of a summer night in the country is a silence to which you can listen; " soft stillness and the night become the touches of sweet harmony. " Come out in this musical silence for awhile if you " want to hear the old band play; " listen to it night after night, until you have learned to love this melodious stillness, and then if you wish, go back to brick walls and paved streets, and lie down to be lulled to sleep by the varied pleasing of rattling hacks, crashing trucks, thundering fire engines and jingling trolley bells.

It is pleasant, as we attend the opera night after night, to note the advent of old favorites. Our artists teach their children to sing and play so exactly like themselves that we scarcely realize we have a new cast every season. We think of it and speak of it, perhaps, in the closing days of summer. The music, I grant you, is somewhat melancholy in the autumn time. There will come some sharp, keen night when the orchestra is very meager. Only a few hardy little musicians appear. And they do not play very long; they cut the opera in every scene, and play only long enough, probably, to save the box receipts, then they pack up their instruments and hurry away to the warmest corners of stack yard and stubble field. We observe on these nights that the voices of the soloists display no hoarseness, however. So long as they do sing, they sing their best.

But in spite of that, the autumnal performance on the whole is pathetic. For they choose mournful themes; they sing of the golden summer that is gone, and their music shudders with the dread of frosty nights and the cruel winter that is coming; they play dirges for their dead comrades; they sing of purple aster and royal golden-rod; the plumy lances of the iron weed in old meadows; the yellow prim-

rose, gleaming like stars in the gray twilight; the ghostly
thistle-down,drifting over the reedy marshes where the fire-
flies died; of grotesque shadows in the old stump lot; of
cold winds, creeping with eerie whispers across the fields
where the corn stands in ragged shocks with stiffened blades;
of wheeling colonies of summer birds that flecked the fields
with restless shadows as they gathered the clans together
and sped away to the gayety of the winter resorts; of faded
ferns in the glens, of withered grasses in the fence corners
and blighted flowers in the old-fashioned gardens, until at
last the merry voices cease, all the daughters of music are
brought low, the last little soloist sings his good-bye song
with a brave little trill in his far-reaching voice, and goeth
the way of all grasshoppers.   *   *   *   *

So he sings for us in the lengthening nights. And as he
sings, some there are in his audience who hear as in a dream,
the songs he sung on yester eve; songs of that happy Past,
" whose yesterdays look backward with a smile. " To them
his strident solo is a talisman that opens wide the doors of
Memoryland, with the old walks we only take when time is
swifter than a thought and longer than eternity.

Down winding paths beneath the whispering oaks;
through tangled grasses in the orchard glooms; across the
foot-bridge where the brook goes singing softly all night
long; through forest vistas, where the sunset loiters with
its benediction to the day— all the dear paths that only
lovers know and love; even by shadowed ways that lead
through valleys where the damps are chill; through desert
paths of tears, and rankling pain, where Marah's waters
darken in the solemn pools; and all the way and all the
time the clasp of a fluttering hand, the gleam of starlight
in the love-lit eyes. Until, at last, the song and the dream
lead on to where the singing brook, its laughter silenced
and its music hushed, deepens into the darkly flowing river

and in the morning light that lights our sun, the shadows pass away forever.

Ah, katydid, in other worlds than ours you must have sung and learned new melodies since all the days were gold and all the world was young. For who, in this bright world of ours, this land of hope and song, this sunlit world of happy hearts and summer skies, could teach your tiny harp these minor chords? Where could you learn on all this laughing earth, that Joy and Sorrow, sisters born of Love, walk ever hand in hand? Where could you learn to sing of tears and loneliness?

"CHIMES from a JESTER's BELLS." ROBERT J. BURDETTE.

THE GARDENER.

And if you ever planted a morning glory seed, which I advise you to do for the sheer pleasure of it— a poor thing brown and hopeless and almost formless in shape or in beauty, but put it in the ground, and the sky will call it, "Come, come!" And if you and I hear what the gardener doth you can hear the morning glory flower saying, "I am coming." It is like the sleepy voice, that is only half awake, not quite half awake, "Who called me? Was I called?" "Hurry, hurry!" says the wind. "I am getting my things on," says the flower. "Oh, hurry, hurry, hurry!" says the sky, and then above the ground comes the flash of leaves. And then, if you care to mark a miracle, all foul and dispirited, and out of humor apparently with all the world, and with self included, and looks clean down, lips clamped together as with an iron band, and the sky says, "Cheer up! Come on up here, I am waiting for you to flower up here," and then the leaves expand, and the sprangles fling out, and the tendrils climb and climb.

Oh, morning glory flower, where are you going, morning glory flower? And the morning glory says, "Into the sky, into the sky, into the sky!" Tendrils fling out, climbing on whatsoever thing there is to climb on, on the wire netting, or the string the child put up, but always climbing into the sky. And the ground says, "You belong down here, you seem to be getting aristocratical. You belong down here. I am your mother." But the morning glory says, "Aye, but the sky is my father. I belong to the sky." And when the summer comes, and the autumn approaches, there is the morning glory with its purple trumpets of flowers and every trumpet, if you had the ear to hear it, and the ear of the poet to listen to what it said, would say, "I belong in the sky." And the gardener believes in the sky.

And then the gardener believes in tending. The gardener knows that the sincerest poetry of life is just digging around in the dirt, just that! Oh, beloved, don't you folks get tired just doing the same thing all the time? Woman, have you ever been known to make a word of remark about the dishwashing coming three times a day? Have you? Have you been heard to say that you didn't so much mind to cook, but that the cleaning up hampered your finer sensibilities and that your æsthetical tendencies were hampered by the dish cloth? And if it came only once a week, not to say three times a day, there might be some comfort in preparing a meal, and the garments are around, and the stockings must be fixed for the feet, and the dinner must be fixed for the lips, and things must be done over and over and over. And I confess that I feel with anybody who gets tired of the eternal reiteration of things. But what is the gardener doing? Oh, what he did yesterday, digging in the dirt, digging in the dirt, planting the seeds, digging in the dirt, tending. Oh, Gardener, blessed Gardener, don't get tired digging in the dirt of my heart. Oh, blessed

Gardener, don't get tired sowing the seeds in my heart. Oh, kind Gardener, don't forget to furnish me a sky. Oh, Gardener, drench me with thy rain, and enswathe me with thy dew. Sweeten my breath with thy south wind's gust, and shine the lamp light of thy stars on my sleeping face, turn the wonder of thy moonlight on the place where we are trying to get into the sky, and waken me with the wonder of thy winsome look along the eastern window of my heart. Oh, Gardener, don't get tired of tending to my garden. He says, " Don't worry, I never will ! "

I would have you mark what seed the Gardener grows. I will talk of the flowers that the Christ Gardener grows in the heart. One of these is the crocus. It is the earliest flower of the lawn. It blooms close against the winter. It barely waits till the last winter wave laps on the shore— and there is the crocus. Thank God, there is a flower that does not wait till spring is here, but grows ere spring has come, gives a prophecy. Some of you people have no call to wait, you are anguish bound, you are winter girt, you look afar, the hills are still clad with snow, the gray skies lower, the falling rain is snowflakes, and you say, " Winter, winter, winter ! " And then the Gardener, so we may not die from the winter, and being winter bound, and storm bound, and snow bound, where the winter's drift is barely vanished displays the crocus blooms. Oh, the Gardener plants in the heart the crocus flower.

And the Gardener plants in the heart the pansies. "Pansies, that's for thoughts, " said Brother Shakespeare. Does the Gardener plant thoughts? Quite true. Do we chance to need flowers, any of them, more than thought flowers ? None. The Gardener is planting thoughts, thoughts of a better life, thoughts of a day undimmed by despair. True. Thoughts of service. True. Thoughts of a life that has no weariness. True. Thoughts of a day that is not dark.

Truly.   Thoughts of a prayer a heart may offer that shall do somebody help.   Thoughts.

And then the Gardener plants heart's ease.   Oh, maybe you need that flower — heart's ease.   What ails your fingers beloved, that you clutch them so tight?   What ails your breath that it stops and then hastens like the beating of a diseased heart?   What ails your voice that it breaks like an instrument out of tune?   What ails your hand that when you reach out to a friend, then all of a sudden you turn your face away and your hand shakes, and you say " Excuse me, excuse me? "   Oh, well, you have heartache and you need heart's ease.   And then the Gardener, this beautiful Gardener, this blessed Gardener, he is planting the flower called heart's ease, and it is for the heartening of the nations.   Oh, heart, hast thou this heart's ease flower?

And then this Gardener plants the red rose of love. Every heart hath room for its red rose flower.

And this Gardener plants the amaranth, that is the flower of immortality.   And when day darkens, then we take the amaranth flower of purple and put it up before our sight, and then we know time cometh when the curtain of dark is not put down and when the dull lamp of evening star is snuffed out by daylight.

And then this Gardener plants the flower of the lily, the white flower of a blameless life.   This bad life, yes, and the bleak?   And in that dull drear ground he plants the seed and lo, there is the white flower of a blameless life.   True.

And there is the lily flower of resurrection.   I cannot, I cannot, I cannot pass this place.   I must go in.   What place is this?   It is an acre.   Yes.   Whose is it?   God's acre. And I must go in.   It has winter on it.   And all wonderful enough, when you go in, to find the dull grave ye left and wept across with broken hearts, it is all grown white as the moonlight of June with lilies of the resurrection.

BISHOP JAMES A. QUAYLE.

THE THIRD STEP IN RENDERING.
NARRATIVE STYLE.

A Narrative is a connected account of events related as a story, an incident or an event. This style may include Anecdotes, Histories, Biographies and Travels.

The Narrative style is closely related to the Conversational style, therefore directions for rendering that style may be followed in this.

A narration or story must have a Purpose. It may be either to entertain, to instruct or to ennoble. Beside this, the effect the narration is likely to produce must be taken into consideration.

It must have a Unity to be preserved throughout, with the unimportant subordinate to the central idea.

It must be Complete that the mind may be satisfied.

In relating an Anecdote, reserve the point till all the circumstances are related. Remember : " Brevity is the soul of wit. "

Successful story telling is a rare and charming gift. Simple narration seems to be the easiest thing possible, yet few are able to successfully tell a good story. Young and old alike are interested in stories. A story appropriate and in harmony with the occasion is seldom out of place.

Simple events may be told in the order of their happening, leaving out parts that do not bear on the story. Describing minutely all details is tedious to the listener.

Train the mind to select readily the essentials, leaving out the unessential.

Suggestions found in the chapter on Imagination will be found helpful at this point. It treats of how the mind may take up the bare facts and through the imagination re-create them with the aid of the fancy, in this way creating in commonplace happenings a new life and interest, always, of course, keeping within the bonds of truth, unless the story is a novel. The culture of the imagination aids original story telling and in rendering stories written by others. In reading, the mind must first secure the facts, the events, as they happened, as nearly as possible. Then use such material as if an actual experience, when the mind may do the re-creative work, coloring the expression with the personality of the reader, where he may respond showing his attitude toward all the incidents he narrates.

The aged, because of a large experience are especially narrative in style.

"The poor, the rich, the valliant, and the sage,
The boasting youth, and narrative old age. "

RIDING ON A CROCODILE.

By the time the cayman was within two yards of me, I saw he was in a state of fear and perturbation. I instantly dropped the mast, sprung up and jumped on his back, turn_ing half round as I vaulted, so that I gained my seat with my face in a right position. I immediately seized his fore_legs and by main force twisted them on his back; thus they served for a bridle. He now seemed to have recovered from his surprise, and, probably fancying himself in hostile company, began to plunge furiously and lashed the sand with his long and powerful tail. I was out of reach of it by being near his head. He continued to plunge and strike and made my seat very uncomfortable. It must have been a fine sight for an unoccupied spectator.

The people roared out in triumph, and were so vociferous, that it was some time before they heard me tell them to pull me and my beast of burden further inland. I was apprehensive the rope might break and then there would have been every chance of going down to the regions under the water with the cayman.

The people dragged us about forty yards on the sand. It was the first and last time I was ever on a cayman's back. Should it be asked how I managed to keep my seat, I would answer, I hunted some years with Lord Darlington's fox hounds.

CHARLES WATERTON.

ADVENTURE WITH A PYTHON.

That moment the negro next to me seized the lance and held it firm in its place while I dashed head foremost into the den to grapple with the snake, and to get hold of his tail before he could do any mischief.

On pinning him to the ground with the lance, he gave a tremendous loud hiss, and the little dog ran away, howling as he went. We had a sharp fray in the den, the rotten sticks flying on all sides, and each party struggling for the superiority. I called out to the second negro to throw himself upon me as I found I was not heavy enough. He did so, and his additional weight was of great service. I had now got firm hold of his tail, and after a violent struggle or two, he gave in, finding himself overpowered. This was the moment to secure him. So while the first negro continued to hold the lance firm to the ground, and the other was helping me, I contrived to unloose my braces and with them tied up the snake's mouth.

The snake finding himself in an unpleasant situation, tried to better himself, and set resolutely to work, but we overpowered him. It measured fourteen feet and was of great thickness. We contrived to make him twist himself around the shaft of the lance, and then prepared to convey him out of the forest. 1 stood at his head and held it firmly under my arm, one negro supported the belly, and the other the tail. In this order we began to move slowly towards home, and reached it after resting ten times.

CHARLES WATERTON.

A " SASSY " CORPSE.

Jehoida Brown and his good wife Abigail had been members of the Wekamen Baptist church for many years. Jehoida was a deacon and his wife was all that except the name. About this time an uncertain number of spooks appeared in and about Wekamen and Wahoo and became obtrusively familiar and oppressively impertinent in the affairs of the community. Abigail was sure she had seen the trailing skirts of one or two and she became at once a confirmed, zealous, and " rantankerous " spiritualist. She was not only interested, but on terms of constant social intercourse with the uncanny denizens of " Spookland. "

In the course of time " Deekin " Brown died. Abigail had 'still remaining in her soul a fragment of respect for the "Deekin's" religious convictions and church affiliations so she sent for Elder Donnelly — for years the " Deekin's " pastor — to come and officiate in the funeral.

When the hour for the services arrived the spiritual and spirited Abigail declared " on her conscience " she would not listen to the Elder's nonsense; but she would retire to a private room where she could commune with the "sperit" of her dear companion while the minister was entertaining and comforting the neighbors and mourners with an endless funeral "sarmin."

The Elder delivered the usual homily on such occasions—dilating on the virtue and piety of the departed Deacon and closing with a descriptive bird's-eye of his present home, condition, and business. The "Deekin" he said, was in glory, was perfectly happy, and "singin' among the An-gels," (forgetful of his late spouse.) He closed the "sarmin" leaving the "Deekin" in the midst of some entrancing lyric — oblivious to all mundane interests.

As the meeting was being dismissed, the widow rushed out of her "private room." She had been quite attentive to the Elder's "sarmin" notwithstanding the presence of the visiting "sperit" of Mr. Brown. She called a halt in the movement of the congregation and pre-emptorily ordered them seated a moment. As it was "her funeral" and they were there to accomodate her, the people sat down.

In a sharp and acrid tone of voice she declared that Elder Donnely had lied through his whole "sarmin." She had been in communion with the "Deekin" during the whole time; he was not among the Angels; but with her. He was "not singin' neither," but nebulously hovering over Abigail's head. She added that the "Deekin" sent a message that he did not want Elder Donnely to lie about him; he — the Elder — "better go home and tend to his own business." Such she said was the message of "Deekin" Brown to his friends and the Elder.

Elder Donnely rose with a sad countenance which he partially covered with a red bandana; in a doleful tone of voice, and a suspicion of a make-believe tear in one eye he declared with his rich Irish brogue:

" Oi have preached many a fun'ral sarmin; but the Lord knows this is the first time I've been *sassed* by the corpse for me effort. "

Then the procession moved on.

Rev H. O. ROWLANDS.

WEE DAVIE.

" Wee Davie " was the only child of William Thorburn, blacksmith. He had reached the age at which he could venture, with prudence and reflection, on a journey from one chair to another; his wits kept alive by maternal warnings of " Tak care, Davie; mind the fire, Davie. " When the journey was ended in safety, and he looked over his shoulder with a crow of joy to his mother, he was re warded, in addition to the rewards of his own brave and adventurous spirit, by such a smile as equalled only his own, and by the well-merited approval of " Weel done, Davie ! "

Davie was the most powerful member of the household. Neither the British fleet, nor the French army, nor the Armstrong gun had the power of doing what Davie did. They might as well have tried to make a primrose grow or a lark sing!

He was for example a wonderful stimulus to labor. The smith had been rather disposed to idleness before his son's arrival. He did not take to his work on cold mornings as he might have done, and was apt to neglect many opportunities, which offered themselves, of bettering his condition; and Jeanie was easily put off by some plausible objection when she urged her husband to make an additional honest penny to keep the house. But " the bairn " became a new motive to exertion; and the thought of leaving him and Jeanie more comfortable, in case sickness laid the smith aside, or death took him away, became like a new sinew to his powerful arm, as he wielded the hammer and made it ring the music of hearty work on the sounding anvil. The meaning of benefit-clubs, sick-societies, and penny-banks was fully explained by " wee Davie. "

Davie also exercised a remarkable influence on his father's political views and social habits. The smith had been fond of debates on political questions: and no more sonorous growl of discontent than his could be heard against the " powers that be, " the injustice done to the masses, or the misery which was occasioned by class legislation. He had also made up his mind not to be happy or contented, but only to endure life as a necessity laid upon him, until the required reforms in church and state, at home and abroad, had been attained. But his wife, without uttering a syllable on matters which she did not even pretend to understand; by a series of acts *out* of Parliament; by reforms in household arrangements; by introducing good *bills* into her own House of Commons; and by a charter, whose points were very commonplace ones — such as a comfortable meal, a tidy home, a clean fireside, a polished grate, above all, a cheerful countenance and womanly love — by these *radical* changes she had made her husband wonderfully fond of his home. He was, under this teaching, getting too contented for a patriot, and too happy for a man in an ill-governed world. His old companions at last could not coax him out at night. He was lost as a member of one of the most philosophical clubs in the neighborhood. " His old pluck, " they said, " was gone. " The wife, it was alleged by the patriotic bachelors, had " cowed " him, and driven all the spirit out of him. But " wee Davie " completed this revolution. I shall tell you how.

One failing of William's had hitherto resisted Jeanie's silent influence. The smith had formed the habit, before

he was married, of meeting a few companions, " just in a
friendly way," on pay-nights at a public-house. It was
true that he was never what might be called a drunkard—
never lost a day's work — never was the worst for liquor,
etc. But, nevertheless, when he entered the snuggery in
Peter Wilson's whisky-shop, with the blazing fire and comfortable atmosphere ; and when, with half-a-dozen talkative,
and to him, pleasant fellows and old companions, he sat
around the fire, and the glasses circulated ; and the gossip of the week was discussed ; and racy stories were told :
and one or two songs sung, linked together by memories
of old merry-meetings ; and current jokes were repeated
with humor, of the tyrannical influence which some would
presume to exercise on " innocent enjoyment " — then
would the smith's brawny chest expand, and his face beam,
and his feelings become malleable, and his sixpences begin to melt, and flow out in generous sympathy into Peter
Wilson's fozy hand, to be counted greedily beneath his
sodden eyes. And so it was the smith's wages were always lessened by Peter's gains. His wife had her fears—
her horrid anticipations — but did not like, even to her
husband, to hint at anything so dreadful as what she
in her heart dreaded. She took her own way, however, to
win him to the house and to good, and gently insinuated
wishes rather than expressed them. The smith, no doubt,
she comforted herself by thinking, " was only merry,"and
never ill-tempered or unkind— " yet at times,— and then,
what if — ! " Yes. Jeanie, you are right! The demon
sneaks into the house by degrees, and at first he may be
kept out, and the door shut upon him ; but let him only
once take possession, then he will keep it, and will keep it
and shut the door against everything pure, lovely, and of
good report — barring it against thee and " wee Davie, "
ay, and One who is best of all — and will fill the house

with sin and shame, with misery and despair! But " wee Davie, " with his arm of might, drove the demon out. It happened thus:

One evening when the smith returned home so that " you could *know it* on him, " Davie toddled forward; and his father, lifting him up, made him stand on his knee. The child began to play with the locks of the Sampson, to pat him on the cheek, and to repeat with glee the name of " dad-a. " The smith gazed on him intently, and with a peculiar look of love, mingled with sadness. " Isn't he a bonnie bairn? " asked Jeanie, as she looked over her husband's shoulder at the child, nodding and smiling to him. The smith spoke not a word, but gazed intently on his boy, while some sudden emotion was strongly working in his countenance.

" It's done! " he at last said, as he put the child down.

" What's wrang? what's wrang? " exclaimed his wife as she stood before him, and put her hands round his shoulders, bending down until her face was close to his.

" Everything is wrang, Jeanie. "

" Willie, what is't? are ye no weel?— tell me what's wrang wi' you! — oh, tell me! " she exclaimed in evident alarm.

" It's a' right noo. " he said, rising up and seizing the child. He lifted him to his breast and kissed him. Then looking up he said, " Davie has done it, along wi' you, Jeanie. Thank God, I am a free man! "

His wife felt awed, she knew not how.

" Sit doon, " he said, as he took out his handkerchief, and wiped away a tear from his eye, " and I'll tell you a' aboot it. "

Jeanie sat on a stool at his feet, with Davie on her knee. The smith seized the child's little hand in one of his own and with the other took his wife's.

" I hav'na been what ye may ca'a drunkard, " he said, slowly, and like a man abashed, " but I hae been often as I shouldna have been, and as, wi' God's help, I never, never will be again ! "

" Oh ! " exclaimed Jeanie.

" It's done, it's done ; as I'm a leevin man, it's done ! But dinna greet, Jeanie.   Thank God for you and Davie my best blessings. "

" Except Himself ! " said Jeanie, as she hung on her husband's neck.

" And noo, woman, " replied the smith, " nae mair about it ; it's done.   Gie wee Davie a piece, and get the supper ready. "

Norman Macleod.

ELIZABETH.

Now was the winter gone, and the snow ; and Robin
        the Redbreast,
Boasted on bush and tree it was he, it was he and no other
That had covered with leaves the Babes in the Wood,
        and blithely
All the birds sang with him, and little cared for his boasting,
Or for his Babes in the Wood, or the Cruel Uncle, and only
Sang for the mates they had chosen,   and cared for the
        nests they were building.
With them, but more sedately and meekly, Elizabeth Haddon
Sang in her inmost heart, but her lips were silent and
        songless.
Thus came the lovely spring with a rush of blossoms and
        music,
Flooding the earth with flowers, and the air with melodies
        vernal.

Then it came to pass, one pleasant morning, that slowly
Up the road there came a cavalcade, as of pilgrims,
Men and women, wending their way to the Quarterly
      Meeting
In the neighboring town ; and with them came riding
      John Estaugh.
At Elizabeth's door they stopped to rest, and alighting
Tasted the currant wine, and the bread of rye, and the honey
Brought from the hives, that stood by the sunny wall of
      the garden ;
Then remounted their horses, refreshed, and continued
      their journey,
And Elizabeth with them, and Joseph, and Hannah the
      housemaid.
But, as they started, Elizabeth lingered a little, and leaning
Over her horse's neck, in a whisper said to John Estaugh:
" Tarry awhile behind, for I have something to tell thee,
Not to be spoken lightly, nor in the presence of others;
Them it concerneth not, only thee and me it concerneth. "
And they rode slowly along through the woods, conversing
      together.
It was pleasant to breathe the fragrant air of the forest ;
It was pleasant to live on that bright and happy May morning!

Then Elizabeth said, though still with a certain reluctance
As if impelled to reveal a secret she fain would have guarded;
" I will no longer conceal what is laid upon me to tell thee;
I have received from the Lord a charge to love thee, John
      Estaugh. "

And John Estaugh made answer, surprised by the words
      she had spoken,
" Pleasant to me are thy converse, thy ways, thy meekness
      of spirit;

Pleasant thy frankness of speech, and thy soul's immacu-
       late whiteness,
Love without dissimulation, a holy and inward adorning.
But I have yet no light to lead me, no voice to direct me.
When the Lord's work is done, and the toil and the labor
       completed
He hath appointed to me, I will gather into the stillness
Of my own heart awhile, and listen and wait for his guid-
       ance. "

Then Elizabeth said, not troubled nor wounded in spirit,
 "So is it best, John Estaugh.   We will not speak of it
       further.
It hath been laid upon me to tell thee this, for to-morrow
Thou art going away, across the sea, and I know not
When I shall see thee more; but if the Lord hath decreed it,
Thou wilt return again to seek me here and to find me. "
And they rode onward in silence, and entered the town
       with the others.

Ships that pass in the night, and speak each other in passing,
Only a signal shown and a distant voice in the darkness ;
So on the ocean of life we pass and speak one another,
Only a look and a voice, then darkness again and a silence.

Now went on as of old the quiet life of the homestead.
Patient and unrepining Elizabeth labored, in all things
Mindful not of herself, but bearing the burdens of others
Always thoughtful and kind and untroubled ; and Hannah
       the housemaid
Diligent early and late, and rosy with washing and scouring,
Still as of old disparaged the eminent merits of Joseph,
And was at times reproved for her light and frothy behavior,
For her shy looks, and her careless words, and her evil
       surmisings,

Being pressed down somewhat, like a cart with sheaves
    overladen,
As she would sometimes say to Joseph, quoting the Scriptures.

Meanwhile John Estaugh departed across the sea, and
    departing
Carried hid in his heart a secret sacred and precious,
Filling its chambers with fragrance, and seeming to him in
    its sweetness
Mary's ointment of spikenard, that filled all the house with
    its odor.
O lost days of delight, that are wasted in doubting and
    waiting !
O lost hours and days in which we might have been happy !
But the light shone at last, and guided his wavering foot-
    steps,
And at last came the voice, imperative, questionless, certain.

Then John Estaugh came back o'er the sea for the gift
    that was offered,
Better than houses and lands, the gift of a woman's affection.
And on the First Day that followed, he rose in the Silent
    Assembly,
Holding in his strong hand a hand that trembled a little,
Promising to be kind and true and faithful in all things.
Such were the marriage-rites of John and Elizabeth Estaugh.

And not otherwise Joseph, the honest, the diligent servant,
Sped in his bashful wooing with homely Hannah the house-
    maid ;
For when he asked her the question, she answered, "Nay;"
    and then added
" But thee may make believe, and see what will come of
    it, Joseph. "
" ELIZABETH. " PARTS III & IV   H. W. LONGFELLOW.

FOURTH STEP IN RENDERING.
DESCRIPTIVE STYLE.

To Describe is to represent by drawing ; a represen-tation by words or other signs. The figure to be delin-eated may be that which appeals to the eye : objects, persons, places.

The person who gives the description must, like a photographer, select a definite view-point and hold it unchanged for one picture lest the impression be indistinct. If the view-point is large and distant, a change may be allowed, otherwise but one impression should be given. The essential characteristics must be brought out. Take advantage of proper background, contrasts and comparisons. Use carefully and skillfully such words as will awaken mental pictures: for example, make use of words giving color, brilliancy and life.

Call attention to the various points to be brought out in such an order as to be easily grasped by the listener. Naturally the mind looks, first at the picture as a whole, next the parts, then the relation of one part to another, last, selects that which seems most important.

As the speaker presents his mental picture to his lis-teners he too should look at his picture as well as at his auditors. Both speaker and listeners inspect it together, so it cannot be placed between speaker and audience.

The Descriptive Style is closely related to the Conversational Style; because of this, the suggestions for rendering the Conversational Style may be applied to the Descriptive.

As in the Narrative Style so in the Descriptive Style there must be a Purpose. The Unity must be preserved. See that the picture is properly focused. It must be well balanced and complete. It must be brief and well concentrated so a mind that has given no previous thought to it may grasp all readily like a picture. Enter into the description as if it is something new that you only know.

It is of importance to note at this point that knowing in an abstract way is cold and uninteresting, and has little power to influence or move; knowing things in a concrete way leads to life and action. Abstract and general ideas have no power to move the emotions, while the presenting of definite, actual ideas may be grasped first by the mind of the speaker after which he may move his listeners profoundly. We may illustrate what we mean by general ideas as compared with the particular by calling attention to the fact that we may hear, almost unmoved, of some great disaster, some horror costing hundreds of lives, while a definite description of one child perishing in some accident moves us profoundly, even to tears. Attention to what is barely suggested here will enable the speaker to make use of concrete rather than the abstract, particular rather than general ideas.

Where ideas of a *general* character must be used in the readings, the reader must *create* vivid mental pictures for himself, in this way adding reality and life. The following may serve to illustrate the mental action in creating real, concrete ideas from what is generally mere words.

Let the student read " The Ocean, " by Lord Byron.

"Thou glorious mirror, " — Let the mind behold a vast, glassy surface, wherein, in turn, is reflected tempest, calm,

convulsed, breeze, gale, storm, ice, and " dark heaving. "
Following these definite reflections in this vast mirror, the
mind passes to the invisible, mystic, which cannot be described.   But as the mind sees definite pictures of the surface of the water as the different word pictures are presented — pictured in detail, as if to reproduce in a painting, the
listener will feel the force of something alive and interesting.   Herein is art.   Each artist must create his own ideals.
He may introduce into this series of ocean views, boats, ships,
clouds, rocks or anything to make it exist in mind as an
object, concrete,— not abstract or considered apart from
a particular object.

> Thou glorious mirror, where the Almighty's form
> Glasses itself in tempests ; in all time,
> Calm or convulsed — in breeze, or gale or storm,
> Icing the pole, or in the torrid clime
> Dark-heaving ;— boundless, endless and sublime —
> The image of Eternity — the throne
> Of the Invisible ; even from out thy slime —
> The monsters of the deep are made ; each zone
> Obeys thee : thou goest forth, dread, fathomless, alone.

Says Dr. Campbell concerning the importauce of clearness : " If the medium through which we look at any object is perfectly transparent, our whole attention is fixed on
the object ; we are scarcely sensible that there is a medium which intervenes, and we can hardly be said to perceive
it, but if there is a flaw in the medium, if we see through
it but dimly, if the object is imperfectly represented, or if
we know it to be misrepresented, our attention is immediately taken off the object to the medium. . . . . .
A discourse, then, excells in perspicuity when the subject
engrosses the attention of the hearer, and the language is

so little minded by him that he can scarcely be said to be conscious it is through the medium he sees the speaker's thoughts. "

The descriptive studies following are of an objective character. Care has been exercised in selecting such short and easy studies as have one simple picture to portray. Let the student form a complete mental image of each of the following studies. After careful study and concentration of the mind upon it, read your study to some one asking them, in turn, to describe to you the picture the reading has suggested to them. Practice of this kind will enable the pupil to know if he has ability to project mental pictures into the minds of others.

Objective studies with one prominent picture are given here. Subjective studies with one leading feeling come under the step headed Lyrics.

Experience has proven the objective studies,— pictures, and the subjective,— manifesting feeling are most helpful.

WASHINGTON.

George Washington's personal appearance was in harmony with his character; it was a model of manly strength and beauty. He was about six feet two inches in height and his person well proportioned,— in the earlier part of life, rather spare, and never too stout for action and graceful movement. The complexion inclined to the florid ; the eyes blue and remarkably far apart; a profusion of brown hair was drawn back from the forehead, highly powdered, according to the fashion of the day, and gathered in a bag behind. He was scrupulously neat in his dress, and while in camp, though he habitually left his tent at sunrise, he was usually dressed for the day.   EVERETT.

JOHN BURNS OF GETTYSBURG.

Just where the tide of battle turns
Erect and lonely stood old John Burns.
How do you think the man was dressed?
He wore an ancient long buff vest,
Yellow as saffron — but his best;
And buttoned over his manly breast,
Was a bright blue coat with a rolling collar,
And large, gilt buttons — size of a dollar;
He wore a broad brimmed, bell-crowned hat,
White as the locks on which it sat.
But Burns unmindful of jeer and scoff,
Stood there picking the rebels off —
With his long, brown rifle and bell-crowned hat,
And the swallow-tails they were laughing at.
In fighting the battle, the question's whether
You'll show a hat that's white, or a feather!

BRETE HARTE.

JOHN HANCOCK.

One raw morning in spring, the town militia came together before daylight " for training. " A great tall man, with a large head and a high, wide brow, their captain,— one who had " seen service ",— marshalled them into line, numbering but seventy, and bade every man to load his piece with powder and ball. " I will order the first man shot that runs away, " said he, when some faltered.

" Don't fire unless fired upon, but if they want to have a war, let it begin here. "

You know what followed ; those farmers and mechanics " fired the shot that was heard round the world. "

THEODORE PARKER.

EVANGELINE.

Somewhat apart from the village, and nearer the Basin
    of Minas,
Benedict Bellefontaine, the wealthiest farmer of Grand-Pre,
Dwelt on his goodly acres; and with him, directing his
    household,
Gentle Evangeline lived, his child, and the pride of the
    village.
Stalworth and stately in form was the man of seventy winters;
Hearty and hale was he, an oak that is covered with snow-
    flakes;
White as the snow were his locks, and his cheeks as brown
    as the oak-leaves.
Fair was she to behold, that maiden of seventeen summers.
Black were her eyes as the berry that grows on the thorn by
    the wayside,
Black, yet how softly they gleamed neath the brown shade
    of her tresses!
Sweet was her breath as the breath of kine that feed in
    the meadows.
Fairer was she when, on Sunday morn, while the bell from
    its turret
Sprinkled with holy sounds the air, as the priest with his
    hyssop
Sprinkles the congregation, and scatters blessings upon them,
Down the long street she passed, with her chaplet of beads
    and her missal,
Wearing her Norman cap, and her kirtle of blue, and the
    ear-rings,
Brought in the olden time from France, and since, as an
    heirloom,
Handed down from mother to child, through long generations.
But a celestial brightness — a more ethereal beauty —

Shone on her face and encircled her form, when after con-
        fession,
Homeward serenely she walked with God's benediction
        upon her.
When she had passed, it seemed like the ceasing of exqui-
        site music.

H. W. LONGFELLOW.

MARY.

Of the new-comers, there was a group over by the south
wall, consisting of a man, a woman, and a donkey, which
requires extended notice. The man stood by the animal's
head, holding a leading-strap. . . . The donkey ate
leisurely from an armful of green grass, of which there
was an abundance in the market. In its sleepy content,
the brute did not admit of disturbance from the bustle and
clamor about; no more was it mindful of the woman sitting
upon its back in a cushioned pillion. An outer robe of
dull woolen stuff completely covered her person, while a
white wimple veiled her head and neck. . . . . .
The sun streamed garishly over the stony face of the
famous locality, and under its influence Mary, the daughter
of Joachim, dropped the wimple entirely, and bared her
head. . . . She was not more than fifteen. Her form,
voice, and manner belonged to the period of transition from
girlhood. Her face was perfectly oval, her complexion
more pale than fair. The nose was faultless; the lips slightly parted, were full and ripe, giving to the lines of the
mouth warmth, tenderness, and trust; the eyes were blue
and large, and shaded by drooping lids and long lashes;
and, in harmony with all, a flood of golden hair, in the
style permitted to Jewish brides, fell unconfined down her
back to the pillion on which she sat. The throat and

neck had the downy softness sometimes seen, which leaves the artist in doubt whether it is an effect of contour or color. To these charms of feature and person were added others more indefinable — an air of purity which only the soul can impart, and of abstraction natural to such as think of things impalpable. Often, with trembling lips, she raised her eyes to heaven, itself not more deeply blue; often she crossed her hands upon her breast, as in adoration and prayer; often she raised her head like one listening eagerly for a calling voice. Now and then, midst his slow utterance, Joseph turned to look at her, and, catching the expression kindling her face as with light, forgot his theme, and with bowed head, wondering, plodded on.

" Ben-Hur. " Lew. Wallace.

PRISCILLA.

So through the Plymouth woods John Alden went on
    his errand ;
Heard, as he drew near the door, the musical voice of
    Priscilla
Singing the hundredth Psalm, the grand old Puritan anthem,
Then, as he opened the door, he beheld the form of the
    maiden
Seated beside her wheel, and the carded wool like a snow-drift
Piled at her knee, her white hands feeding the ravenous
    spindle,
While with her foot on the treadle she guided the wheel in
    its motion.
Open wide on her lap lay the well-worn psalm-book of
    Ainsworth,
Printed in Amsterdam, the words and the music together,
Rough-hewn, angular notes, like stones in the wall of a
    churchyard,

Darkened and overhung by the running vines of the verses.
Such was the book from whose pages she sang the old Pu-
  ritan anthem,
She, the Puritan girl, in the solitude of the forest,
Making the humble house and the modest apparel of home-
  spun
Beautiful with her beauty, and rich with the wealth of her
  being!
"COURTSHIP OF MILES STANDISH." H. W. LONGFELLOW.

ROMOLA.

" Ah, you are come back, Moso. It is well. We have wanted nothing. "

The voice came from the farther end of a long, spacious room, surrounded with shelves, on which books and antiquities were arranged in scrupulous order. Here and there on separate stands in front of the shelves, were placed a beautiful feminine torso; a headless statue, with an uplifted muscular arm wielding a bloodless sword; rounded, dimpled, infantine limbs severed from the trunk, invited the lips to kiss the cold marble; some well preserved Roman busts; and two or three vases from Magna Grecia. A large table in the centre was covered with antique bronze lamps and small vessels in dark pottery. The color of these objects was chiefly pale or somber; the vellum bindings, with their deep ridged backs, gave little relief to the marble, livid with long burial: the once splendid patch of carpet at the farther end of the room had long been worn to dimness; the dark bronzes wanted sunlight upon them to bring out their tinge of green, and the sun was not yet high enough to send gleams of brightness through the narrow windows that looked on the Via di Bardi.

The only spot of bright color was made by the hair of a tall maiden of seventeen or eighteen, who was standing before a carved leggio, or reading desk, such as is often seen in the choirs of Italian churches. The hair was of reddish gold color, enriched by an unbroken small ripple, such as may be seen in the sunset clouds on grandest autumnal evenings. It was confined by a black fillet above her ears, from which it rippled forward again, and made a natural veil for her neck above her square-cut gown of black serge. Her eyes were bent on a large volume placed before her : one long white hand rested on the reading desk, and the other clasped the back of her father's chair.

The blind father sat with head uplifted and turned a little aside towards his daughter, as if he were looking at her. His delicate paleness, set off by the black velvet cap, which surmounted his drooping white hair, made all the more perceptible the likeness between his aged features and those of the young maiden, whose cheeks were also without any tinge of the rose. There was the same refinement of brow and nostril in both, counterbalanced by a firm mouth and powerful chin, which gave an expression of proud tenacity and latent impetuousness; an expression carried out in the backward poise of the girl's head, and the grand line of her neck and shoulders. It was a type of face of which one could not venture to say whether it would inspire love or only that unwilling admiration which is mixed with dread; the question must be decided by the eyes, which often seem charged with a more direct message from the soul. But the eyes of the father had long been silent, and the eyes of the daughter were bent on the Latin pages of " Politian's Miscellanea " from which she was reading aloud.

GEORGE ELIOT.

SENECA LAKE.

On thy fair bosom, silver lake,
  The white swan spreads his snowy sail,
And round his breast the ripples break,
  As down he bears before the gale.

On thy fair bosom, waveless stream,
  The dipping paddle echoes far,
And flashes in the moonlight gleam,
  And bright reflects the polar star.

The waves along thy pebbly shore,
  As blows the north wind, heave their foam,
And curl around the dashing oar,
  As late the boatman hies him home.

How sweet, at set of sun, to view
  Thy golden mirror spreading wide,
And see the mist of mantling blue
  Float round the distant mountain's side!

At midnight hour, as shines the moon,
  A sheet of silver spreads below,
And swift she cuts, at highest noon,
  Light clouds, like wreaths of purest snow.

On thy fair bosom, silver lake,
  Oh! I could ever sweep the oar,
When early birds at morning wake,
  And evening tells us toil is o'er.

                    JAMES G. PERCIVAL.

THE SNOW ANGEL.

The sleigh bells danced that winter night;
Old Brattleboro rang with glee;
The windows overflowed with light;
Joy ruled each hearth and Christmas tree,
But to one the bells and mirth were naught:
His soul with deeper joy was fraught.
He waited until the guests were gone
He waited to dream his dream alone;
And the night wore on.

Alone he stands in the silent night;
He piles the snow in the village square;
With spade for a chisel, a statue white
From the crystal quarry rises fair.
No light save the stars to guide his hand,
But the image obeys his soul's command.
The sky is draped with fleecy lawn,
The stars grow pale in the early dawn,
But the lad toils on.

And lo! in the morn the people came
To gaze at the wondrous vision there;
And they call it " The Angel, " divining its name,
For it came in silence and unaware.
It seemed no mortal hand had wrought
The uplifted face of prayerful thought;
But its features wasted beneath the sun;
Its life went out ere the day was done;
And the lad dreamed on.

And his dream was this :   In the years to be
I will carve the Angel in lasting stone;
In another land beyond the sea
I will toil in darkness, I will dream alone,
While others sleep I will find a way
Up through the night to the light of day.
There's nothing desired beneath star or sun
Which patient genius has not won.
And the boy *toiled* on.

The years go by.   He has wrought with might.
He has gained renown in a land of art;
But the thought inspired that Christmas night
Still kept its place in the sculptor's heart;
And the dream of the boy that melted away
In the light of the sun that winter day,
Is embodied at last in enduring stone,
Snow Angel in marble — his purpose won;
And the man toils on.

WALLACE BRUCE.

KAATSKILL ON THE HUDSON.

Whoever has made a voyage up the Hudson, must remember the Kaatskill mountains.   They are a dismembered branch of the great Appalachian family, and are seen far away to the west of the river, swelling up to a noble height, and lording it over the surrounding country. Every change of season, every change of weather, indeed, every hour of the day produces some change in the magical lines and shapes of these mountains; and they are regarded by the good wives far and near as perfect barometers.   When the weather is fair and settled, they are clothed in blue and purple, and print their bold outlines on the clear, evening sky; but sometimes when the rest of the landscape is cloudless, they will gather a hood of gray vapor about their summits, which in the last rays of the setting sun, will glow and light up like a crown of glory.

WASHINGTON IRVING.

EL CAPITAN.

The most impassive granite wonder in the Yosemite Valley is the great rock, El Capitan, gray in the shadow, and white in the sun. Standing out a vast cube with a half mile front, a half mile side, three-fifths of a mile high, and seventy-three hundred feet above the sea, it is almost the crowning triumph of solid geometry. Well did the Indians name him Tu-touch-ah-nu-lah,— Great Chief of the Valley. When you reach the valley he towers above you in the left. He grows grander and more solemn every step of the way. When you stand beneath him he blots out the world; when you stand near the base he blots out the sky. Get as far from him as you can, he never diminishes. He follows you as you go. He is the overwhelming presence of the place. You never tire seeing the eastern sunshine move down the front like a smile on a human face. You never tire seeing the great shadows roll out across the broad meadows as the sun descends and rises like the tide in the Fundy's Bay, till the valley is half filled with night, and the tips of the tall trees are dipped like pens in ink. You never weary watching a light from a moon you cannot see, as it silvers the cornices and brightens the dusky front, as if wizards were painting their way down without a stage or scaffold. A dark spot starts out in the light. It turns into a great cedar.   Pines that stand about the base resemble shrubs along a garden wall, though they are two hundred feet high.   A few men have crept out to the eaves of El Capitan, looked over, crept back again.   Little white clouds sail silently toward the lofty eaves and are gone as if to a dovecote in a garret.   And yet the earthquake in 1872 rocked him like a cradle.   The clocks in the valley all stopped as though, when El Capitan was moved, then " time shall be no more. "

BAYARD TAYLOR.

MORNING.

As we proceeded, the timid approach of twilight became more perceptible; the intense blue of the sky began to soften; the smaller stars, like little children, went first to rest; the sister beams of the Pleiades soon melted together; but the bright constellations of the west and north remained unchanged.   Steadily the wondrous transfiguration went on.   Hands of angels hidden from mortal eyes shifted the scenery of the heavens; the glories of night dissolved into the glories of the dawn.   The blue sky turned more softly gray; the great watch-stars shut up their holy eyes; the east began to kindle.   Faint streaks of purple soon blushed along the sky: the whole celestial concave was filled with the inflowing tides of the morning light, which came pouring down from above in one great ocean of radiance; till at length, as we reached the Blue Hills, a flash of purple fire blazed out from above the horizon, and turned the dewy tear-drops of flower and leaf into rubies and diamonds.   In a few seconds the everlasting gates of the morning were thrown wide open, and the lord of day, arrayed in glories too severe for the gaze of man, began his state.

EDWARD EVERETT.

NIGHT.

A mysterious darkness creeps over the face of nature; the beautiful scenes of earth are slowly fading, one by one.

He raises his gaze toward heaven; and lo ! a silver crescent of light, clear and beautiful hanging in the western sky, meets his astonished gaze. The young moon charms his vision, and leads him upward to her bright attendants which are now stealing, one by one, from out the deep blue sky. The solitary gazer bows, wonders and adores.

The hours glide by; the silver moon is gone; the stars are rising, slowly ascending the heights of heaven and solemnly sweeping downward in the stillness of the night. A faint streak of rosy light is seen in the east; it brightens; the stars fade, the planets are extinguished; the eye is fixed in mute astonishment on the glowing splendor, till the first rays of the returning sun dart their radiance on the earth.

O. M. MITCHELL.

THE OAK.

Beware a speedy friend, the Arabian said,
And wisely was it he advised distrust:
The flower that blossoms earliest fades the first.
Look at yon Oak that lifts its stately head,
And dallies with the autumnal storm, whose rage
Tempests the great sea-waves; slowly it rose,
Slowly its strength increased through many an age
And timidly did its light leaves disclose,
As doubtful of the spring, their palest green.
They to the summer cautiously expand,
And by the warmer sun and season bland
Matured, their foliage in the grove is seen,
When the bare forest by the wintry blast is swept,
Still lingering on the boughs the last.   SOUTHEY.

AN IDYL.

I saw her first on a day in spring,
  By the side of a stream, as I fished along,
And loitered to hear the robins sing,
  And guessed at the secret they told in song.

The apple-blossoms, so white and red,
  Were mirrored beneath in the streamlet's flow;
And the sky was blue far overhead,
  And far in the depths of the brook below.

I lay half hid by a mossy stone
  And looked in the water for flower and sky.
I heard a step — I was not alone:
  And a vision of loveliness met my eye.

I saw her come to the other side,
  And the apple-blossoms were not more fair;
She stooped to gaze in the sunlit tide,
  And her eyes met mine in the water there.

She stopped in timid and mute surprise,
  And that look might have lasted till now, I ween;
But, modestly dropping her dove like eyes,
  She turned her away to the meadow green.

I stood in wonder and rapture lost
  At her slender form and her step so free,
At her raven locks by the breezes tossed,
  As she kicked up her heels in the air for glee.

The apple-blossoms are withered now,
  But the sky, and the meadow, and stream, are there;
And whenever I wander that way I vow
  That some day I'll buy me that little black mare.

                              C. G. BUCK.

THE PRIMROSE OF THE ROCK.

A rock there is whose lonely front
   The passing traveller slights;
Yet there the glow-worms hang their lamps
   Like stars, at various heights;
And one coy Primrose to that Rock
   The vernal breeze invites.

What hideous warfare hath been waged,
   What kingdoms overthrown,
Since first I spied that Primrose-tuft
   And marked it for my own
A lasting link in Nature's chain
   From highest heaven let down!

The flowers, still faithful to the stems,
   Their fellowship renew;
The stems are faithful to the root,
   That worketh out of view;
And to the rock the root adheres
   In every fibre true.

WORDSWORTH.

THE VIOLET.

The violet in her green-wood bower,
   Where birchen boughs with hazels mingle,
May boast itself the fairest flower
   In glen, or copse, or forest dingle.

Though fair her gems of azure hue,
   Beneath the dew-drop's weight reclining,
I've seen an eye of lovelier hue,
   More sweet through wat'ry lustre shining.

SCOTT.

THE DANDELION.

Dear common flower, that grow'st beside the way,
Fringing the dusty road with harmless gold,
First pledge of blithesome May,
Which children pluck, and, full of pride, uphold,
High hearted buccaneers, o'erjoyed that they
An El Dorado in the grass have found,
Which not the rich earth's ample round
May match in wealth, thou art more dear to me
Than all the prouder summer blooms may be.

How like a prodigal doth nature seem,
When thou, for all thy gold, so common art!
Thou teachest me to deem
More sacredly of every human heart,
Since then reflects in joy its scanty gleam
Of heaven, and could some wondrous secret show,
Did we but pay the love we owe.
And with a child's undoubting wisdom look,
On all these pages of God's book.

LOWELL.

FLOWERS.

Ere yet our course was graced with social trees
It lacked not old remains of hawthorn bowers,
Where small birds warbled to their paramours;
And, earlier still, was heard the hum of bees;
I saw them ply their harmless robberies,
And caught the fragrance which the sundry flowers,
Fed by the stream with soft perpetual showers,
Plenteously yielded to the fragraut breeze.
There bloomed the strawberry of the wilderness;
The trembling eyebright showed her sapphire blue,
The thyme her purple, like the blush of Even;

And if the breath of some to no caress
Invited, forth they peeped so fair to view,
All kinds alike seemed favorites of Heaven.

WORDSWORTH.

THE BUTTERFLY.

I've watch'd you now a full half-hour,
Self-poised upon that yellow flower;
And, little Butterfly! indeed
I know not if you sleep or feed.
How motionless! — not frozen seas
More motionless! and then
What joy awaits you, when the breeze
Hath found you out among the trees,
And calls you forth again!

This plot of orchard-ground is ours:
My trees they are, my Sister's flowers;
Here rest your wings when they are weary;
Here lodge as in a sanctuary!
Come often to us, fear no wrong;
Sit near us on the bough!
We'll talk of sunshine and of song,
And summer days, when we were young;
Sweet childish days, that were as long
As twenty days are now.

WORDSWORTH.

LICHENS AND MOSSES.

Lichen and mosses (though these last in their luxuriance are deep and rich as herbage, yet both for the most part humblest of the green things that live) — how of these?

Meek creatures! the first mercy of the earth, veiling with hushed softness its dintless rocks; creatures full of pity, covering with strange and tender honor the scarred disgrace of ruin,— laying quiet fingers on the trembling stones, to teach them rest.   No words, that I know of, will say what these mosses are.   None are delicate enough, none perfect enough, none rich enough.   How is one to tell of the rounded bosses of furred and beaming green — the starred divisions of rubied bloom, fine-filmed, as if the Rock Spirits could spin porphyry as we do glass — the traceries of intricate silver, and fringes of amber, lustrous, arborescent, burnished through every fibre into fitful brightness and glossy traverses of silken change, yet all subdued and pensive, and framed for simplest, sweetest offices of grace. They will not be gathered, like the flowers, for chaplet or love-token; but of these the wild bird will make its nest, and the wearied child his pillow.   .

And, as the earth's first mercy, so they are its last gift to us.   When all other service is vain, from plant and tree, the soft mosses and gray lichen take up their watch by the headstone. The woods, the blossoms, the gift-bearing grasses, have done their parts for a time, but these do service forever.   Trees for the builder's yard, flowers for the bride's chamber, corn for the granary, moss for the grave.

Yet as in one sense the humblest, in another they are the most honored of the earth-children.   Unfading, as motionless, the worm frets them not, and the autumn wastes not. Strong in lowliness, they neither blanch in heat nor pine in frost. To them, slow-fingered, constant-hearted, is entrusted the weaving of the dark, eternal, tapestries of the hills; to them, slow-penciled, iris-dyed, the tender framing of their endless imagery.   Sharing the stillness of the unimpassioned rock, they share also its endurance; and while the winds of departing spring scatter the white hawthorn blossom like drifted snow, and summer dims on the parched meadow the drooping of its cowslip-gold,— far above, among the mountains, the silver lichen spots rest, star-like, on the stone, and the gathering orange-stain upon the edge of yonder western peak reflects the sunsets of a thousand years.

JOHN RUSKIN.

LAKE OTSEGO.

On all sides, wherever the eye turned, nothing met it but the mirror-like surface of the lake, the placid view of heaven, and the dense setting of woods. So rich and fleecy were the outlines of the forest, that scarce an opening could be seen: the whole visible earth, from the rounded mountain-top to the water's edge, presenting one unvaried line of unbroken verdure. As if vegetation were not satisfied with a triumph so complete, the trees overhung the lake itself, shooting out towards the light; and there were miles along its eastern shore where a boat might have pulled beneath the branches of dark Rembrandt-looking hemlocks, quivering aspens, and melancholy pines. In a word, the hand of man had never yet defaced or deformed any part of this native scene, which lay bathed in the sunlight, a glorious picture of affluent forest grandeur, softened by the balminess of June, and relieved by the beautiful variety afforded by the presence of so broad an expanse of water.

COOPER.

THE LOVELY SHELL.

See what a lovely shell,
Small and pure as a pearl,
Lying close to my foot,

Frail, but a work divine,
Made so fairily well
With delicate spire and whorl,
How exquisitely minute,
A miracle of design!

What is it? a learned man
Could give it a clumsy name.
Let him name it who can,
The beauty would be the same.

The tiny cell is forlorn,
Void of the little living will
That made it stir on the shore.
Did he stand at the diamond door
Of his house in a rainbow frill?
Did he push, when he was uncurl'd,
A golden foot or a fairy horn
Thro' his dim water-world?   TENNYSON.

ON THE ST. LAWRENCE RIVER.

Faintly as tolls the evening chime,
Our voices keep tune and our oars keep time.
Soon as the woods on the shore look dim,
We'll sing at St. Ann's our parting hymn.
Row, brothers, row, the stream runs fast,
The Rapids are near, and the daylight's past!

Why should we yet our sail unfurl?
There is not a breath the blue wave to curl!
But when the wind blows off the shore,
Oh! sweetly we'll rest our weary oar.
Blow, breezes, blow, the stream runs fast,
The Rapids are near, and the daylight's past.

Utawas' tide! this trembling moon
Shall see us float over thy surges soon.
Saint of this green Isle! hear our prayers.
Oh! grant us cool heavens and favoring airs.
Blow, breezes, blow, the stream runs fast,
The Rapids are near, and the daylight's past!

MOORE.

NIGHT.

The sky is overcast
With a continuous cloud of texture close,
Heavy and wan, all whitened by the Moon,
Which through that veil is indistinctly seen,
A dull, contracted circle, yielding light
So feebly spread, that not a shadow falls,
Checkering the ground — from rock, plant, tree or
Tower, at length a pleasant instantaneous gleam
Startles the pensive traveler while he treads
His lonesome path, with unobserving eye
Bent earthwards; he looks up — the clouds are split
Asunder :— and above his head he sees
The clear Moon, and the glory of the heavens.
There, in a black–blue vault she sails along,
Followed by multitudes of stars, that, small
And sharp, and bright, along the dark abyss
Drive as she drives: how fast they wheel away,
Yet vanish not!— the wind is in the tree,
But they are silent;— still they roll along
Immeasurably distant; and the vault,
Built round by those white clouds, enormous clouds,
Still deepens its unfathomable depth.
At length the Vision closes; and the mind,
Not undisturbed by the delight it feels, which
Slowly settles into peaceful calm. WORDSWORTH.

A COTTAGE.

I knew by the smoke, that so gracefully curled
      Above the green elms, that a cottage was near;
And I said, ' If there's peace to be found in the world,
      A heart that was humble might hope for it here!'

It was noon, and on flowers that languished around
      In silence reposed the voluptuous bee;
Every leaf was at rest, and I heard not a sound
      But the woodpecker tapping the hollow beech-tree.

And ' Here in this lone little wood, ' I exclaimed,
      With a maid who was lovely to soul and to eye,
Who would blush when I praised her, and weep if I
            blamed,
      How blest could I live, and how calm could I die!
                                    MOORE.

THE FIRE-FLY.

This morning, when the earth and sky
      Were burning with the blush of spring,
I saw thee not, thou humble fly!
      Nor thought upon thy gleaming wing.

But now the skies have lost their hue,
      And sunny lights no longer play,
I see thee, and I bless thee too
      For sparkling o'er the dreary way.

Oh! let me hope that thus for me,
      When life and love shall lose their bloom,
Some milder joys may come, like thee,
      To light, if not to warm the gloom!
                                    MOORE.

A WATER-FOWL.

Mark how the feathered tenants of the flood,
With grace of motion that might scarcely seem
Inferior to angelical, prolong
Their curious pastime! shaping in mid air
(And sometimes with ambitious wing that soars
High as the level of the mountain-tops)
A circuit ampler than the lake beneath —
Their own domain; but ever, while intent
On tracing and retracing that large round,
Their jubilant activity evolves
Hundreds of curves and circlets, to and fro,
Upward and downward, progress intricate
Yet unperplexed, as if one spirit swayed
Their indefatigable flight.   'Tis done —
Ten times, or more, I fancied it had ceased;
But lo ! the vanished company again
Ascending: they approach — I hear their wings,
Faint, faint at first; and then an eager sound,
Past in a moment — and as faint again !
They tempt the sun to sport amid their plumes:
They tempt the water, or the gleaming ice,
To show them a fair image; 'tis themselves,
Their own fair forms, upon the glimmering plain,
Painted more soft and fair as they descend
Almost to touch ;— then up again aloft,
Up with a sally and a flash of speed,
As if they scorned both resting-place and rest !

WORDSWORTH.

THE HAWK.

Who but hails the sight with pleasure
When the wings of genius rise
Their ability to measure

With great enterprise ;
But in man was ne'er such daring
As yon Hawk exhibits, pairing
His brave spirit with the war in
  The stormy skies!

Mark him, how his power he uses,
Lays it by, at will resumes !
Mark, ere for his haunt he chooses
  Clouds and utter glooms !
There, he wheels in downward mazes
Sunward now his flight he raises,
Catches fire, as seems, and blazes
  With uninjured plumes !

WORDSWORTH.

THE GREEN LINNET.

Beneath these fruit-tree boughs that shed
Their snow-white blossoms on my head
With brightest sunshine round me spread
  Of spring's unclouded weather,
In this sequestered nook how sweet
To sit upon my orchard-seat !
And birds and flowers once more to greet,
  My last year's friends together.

One have I marked, the happiest guest
In all this covert of the blest :
Hail to Thee, far above the rest
  In joy of voice and pinion !
Thou, Linnet ! in thy green array,
Presiding Spirit here to-day,
Dost lead the revels of the May ;
  And this is thy dominion.

While birds, and butterflies and flowers,
Make all one band of paramours,
Thou, ranging up and down the bowers,
      Art sole in thy employment:
A Life, a Presence like the Air,
Scattering thy gladness without care
Too blest with any one to pair ;
      Thyself thy own enjoyment.

Amid yon tuft of hazel trees,
That twinkle to the gusty breeze,
Behold him perched in ecstacies,
      Yet seeming still to hover ;
There ! where the flutter of his wings
Upon his back and body flings
Shadows and sunny glimmerings,
      That cover him all over.

My dazzled sight he oft deceives,
A brother of the dancing leaves ;
Then flits, and from the cottage-eaves
      Pours forth his song in gushes,
As if by that exulting strain
He mocked and treated with disdain
The voiceless Form he choose to feign,
      While fluttering in the bushes.
                WORDSWORTH.

THE SHIP.

She comes majestic with her swelling sails
The gallant Ship ; along her watery way
Homeward she drives before the favoring gales.
Now flirting at their length the streamers play,
And now they ripple with the ruffling breeze.

Hark to the sailors' shouts ! the rocks rebound,
Thundering in echoes to the joyful sound.
Long have they voyaged o'er the distant seas :
And what a heart-delight they feel at last,
So many toils, so many dangers past,
To view the port desired, he only knows
Who on the stormy deep for many a day
Hath tost, aweary of his watery way,
And watch'd, all anxious, every wind that blows.

SOUTHEY.

THE SPINNING WHEEL.

Swiftly turn the murmuring wheel !
Night has brought the welcome hour
When the weary fingers feel
Help, as if from fairy power ;
Dewy night o'ershades the ground ;
Turn the swift wheel round and round !
Now, beneath the starry sky,
Couch the widely-scattered sheep ;
Ply the pleasant labor, ply !
For the spindle, while they sleep,
Runs with speed more smooth and fine,
Gathering up a trustier line.
Short lived likings may be bred
By a glance from fickle eyes ;
But true love is like the thread
Which the kindly wool supplies,
When the flocks are all at rest
Sleeping on the mountain's breast.

WORDSWORTH.

RAINBOW FALLS IN WATKINS GLEN.

Watkins Glen consists properly of a number of glens or sections rising one above another, forming a series of rocky arcades, galleries and grottoes, subterranean at times, and again widening out into vast amphitheatres. It comprises a superficial area of nearly five hundred acres; its general course is east and west; its tortuous length extends over three miles, and its total ascent to the summit of the mountain above is eight hundred feet. This Great Natural Wonder is located at the head of the beautiful Seneca Lake, where is presented a charming combination picture of glen, mountain, lake and valley.

Triple Cascade and Rainbow Falls is thought by many to be the finest in the glen. As its name indicates, it is formed of three portions, one above another, each different in form from the others and making a beautiful combination. Directly opposite the Triple Cascade a little brook leaps over the brow of the great cliff nearly four hundred feet high, down into the glen, trickling over the irregular surface of the rock until it reaches a point thirty feet above the footpath, where it falls on a projecting rock, the edge of which is curved outward to form a shelf, this edge or shelf is in a crescent form. The water descends in a myriad of tiny threads and drops, forming a sparkling crystal veil. While standing here and looking out through the misty curtain, the novelty of the position and the peculiar beauty that the radiant raindrops impart to everything viewed through them, fill us with wonder. It is beautiful beyond description. In the afternoon, when fair weather prevails, the rays of the sun fall into the gorge. The enraptured visitor looking through the veil may behold two most beautiful rainbows, a primary and a secondary, a sight that once enjoyed can never be forgotten.

FIFTH STEP IN RENDERING.
FORMING PICTURES.

In this step the individual characters, scenes, situations and objects found in selections to be rendered should be treated as directed in the Descriptive Style, with all pictures of the study combined into a composite whole, with scenes and characters, properly placed as to rank, and with effective background and lights.

In working up the following studies, first gather in the full meaning of the selection : and often as much thought and study may be given to the reading of a study as the author has given in writing it. In such a case it may be said : " Of equal honor with him who writes a grand poem is he who reads it grandly."

After securing a full comprehension of the study, its purpose, aim and UNITY, divide it into acts and scenes and action of the characters. Picture the whole as if on a large canvas. Become familiar with it so as to tell it in your own language. Your fancy may add some little details or slight some unimportant points.

Place in a high light the central idea even as the photographer focuses his camera on the point of chief interest. He may focus either on the person or the background. The result is governed by the focus. In rendering, distinguish between essentials and accidentals. Let all lend itself to the essential, the unity. Giving essentials prominence is strength : accidentals, weakness.

It has been said, " Every one is mentally Consumptive whose powers of imagination are weak, for fancy is the lungs of the mind. "

The Imagination, as well as the other great factors of the mind, Memory, Reason etc. may be so cultivated as to be of most practical value and to afford æsthetic pleasure as well. Through the culture of the Imagination is found a mighty means of training individuals from the condition of animal nature to that of spirit. Through its culture benevolent feelings and broad sympathies are developed. It is a well known fact that artists along the various lines are, as a class, most benevolent. Through an awakened imagination it is possible to feel, *really* for the unfortunate, to take their place, assume such character and act it. On the other hand the people who astonish with bluntness, selfishness and cruelty, because of feeble imaginative powers are unable to go out of self and take another person's place, but are self-centered.

This precious faculty, the Imagination, should be cultivated rather than repressed or allowed to run wild. When properly trained, it becomes an aid in quickening all the other mental faculties, and whipping the naturally sluggish brain into action.

The material for the Imagination is held by Memory. Memory through the aid of Perception collects and holds the images. The Imagination rearranges this material to please the taste or fancy of the individuality. A person with small imaginative powers represents the bare image as memory holds it — the exact facts. A person with a large, active imagination would rearrange the facts, give effective touches here and there, expressions which are the choice of his own soul ; so when the image reaches the attention of the listener it is a new creation, a child of the speaker's personality, breathing with his own life.

The mental action of the person who presents the *exact*

image or impression, just as he saw it, may be likened to a photographer who makes his exposure haphazard, taking in all detail with realistic fidelity, the unsightly and beautiful.

The mental action of the person who takes into his mind the exact image and turns it over, selecting and rejecting to please his own fancy, may recreate from his own personality (always keeping within the bounds of truth) that which is original and colored with his individuality. The expression may be made artistic even as a painting by a master who has selected only that in harmony with his theme, finishing all with touches of the ideal rather than the exactness of the real. The impression made on the mind of the listener by the realistic is a feeling of having been annoyed by much that is uninteresting, while the impression made by the artistic is most gratifying and lasting.

The speaker with bare material facts tires and confuses the mind of the listener. The speaker who possesses the magical power of entering into the realm of the ideal, and as he appeals to the ideal, charms and entrances the listener.

There are three distinct classes of readers and speakers. The most tedious —the least interesting is the speaker who gives words simply. The second class is more entertaining and is able to hold the attention of his listeners. He presents ideas instead of words and creates realistic, well-defined pictures. He gives much that is satisfying. The third gives that which is the artistic creation of his own mind and heart. With a noble personality, he charms and fascinates and gives that which cannot be forgotten. The last named gives the most for he gives with his reading, himself.

The development of all the powers of the mind, Imagination no less than Reason, depends on judicious exercise.

Ample exercise for the culture of the Imagination of a vigorous and wholesome character may be found in the broad fields of Nature, Literature, Music, Art and Religion.

The mind should search for its ideal material to use in building its own creations. Search for images in all forms of Life, Nature, Literature, Music, Art, Religion.

The memory should be exact in its action. The greater the store of ideals, images, memory gems, the richer the experience, the greater will be the resources at hand for new creations and the more expert will become the faculty of the Imagination in using its store.

Train the mind to reflect. Create ideal scenes and characters. Think out such matters definitely, even as an artist. Give careful attention to the minute as well as the great.

In rendering the writings of others, let the imagination play its part that you may not read words, but give ideas, even experiences, participating heartily in that rendered.

Study that which is vast and sublime and that which is delicate and ethical.

Study the characters portrayed by Dickens, Shakespeare and other writers. Become familiar with the notable characters of the Bible and History. Meditate on models of excellence till you feel the influence and inspiration of their living presence.

Literary companions afford excellent entertainment and profit when through fancy they are endowed with life, so in this way one need never lack for companionship.

With a well trained Imagination, there is little danger of IMITATION. The reader has such wealth of his own ideas there is no room for borrowed ways. The listener feels there is an abundance, a wealth in a personality that can give lavishly.

With well-defined pictures living and glowing in the mind at the moment of utterance, it is not uncertain that something may take place quite as positive and wonderful as wireless telegraphy, even mental photography. With thought, which some tell us is the greatest force in the universe, there seems to be power in certain minds to flash an idea or picture into the minds of others as it is in his own mind, making the listener conscious of his exact thought and feeling. On the other hand, it is not difficult to detect hollow words with no ideas back of them. Such words are vacant and empty like the stare of an idiot. When such a reader arises and calls for attention the minds of his listeners are invited to a feast only to be deluded with empty plates.

The art of having something to give may be learned, and the host who takes pains to prepare his repast and serve it with a lavish hand may spread a feast to delight and satisfy the minds of his guests, a feast of good things not soon to be forgotten.

Through the culture of the Imagination comes the much coveted grace of self-forgetfulness, so necessary in the public speaker. As the attention is fixed on the ideas to be given instead of self and what the audience may think, in giving the undivided attention to the thought is a refuge for self to hide behind the thought, gaining ease and freedom.

The feelings play an important part in stimulating the imagination. We may never go beyond what we have experienced in real feeling, yet we may so associate what is similar making it near experience.

Under the sublime and beautiful, one may rise into the realm of the ideal.

According to Sully we may classify the Imagination as Constructive, Receptive, Creative. Constructive—Reproduction of images. Ability to elaborate new images.
Receptive — as in reading (studying) a poem.
Creative — as the poet creating the poem,— complex.
Aids : Knowing things. Acquiring knowledge. Emotious.

KING ROBERT OF SICILY.

Robert of Sicily, brother of Pope Urbane
And Valmond, Emperor of Allemaine,
Appareled in magnificent attire,
With retinue of many a knight and squire,
On St. John's eve, at vespers, proudly sat
And heard the priests chant the Magnificat.
And as he listened, o'er and o'er again
Repeated like a burden or refrain,
He caught the words, " *Deposuit potentes*
De sede et exaltavit humiles " ;
And slowly lifting up his kingly head,
He to a learned clerk beside him said,
" What mean these words ? "   The clerk made an-
                swer meet,
   " He has put down the mighty from their seat,
And has exalted them of low degree. "
Thereat King Robert muttered scornfully,
" 'Tis well that such seditious words are sung
Only by priests and in the Latin tongue;
For unto priests and people be it known,
There is no power can push me from my throne ! "
And leaning back, he yawned and fell asleep,
Lulled by the chant monotonous and deep.

When he awoke it was already night;
The church was empty, and there was no light,
Save where the lamps that glimmered few and faint,
Lighted a little space before some saint.
He started from his seat and gazed around,
But saw no living thing and heard no sound.
He groped towards the door, but it was locked;
He cried aloud, and listened, and then knocked,
And uttered awful threatenings and complaints,

And imprecations upon men and saints.
The sounds re-echoed from the roof and walls
As if dead priests were laughing in their stalls.

At length the sexton, hearing from without
The tumult of the knocking and the shout,
And thinking thieves were in the house of prayer,
Came with his lantern, asking, "Who is there?"
Half choked with rage, King Robert fiercely said,
"Open: 't is I, the King! Art thou afraid?"
The frightened sexton, muttering, with a curse,
"This is some drunken vagabond, or worse!"
Turned the great key and flung the portal wide;
A man rushed by him at a single stride,
Haggard, half naked, without hat or cloak,
Who neither turned, nor looked at him, nor spoke,
But leaped into the blackness of the night
And vanished like a spectre from his sight.

Robert of Sicily, brother of Pope Urbane
And Valmond, Emperor of Allemaine,
Despoiled of his magnificent attire,
Bareheaded, breathless, and besprent with mire,
With sense of wrong and outrage desperate,
Strode on and thundered at the palace gate;
Rushed through the court–yard, thrusting in his rage
To right and left each seneschal and page,
And hurried up the broad and sounding stair,
His white face ghastly in the torches' glare.
From hall to hall he passed with breathless speed:
Voices and cries he heard, but did not heed,
Until at last he reached the banquet room,
Blazing with light and breathing with perfume.

There on the dais sat another king,

Wearing his robes, his crown, his signet-ring,
King Robert's self in feature, form and height,
But all transfigured with angelic light!
It was an Angel; and his presence there
With a divine effulgence filled the air,
An exaltation piercing the disguise,
Though none the hidden Angel recognize.

A moment speechless, motionless, amazed,
The throneless monarch on the Angel gazed,
Who met his look of anger and surprise
With the divine compassion of his eyes;
Then said, " Who art thou? and why com'st thou
        here? "
To which King Robert answered with a sneer,
" I am the King, and come to claim my own
From an impostor, who usurps my throne! "
And suddenly, at these audacious words,
Up sprang the angry guests, and drew their swords!
The Angel answered with unruffled brow,
" Nay, not the King, but the King's Jester, thou
Henceforth shalt wear the bells and scalloped cape,
And for thy counsellor shalt lead an ape;
Thou shalt obey my servants when they call,
And wait upon my henchmen in the hall! "

Deaf to King Robert's threats and cries and prayers,
They thrust him from the hall and down the stairs;
A group of tittering pages ran before,
And as they opened wide the folding-door,
His heart failed, for he heard, with strange alarms,
The boisterous laughter of the men-at-arms,
And all the vaulted chamber roar and ring
With the mock plaudits of " Long live the King! "
Next morning, waking with the day's first beam,

He said within himself, " It was a dream ! "
But the straw rustled as he turned his head,
There were the cap and bells beside his bed,
Around him rose the bare discolored walls,
Close by, the steeds were champing in their stalls,
And in the corner, a revolting shape,
Shivering and chattering sat the wretched ape.
It was no dream; the world he loved so much
Had turned to dust and ashes at his touch !

Days came and went; and now returned again
To Sicily the old Saturnian reign ;
Under the Angel's governance benign
The happy island danced with corn and wine,
And deep within the mountain's burning breast
Enceladus, the giant, was at rest.

Meanwhile King Robert yielded to his fate,
Sullen and silent and disconsolate,
Dressed in the motley garb that Jesters wear,
With look bewildered and a vacant stare,
Close shaven above the ears, as monks are shorn,
By courtiers mocked, by pages laughed to scorn,
His only friend the ape, his only food
What others left,— he still was unsubdued.
And when the Angel met him on his way,
And half in earnest, half in jest, would say,
Sternly, though tenderly, that he might feel
The velvet scabbard held a sword of steel,
" Art thou the King ? " the passion of his woe
Burst from him in resistless overflow,
And, lifting high his forehead, he would fling
The haughty answer back " I am, I am the King ! "

Almost three years were ended; when there came

Ambassadors of great repute and name
From Valmond, Emperor of Allemaine,
Unto King Robert, saying that Pope Urbane
By letter summoned them forthwith to come
On Holy Thursday to his city of Rome.
The Angel with great joy received his guests,
And gave them presents of embroidered vests,
And velvet mantles with rich ermine lined,
And rings and jewels of the rarest kind.
Then he departed with them o'er the sea
Into the lovely land of Italy,
Whose loveliness was more resplendent made
By the mere passing of that cavalcade,
With plumes, and cloaks, and housings, and the stir
Of jeweled bridle and of golden spur.

And lo! among the menials, in mock state,
Upon a piebald steed, with shambling gait,
His cloak of fox-tails flapping in the wind,
The solemn ape demurely perched behind,
King Robert rode, making huge merriment
In all the country towns through which they went.

The Pope received them with great pomp and blare
Of bannered trumpets, on Saint Peter's square,
Giving his benediction, and embrace,
Fervent, and full of apostolic grace.
While with congratulations and with prayers
He entertained the Angel unawares.

Robert, the Jester, bursting through the crowd,
Into their presence rushed, and cried aloud,
" I am the King! Look, and behold in me
Robert, your brother, King of Sicily!
This man, who wears my semblance to your eyes,
Is an impostor in a king's disguise.

Do you not know me? does no voice within
Answer my cry, and say we are akin? "
The Pope in silence, but with troubled mien,
Gazed at the Angel's countenance serene;
The Emperor, laughing said, " It is strange sport
To keep a madman for thy Fool at court! "
And the poor, baffled Jester in disgrace
Was hustled back among the populace.

In solemn state the Holy Week went by,
And Easter Sunday gleamed upon the sky;
The presence of the Angel, with its light,
Before the sun rose, made the city bright,
And with new fervor filled the hearts of men,
Who felt that Christ indeed had risen again.
Even the Jester, on his bed of straw,
With haggard eyes the unwonted splendor saw,
He felt within a power unfelt before,
And, kneeling humbly on his chamber floor,
He heard the rushing garments of the Lord
Sweep through the silent air, ascending heavenward.

And now the visit ending, and once more
Valmond returning to the Danube's shore,
Homeward the Angel journeyed, and again
The land was made resplendent with his train,
Flashing along the towns of Italy
Unto Salerno, and from thence by sea.
And when once more within Palermo's wall,
And, seated on the throne in his great hall,
He heard the Angelus from convent towers,
As if the better world conversed with ours,
He beckoned to King Robert to draw nigher,
And with a gesture bade the rest retire;
And when they were alone, the Angel said,

" Art thou the King? " Then, bowing down his head,
King Robert crossed both hands upon his breast,
And meekly answered him : " Thou knowest best !
My sins as scarlet are ; let me go hence,
And in some cloister's school of penitence,
Across those stones, that pave the way to heaven,
Walk barefoot, till my guilty soul be shriven ! "

The Angel smiled, and from his radiant face
A holy light illumined all the place,
And through the open window, loud and clear,
They heard the monks chant in the chapel near,
Above the stir and tumult of the street :
" He has put down the mighty from their seat,
And has exalted them of low degree ! "
And through the chant a second melody
Rose like the throbbing of a single string ;
" I am an Angel, and thou art the King! "

King Robert, who was standing near the throne,
Lifted his eyes, and lo! he was alone!
But all apparelled as in days of old,
With ermined mantle and with cloth of gold ;
And when his courtiers came, they found him there
Kneeling upon the floor, absorbed in silent prayer.

HENRY W. LONGFELLOW.

WORDS LIKE ARROWS.

My own eyes filled with tears, when I saw that hers were
closed. I had stopped in the village to ask about her, but
no one had told me she was blind.

" May I come in? " I swung the open gate with a
little premeditated clatter.

She smiled ever so sweetly. " Yes, indeed, come in.

I shall be very glad to see you. "

Glad *to see* me.   The pathos of the word stung me as I walked the flower-bordered path to the garden bench where she was sitting in the mellow June sunshine which turned her soft white hair to glistening silver.

" Will you sit down ? "   She made room for me beside her and reached out her hand for mine.   " You see now. adays hands help me to get acquainted.   Ah, yours is soft and white I know, not hard and brown like mine.   I always did like a pretty hand, and mine's always been so homely.''

" But it is beautiful to me.   I know it has done so many useful things and many kind deeds. "

" And yours?   It's fine and soft, but it isn't a lazy hand. I feel the strength and firmness in it.   I am quite a dab at reading hands. "   She laughed gently.   " Now tell me truly, it isn't a lazy hand, is it? "

" No ; not lazy, but I'm awfully afraid it has been a very selfish hand. "

" Ah, my dear, that's the way we all feel.   None of us are what we'd like to be, but it won't do to judge ourselves. Why, do you know, if I was to sit in judgment on myself I'd — why I'd sentence myself to everlasting unhappiness. "

" Oh no, you mustn't say so. "

But I'm not judging myself, dear.   I am leaving that to one who is much more loving and forgiving to us poor mortals than we can be to ourselves. "

She loosened the lingering hold of my hand which had thrilled me through and through and softly stroked the folds of my gown.

"Silk : not the shiny kind, but soft and rich. Is it black?"

" No, grey for travelling. "

" You came from the city.   I thought when you first spoke you were probably a summer boarder.   They're always real neighborly, but somehow you talk different from most of them. "

" I have been in England for a long while. You know they speak differently over there. Perhaps I have picked up the English accent, and it's said the soft climate there affects the voice. "

" My youngest daughter used to want to go to England. She talked a lot about it. "

" Did she ? " I asked with the greatest interest.

" Yes; she kind o' reached out for travel and books and pictures. She could paint quite tasty pictures herself. Would you like to see the one she did of the little school-house and the brook? Her father had it framed for me the Christmas before he died. He got it down out of the attic where she'd put it when —— But wouldn't you like to see it ? "

" Yes ; if I may, after a while. "

" You see, James her father, was president of the school board. Daisy was the brightest girl in school — everybody said so — and so it was kind of appropriate for her to make a picture of the old red building. I often wish she could see how fine it looks hanging over the mantel in the parlor. I generally rub my hands over it once or twice a day just to see that it is keeping all right and the gold frame isn't breaking off anywhere. When anybody comes in I usually ask if the paint is keeping bright. You see I set a good deal of store by it. "

" Do you live here alone? " I asked.

" Yes; all by myself. "

" Aren't you lonely ? "

" I can't say that I am ever real lonesome, though of course I do get a little weary of the waiting sometimes. "

Waiting? I asked myself. She couldn't mean that she was hoping or expecting to —— Oh, no she was too brave and cheery.

" Yes; I'm waiting. I've been waiting for years. My sons and my daughters, they're all married and living round here — all but the youngest — on farms mostly, though Lucinda married a preacher, and he often changes churches; that is some comfort, for Lucinda has got convinced herself now that it wouldn't do for me to be moving every whipstitch, so she doesn't ask me to live with her any more. If the others would only quit, I'd be a heap sight happier. I hate to be saying, *no* to my children all the time, and they think I am dreadfully set in my way; and I suppose I am. I just tell them I would not be contented anywhere but right here in the old house where I've lived in since they were all babies. I don't mind having the little maid come every morning from the village to help me, for she's a nice child and I'm teaching her to sew and knit. There is the telephone, too, for company. I had one put in because I've heard how people can talk over them a long distance, and I might, you know, be called up some time from a very long way off. There; I guess I'm getting garrulous. Tell me about yourself. I always like to know about people. "

" Yes; but not yet. First, I should like to know if you feel like telling me about the waiting? "

" I knew when you sat down beside me I'd tell you sooner or later. There's some people I can't help pouring out my heart to, and when I can tell I like to do it for it might help. It's like shooting arrows into the air. You never can tell where words, said to these city folks may land. I remember saying that to a young man that used to come to see me, and he agreed it was true, that words sent out couldn't always go astray — that surely some time the right person would hear them. He gave me a new courage— he was so strong, so helpful. I've always wished he'd come back, but he never has. And — I just go on waiting. "

" What was he like? "

" He was tall and broad-shouldered, with a deep, gentle voice, and his eyes and hair were kind of tawny brown. I remember him very distinctly because he was the last person I saw before my blindness came. He was standing in the garden saying good-bye to me, and I was wondering why such a fine able-bodied man should paint pictures for a living when the darkness began to come. I thought it was just the heat or something, and I didn't say anything about it; but when he was gone I started into the house and I found I was blind. "

" Oh! " I shuddered, " how terribly sudden. "

" Yes, it was sudden, and the worst of it all was that I knew after all my long waiting I'd never see Daisy when she comes back. You see, my dear, I'm waiting for my youngest daughter. Whenever she comes back she'll find her mother waiting for her in the old home. Sometimes I think if she had only been a little more patient when her father refused to let her go to the city to study he might have been brought round to it. But she was determined and enthusiastic, like all young folks I guess. It would be a dull world if they weren't so, wouldn't it? She told him she would surely go some day, and he grew very angry and said dreadful bitter words that he did not mean — oh, I know he didn't mean them. He told her that if she left home against his wishes that would be the end, that she need never come back.

I ought to have spoken up then and made him see how wrong he was, but it was always my way to kind of wait on father's moods, and he usually came round to my way of thinking, sort of dismounting from his high horse in the dark you know. But I've wished many and many a time that I had spoken up and asserted Daisy's rights. That's what I ought to have done, but I guess I was always too peace-loving, and I didn't realise until she was gone that

I might have saved us all a lot of unhappiness, if I'd been a little more high-spirited. When father found she had left without a word he was terribly angry and he wouldn't talk of her to me at all, but I knew afterwards that he tried to trace her in the city, but it was no use. She had disappeared completely. Oh, those were dreary days. "

" Cruel, cruel days, " I cried.

" It wasn't till that last Christmas, when father had the schoolhouse picture framed and hung over the mantel I was sure he was sorry and loving. He couldn't talk about her, but when we sat down before the fire Christmas night he took my hand and said, ' It's some comfort, ain't it, mother?' and I knew just as well as if he had talked a whole chapter that his heart cried out for his baby girl, Daisy, as much as mine did. Somehow we were a good deal happier after that. He died the next fall, and I've been here ever since just waiting. "

" How long ago is that? "

" Almost four years now. "

" Four years? Oh, what a useless tragedy! You know what you said about your words falling like arrows? Well, that young man to whom you told the story repeated it wherever he went, and he was a great wanderer. "

" Why, bless me, did you know him? "

" Yes; I heard him tell the story in a little summer camp of artists on the Scilly Isles, a part of England, you know, and he said moreover that he had vowed that if he ever found your Daisy he would bring her back to you. "

" Did he? God bless him! My, how little and near together this great big, wide-spread world is after all. Just to think you have seen him way off there across the water. "

" And — and how can I tell you? He has kept his word. He has married your Daisy and — "

" Where — where is she? " the dear old voice rang

out with a penetrating agony of hope that stopped my heart's beating for an instant, but I was afraid to speak.

I sank down on the ground at her knee and reached my arms around her waist.

" Where — where is she I say ? "

" Here, marmsie, " I cried in a choking voice, using my old baby-girl name for her.

" My child, my child ! " She passed her hands over my face, and as I rose and took her in my arms and kissed her again and again she murmured, " And sometimes I doubted — I really dared to doubt — the goodness of God. Oh my child, my baby Daisy ! "

Then there was a rattle at the gate and a tall tawny-haired man with the kindest eyes in the world came into the garden and encircled us both in his strong, loving arms.

THE SPHERE.

A DAY IN THE MOUNTAINS.

We commenced our journey to Placid Lake, forty-two miles distant, at daybreak. The mountain air was chill and invigorating, our horses were fresh and we were soon deep in the forest. One who has never experienced it can scarcely appreciate the feeling of isolation that comes over one on finding himself on a narrow trail in the forest surrounded and shut in on all sides by tall pine trees into whose depths he can peer at times but a few yards, yet it is by no means a monotonous isolation for the wood is full of variety and abounds with life. Squirrels and chipmunks chattered and scolded us from the branches of the trees as if they would dispute our right to trespass on the property nature had provided for them. Rabbits scurried across our path. Prairie chickens flew clumsily out of our way to some neighboring boughs from which they watched us with a look

of innocent wonder. Sometimes our trail led us along the
banks of the Big Blackfoot River, sometimes over precipi-
tous mountain spurs, sometimes through deep ravines with
only a narrow passage through the tangled undergrowth,
sometimes across broad valleys looking for all the world
like well-kept Parks with the trees set out singly or in
groups in a beautiful greensward. One of these ideal re-
treats in the heart of the mountains appeared to be a dining-
room for our noonday meal. We sat by the side of a delightful stream of clear, cool water and ate and drank with
a real mountain appetite rendered keen by an early break-
fast and long ride. Our dessert grew all around in a plen-
tiful supply of huckleberries and wild strawberries.

Resuming our journey, our trail now led us up a steep
mountain side, so steep we were obliged to dismount, at times,
and lead our horses. Reaching the crest, we were amply re-
paid for our labor. This vantage afforded us a view of
the surrounding country, or the surrounding forests, mile
upon mile of dense forests as far as the eye could reach
over mountain and valley, one vast ocean of pine trees with
no sign of human life or habitation.

After feasting our eyes awhile we began our descent
of the other side of the mountain, which was almost as difficult as our ascent. On reaching the valley below, two or
three miles of trail through matted thickets and over fallen
trees brought us to the shore of Placid Lake. Our trail lay
along the northern shore. A more beautiful sheet of water
it would be hard to imagine. Surrounded on all sides by
the pine–clad mountains, it is as placid and still as a mirror and like a mirror reflects the dark green of its surroundings till looking from shore to shore it is about impossible
to distinguish between shadow and reality — to tell where
the water leaves off and the wood commences. To make
the picture more perfect a stag stood on the further shore

suspiciously sniffing the air. When one of our horses struck his foot against a rock, the stag bounded off into the depths of the woods.

One hour's ride brought us to the little secluded settlement and the ranch-house where we were to spend the night. The inhabitants do not often get a glimpse of the outside world for they are forty-two miles from the nearest post-office and seventy miles from the nearest railway. The people are simple in their tastes and their wants are few. They live in comparative happiness far from the noise and strife of the commercial world. One can scarcely imagine that such a restful, sequestered, natural retreat could exist in this land of strenuous endeavor.

Our arrival from the outside world caused quite a commotion. We were greeted at the door of the log cabin by the whole family including numerous dogs and cats and other household pets. The children, little, ragged, towheaded urchins wild as their own surroundings, watched us stealthily from behind doors and articles of furniture but instantly disappeared if we chanced to look in their direction. Supper was hastened on our account. And such a supper! steak cut from fresh venison, home-made bread, potatoes and coffee. After our long day's ride in the invigorating mountain air, it tasted good beyond comparison.

After supper we went outside to chat and watch the sunset, the crowning glory of a glorious day in the mountains. Two colossal mountain peaks away in the west with their intervening spaces formed the pillars and gateway through which the sun made his majestic farewell amid a riot of changing glory. In the background behind the mountain portals, massive fleecy clouds had rolled themselves into a gigantic mass of mountain and valley till they looked like some fair, distant land where light and shade combined to make a scene of splendor. A land sunkissed till every cloud–mountain and valley glowed in colors of gold and amber and pink and crimson. Gradually this magnificent cloud–country melted away in more subdued and softer tints, quietly slipping into space till at last one little, lonely silver tipped, roseate tinted cloud remained. This too faded and disappeared. The shadows grew long in the valley. The long-drawn, dismal cry of the coyote rallying for nocturnal adventures and the chill air reminded us that the day was done and we went in to sleep on a forest–made, fragrant bed of pine boughs.

From " A WESTERN TRIP. "   REV. DAVID W. FERRY.

LAKE GRASMERE

Clouds, lingering yet, extend in solid bars
Through the gray west; and lo! these waters, steeled
By breezeless air to smoothest polish, yield
A vivid repetition of the stars;
Jove, Venus, and the ruddy crest of Mars
Amid his fellows beauteously revealed
At happy distance from earth's groaning field,
Where ruthless mortals wage incessant wars.
Is it a mirror? — or the nether Sphere
Opening to view the abyss in which she feeds
Her own calm fires? — But list! a voice is near;
Great Pan himself low-whispering through the reeds,
" Be thankful, thou; for, if unholy deeds
Ravage the world, tranquillity is here! "

WORDSWORTH.

Those evening clouds, that setting ray, and beauteous tints, serve to display their great Creator's praise; then let the short lived thing call'd man, whose life is comprised within a span, to Him his homage raise.   SCOTT.

SIXTH STEP IN RENDERING.

VITAL, ANIMATED PICTURES AND SCENES.

In Vitalized or Animated pictures, have in mind not only a picture but the Scene itself in full, true in action and magnitude. Let the pictures in the mind become reality, then there will be no danger of forcing the voice.

THE SHIPWRECK.

I opened the yard gate and looked into the empty street. The sand, the seaweed, and the flakes of foam were driving by, and I was obliged to call for assistance before I could shut the gate again, and make it fast against the wind.

There was a dark gloom in my lonely chamber, when I at length returned to it; but I was tired now, and getting into bed again, fell into the depths of sleep until broad day; when I was aroused at eight or nine o'clock by some one knocking or calling at my door.

" What is the matter ? "

" A wreck ! close by ! "

" What wreck ? "

" A schooner from Spain or Portugal, laden with fruit and wine. Make haste, sir, if you want to see her ! It's thought down on the beach she'll go to pieces every moment. "

I wrapped myself in my clothes as quickly as I could, and ran into the street, where numbers of people were before me, all running in one direction,— to the beach. I ran the same way, outstripping a good many, and soon came

facing the wild sea. Every appearance it had before presented bore the expression of being *swelled*; and the height
to which the breakers rose and bore one another down, and
rolled in, in interminable hosts, was most appalling.

In the difficulty of hearing anything but wind and waves,
and in the crowd, and the unspeakable confusion, and my
first breathless efforts to stand against the weather, I was so
confused that I looked out to sea for the wreck, and saw
nothing but the foaming heads of the great waves.

A boatman laid a hand upon my arm and pointed. Then
I saw it, close in upon us.

One mast was broken short off, six or eight feet from the
deck, and lay over the side, entangled in a maze of sail and
rigging: and all that ruin, as the ship rolled and beat,—
which she did with a violence quite inconceivable,— beat the
side as if it would stave it in. Some efforts were being
made to cut this portion of the wreck away; for, as the ship,
which was broadside on, turned toward us in her rolling,
I plainly descried her people at work with axes—especially
one active figure, with long curling hair. But a great cry,
audible even above the wind and water, rose from the shore;
the sea, sweeping over the wreck, made a clean breach, and
carried men, spars, casks, planks, bulwarks, heaps of such
toys, into the boiling surge.

The second mast was yet standing, with the rags of a sail,
and a wild confusion of broken cordage, flapping to and fro.
The ship had struck once, the same boatman said, and then
lifted in, and struck again. I understood him to add that
she was parting amidships. As he spoke, there was another
great cry of pity from the beach. Four men arose with the
wreck out of the deep, clinging to the rigging of the remaining mast; uppermost, the active figure with the curling
hair. There was a bell on board; and as the ship rolled and
dashed, this bell rang; and its sound, the knell of those un-

happy men, was borne toward us on the wind. Again we lost her, and again she rose. Two of the four men were gone.

I noticed that some new sensation moved the people on the beach, and I saw them part, and Ham come breaking through them to the front.

Instantly I ran to him, for I divined that he meant to wade off with the rope. I held him back with both arms; and implored the men not to listen to him, not to let him stir from that sand.

Another cry arose, and we saw the cruel sail, with blow on blow, beat off the lower of the two men, and fly up in triumph round the active figure left alone upon the mast. Against such a sight, and against such determination as that of the calmly desperate man, who was already accustomed to lead half the people present, I might as hopefully have entreated the wind.

I was swept away to some distance, where the people a-round me made me stay; urging, as I confusedly perceived, that he was bent on going, with help or without, and that I should endanger the precautions for his safety by troubling those with whom they rested. I saw hurry on the beach, and men running with ropes, and penetrating into a circle of figures that hid him from me. Then I saw him standing alone, in a seaman's frock and trousers, a rope in his hand, another round his body, and several of the best men holding to the latter.

The wreck was breaking up. I saw that she was parting in the middle, and that the life of the solitary man upon the mast hung by a thread. He had a singular red cap on, not like a sailor's cap, but of a finer color; and as the few planks between him and destruction rolled and bulged, and as his death-knell rung, he was seen by all of us to wave this cap. I saw him do it now, and thought I was going distracted, when his action brought an old remembrance to

my mind of a once dear friend, the once dear friend,—
Steerforth.

Ham watched the sea until there was a great retiring
wave; when he dashed in after it, and in a moment was
buffeting with the water, rising with the hills, falling with
the valleys, lost beneath the foam,— borne in toward the
shore, borne on toward the ship.

At length he neared the wreck. He was so near, that
with one more of his vigorous strokes he would be clinging
to it, when a high, green, vast hill-side of water moving on
shoreward from beyond the ship, he seemed to leap up
into it with a mighty bound,— and the ship was gone!

They drew him to my very feet, insensible, dead. He
was carried to the nearest house, and every means of res-
toration was tried; but he had been beaten to death by the
great wave, and his generous heart was stilled forever.

As I sat beside the bed, when hope was abandoned, and
all was done, a fisherman who had known me when Emily
and I were children, and ever since, whispered my name
at the door.

" Sir, will you come over yonder? "

The old remembrance that had been recalled to me was
in his look, and I asked him, " Has a body come ashore? "

" Yes. "

" Do I know it? "

He answered nothing. But he led me to the shore. And
on that part of it where she and I had looked for shells, two
children,— on that part of it where some lighter fragments
of the old boat blown down last night had been scattered
by the wind,—among the ruins of the home he had
wronged,— I saw him lying with his head upon his
arm, as I had often seen him lie at school.

" DAVID COPPERFIELD. "   CHARLES DICKENS.

ERUPTION OF MOUNT VESUVIUS.

" To the lion with the Egyptian. "

With that cry up sprang—on moved — thousands upon thousands! They rushed from the heights — they poured down in the direction of the Egyptian. . . . . The power of the prætor was as a reed beneath the whirlwind; still, at his word the guards had drawn themselves along the lower benches, on which the upper classes sat separate from the vulgar. They made but a feeble barrier — the waves of the human sea halted for a moment to enable Arbaces to count the exact moment of his doom! In despair, and in a terror which beat down even his pride, he glanced his eyes over the rolling and rushing crowd — when, right above them, through the wide chasm which had been left in the velaria, he beheld a strange and awful apparition — he beheld — and his craft restored his courage!

He stretched his hand on high; over his lofty brow and royal features there came an expression of unutterable solemnity and command.

" Behold! " he shouted with a voice of thunder, which stilled the roar of the crowd; " behold how the gods protect the guiltless! The fires of the avenging Orcus burst forth against the false witness of my accusers! "

The eyes of the crowd followed the gesture of the Egyptian, and beheld, with ineffable dismay, a vast vapor shooting from the summit of Vesuvius, in the form of a gigantic pine-tree; the trunk, blackness,— the branches, fire!— a fire that shifted and wavered in its hues with every moment, now fiercely luminous, now of a dull and dying red, that again blazed terrifically forth with intolerable glare!

There was a dead, heart-sunken silence — through which there suddenly broke the roar of the lion, which was echoed back from within the building by the sharper and fiercer

yells of its fellow-beast.   Dread seers were they of the
Burden of the Atmosphere, and wild prophets of the wrath
to come!

Then there arose on high the universal shrieks of women;
the men stared at each other, but were dumb.   At that
moment they felt the earth shake beneath their feet; the
walls of the theatre trembled; and, beyond in the distance,
they heard the crash of falling roofs; an instant more and
the mountain-cloud seemed to roll towards them, dark and
rapid, like a torrent; at the same time, it cast forth from its
bosom a shower of ashes mixed with vast fragments of burning stone!   Over the crushing vines,— over the desolate
streets,— over the amphitheatre itself,— far and wide,—
with many a mighty splash in the agitated sea,— fell that
awful shower!

No longer thought the crowd of justice or of Arbaces;
safety for themselves was their sole thought.   Each turned
to fly — each dashing, pressing, crushing, against the other.
Trampling recklessly over the fallen — amidst groans, and
oaths, and prayers, and sudden shrieks, the enormous crowd
vomited itself forth through the numerous passages.   Whither should they fly?   Some, anticipating a second earthquake,
hastened to their homes to load themselves with their
most costly goods, and escape while it was yet time; others,
dreading the shower of ashes that now fell fast, torrent upon torrent, over the streets, rushed under the roofs of the
nearest houses, or temples, or sheds — shelter of any kind—
for protection from the terrors of the open air.   But darker
and larger, and mightier, spread the cloud above them.
It was a sudden and more ghastly Night rushing upon
the realm of Noon! . . . .   " Gods! — how the darkness
gathers!   Ho, ho;— by yon terrific mountain, what sudden
blazes of lightning!—   Hades is loosed on earth! "

" LAST DAYS OF POMPEII. "   SIR BULWER LYTTON.

THE BURNING OF MOSCOW.

The bright moon rose over the mighty city, tipping with silver the domes of more than two hundred churches, and pouring a flood of light over a thousand palaces and the dwellings of three hundred thousand inhabitants. The weary army sunk to rest, but there was no sleep for Mortier's eyes. Not the gorgeous and variegated palaces and their rich ornaments, nor the parks and gardens and oriental magnificence that everywhere surrounded him, kept him wakeful, but the ominous foreboding that some dire calamity was hanging over the silent capital.   *   *   *

O, it was a scene of woe and fear inconceivable and indescribable! A mighty and closely packed city of houses, and churches, and palaces, wrapped from limit to limit in flames, which are fed by a whirling hurricane, is a sight the world will seldom see.

But this was within the city. To Napoleon, without, the scene was still more sublime and terrific. When the flames had overcome all obstacles, and had wrapped everything in their red mantle, that great city looked like a sea of rolling fire, swept by a tempest that drove it into billows. Huge domes and towers, throwing off sparks like blazing firebrands, now disappeared in their maddening flow, as they rushed and broke high over their tops, scattering their spray of fire against the clouds. The heavens themselves seemed to have caught the conflagration, and the angry masses that swept it rolled over a bosom of fire.

Columns of flame would rise and sink along the surface of this sea, and huge volumes of black smoke suddenly shoot into the air, as if volcanoes were working below. The black form of the Kremlin alone towered above the chaos, now wrapped in flame and smoke, again emerged into view, standing amid this scene of desolation and terror, like Virtue in the midst of a burning world, enveloped but unscathed

by the devouring elements.   Napoleon stood and gazed on
the scene in silent awe.   Though nearly three miles distant,
the windows and walls of his apartments were so hot that
he could scarcely bear his hand against them.

Said he years afterward: " It was a spectacle of a sea
and billows of fire, a sky and clouds of flame, mountains of
red rolling flames, like immense waves of the sea, alternately
bursting forth and elevating themselves to the skies of flame
below.   O. it was the most grand, the most sublime, and the
most terrific sight the world ever beheld. "

Abridged.   J. T. HEADLEY.

VISION OF THE HEAVENLY JERUSALEM.

And he carried me away in the spirit to a great and high
mountain, and showed me that great city, the holy Jerusalem,
descending out of heaven from God, having the glory of
God : and her light was like unto a stone most precious,
even like a jasper stone, clear as crystal; and had a wall
great and high, and had twelve gates, and at the gates twelve
angels, and names written thereon, which are the names of
the twelve tribes of the children of Israel : on the east three
gates; on the north three gates; on the south three gates;
and on the west three gates.   And the wall of the city had
twelve foundations, and in them the names of the twelve
apostles of the Lamb.

And he that talked with me had a golden reed to measure
the city, and the gates thereof, and the wall thereof.   And
the city lieth foursquare, and the length is as large as the
breadth. and he measured the city with the reed, twelve
thousand furlongs.   The length and the breadth and the
height of it are equal.   And he measured the wall thereof,
an hundred and forty and four cubits, according to the measure of a man, that is, of the angel.   And the building of

the wall of it was of jasper: and the city was pure gold, like unto clear glass. And the foundations of the wall of the city were garnished with all manner of precious stones. The first foundation was jasper; the second, sapphire; the third, a chalcedony; the fourth, an emerald; the fifth, sardonyx; the sixth, sardius; the seventh, chrysolyte; the eighth, beryl; the ninth, a topaz; the tenth, a chrysoprasus; the eleventh, a jacinth; the twelfth, an amethyst.

And the twelve gates were twelve pearls; every several gate was of one pearl: and the street of the city was pure gold, as it were transparent glass.

And I saw no temple therein: for the Lord God Almighty and the Lamb are the temple of it. And the city had no need of the sun, neither of the moon, to shine in it; for the glory of God did lighten it, and the Lamb is the light thereof. And the nations of them which are saved shall walk in the light of it: and the kings of the earth do bring their glory and honor into it. And the gates of it shall not be shut at all by day: for there shall be no night there. And they shall bring the glory and honor of the nations into it. And there shall in no wise enter into it anything that defileth, neither whatsoever worketh abomination, or maketh a lie: but they which are written in the Lamb's book of life.

REVELATION XXI. ST. JOHN.

Beneath there sate on many a sapphire throne
The great who had departed from mankind,
A mighty senate; some, whose white hair shone
Like mountain-snow, mild, beautiful, and blind;
Some female forms, whose gestures beamed with mind;
And ardent youths, and children bright and fair;
And some had lyres whose strings were intertwined
With pale and clinging flames.

" REVOLT OF ISLAM. " SHELLEY.

SEVENTH STEP IN RENDERING.
IDEAL PICTURES.

Ideal pictures, or unreal, poetic, fanciful creations of the imagination should be living in the mind vividly, even as the real, substantial pictures. They should be rendered with a touch of delicacy and artistic finesse and poetic suggestiveness, avoiding too much realism.

From the fact that ideal, unreal pictures are not so common as the actual and the real, some minds fail to grasp them so readily. Some of Moore's poems: " Lalla Rookh, " " The Sylph's Ball," and Tennyson's " Merman, " and " Mermaid " present unreal pictures.

Real objects, small and delicate, should be pictured as close at hand and should be portrayed with fitting expression.

THE SEA FAIRIES.

Slow sail'd the weary mariners and saw,
Betwixt the green brink and the running foam,
Sweet faces, rounded arms, and bosoms prest
To little harps of gold; and while they mused,
Whispering to each other half in fear,
Shrill music reach'd them on the middle sea.

Whither away, whither away, whither away? fly no more.
Whither away from the high green field, and the happy
        blossoming shore?
Day and night to the billow the fountain calls:

Down shower the gambolling waterfalls
From wandering over the lea:
Out of the live-green heart of the dells
They freshen the silvery-crimson shells,
And thick with white bells the clover-hill swells
High over the full-toned sea:
O hither, come hither and furl your sails,
Come hither to me and to me:
Hither, come hither and frolic and play;
Here it is only the mew that wails;
We will sing to you all the day:
Mariner, mariner, furl your sails,
For here are the blissful downs and dales,
And merrily merrily carol the gales,
And the spangle dances in bight and bay,
And the rainbow forms and flies on the land
Over the islands free;
And the rainbow lives in the curve of the sand;
Hither, come hither and see;
And the rainbow hangs on the poising wave,
And sweet is the colour of cove and cave,
And sweet shall your welcome be:
O hither, come hither, and be our lords,
For merry brides are we:
We will kiss sweet kisses, and speak sweet words:
Oh listen, listen, your eyes shall glisten
With pleasure and love and jubilee:
When the sharp clear twang of the golden chords
Runs up the ridged sea.
Who can light on as happy a shore
All the world o'er, all the world o'er?
Whither away? listen and stay: mariner, mariner, fly no
    more.

                        TENNYSON.

PARADISE AND THE PERL

One morn a Peri at the gate
Of Eden stood, disconsolate;
And as she listened to the springs
Of life within, like music flowing,
And caught the light upon her wings
Through the half-open portal glowing,
She wept to think her recreant race
Should e'er have lost that glorious place!

" How happy, " exclaimed this child of air,
" Are the holy spirits who wander there,
'Mid flowers that never shall fade or fall!
Though mine are the gardens of earth and sea,
One blossom of heaven outblooms them all! "

The glorious angel who was keeping
The gates of light beheld her weeping;
And, as he nearer drew and listened,
A tear within his eyelids glistened.—
" Nymph of a fair but erring line! "
Gently he said, " one hope is thine.

'Tis written in the book of fate,
The Peri yet may be forgiven,
Who brings to this eternal gate
The gift that is most dear to Heaven!
Go, seek it, and redeem thy sin;
'Tis sweet to let the pardoned in! "

Rapidly as comets run
To the embraces of the sun,
Down the blue vault the Peri flies,
And, lighted earthward by a glance
That just then broke from morning's eyes,

Hung hovering o'er our world's expanse.
Over the vale of Baalbec winging,
　The Peri sees a child at play,
Among the rosy wild-flowers singing,
　As rosy and as wild as they;
Chasing with eager hands and eyes,
The beautiful blue damsel–flies
That fluttered round the jasmine stems,
Like winged flowers or flying gems:
And near the boy, who, tired with play,
Now nestling 'mid the roses lay,
She saw a wearied man dismount
　From his hot steed, and on the brink
Of a small temple's rustic fount
　Impatient fling him down to drink.

Then swift his haggard brow he turned
　To the fair child, who fearless sat—
Though never yet hath day-beam burned
　Upon a brow more fierce than that—
Sullenly fierce—a mixture dire,
Like thunder-clouds of gloom and fire,
In which the Peri's eye could read
Dark tales of many a ruthless deed.

Yet tranquil now that man of crime
(As if the balmy evening time
Softened his spirit) looked and lay,
Watching the rosy infant's play;
Though still, whene'er his eye by chance
Fell on the boy's its lurid glance
　Met that unclouded, joyous gaze,
As torches that have burnt all night
　Encounter morning's glorious rays.

But hark ! the vesper call to prayer,
    As slow the orb of daylight sets,
Is rising sweetly on the air
    From Syria's thousand minarets !
The boy has started from the bed
Of flowers, where he had laid his head,
And down upon the fragrant sod
    Kneels, with his forehead to the south,
Lisping th' eternal name of God
    From purity's own cherub mouth;
And looking, while his hands and eyes
Are lifted to the glowing skies,
Like a stray babe of paradise,
Just lighted on that flowery plain,
And seeking for its home again !

And how felt he, the wretched man
Reclining there — while memory ran
O'er many a year of guilt and strife
That marked the dark flood of his life,
Nor found one sunny resting-place,
Nor brought him back one branch of grace?—
" There was a time, " he said, in mild,
Heart-humbled tones, " thou blessed child !
When young, and haply pure as thou,
I looked and prayed like thee; but now " —
He hung his head; each nobler aim
    And hope and feeling which had slept
From boyhood's hour, that instant came
        Fresh o'er him, and he wept — he wept !

And now ! behold him kneeling there,
By the child's side in humble prayer,
While the same sunbeam shines upon
The guilty and the guiltless one,

And hymns of joy proclaim through heaven
The triumph of a soul forgiven !

'Twas when the golden orb had set,
While on their knees they lingered yet,
There fell a light more lovely far
Than ever came from sun or star —
Upon the tear that, warm and meek,
Dewed that repentant sinner's cheek :
To mortal eye this light might seem
A northern flash or meteor beam ;
But well th' enraptured Peri knew
'Twas a bright smile the angel threw
From heaven's gate, to hail that tear —
Her harbinger of glory near !
" Joy ! joy ! " she cried ; " my task is done —
The gates are passed, and heaven is won ! "

Abridged.   THOMAS MOORE.

TO A SKYLARK.

Hail to thee, blithe spirit —
  Bird thou never wert —
That from heaven or near it
  Pourest thy full heart
In profuse strains of unpremeditated art.

Higher still and higher
  From the earth thou springest,
Like a cloud of fire ;
  The blue deep thou wingest,
And singing still dost soar, and soaring ever
    singest.

In the golden lightning
  Of the sunken sun,
O'er which clouds are bright'ning,
  Thou dost float and run,
Like an unbodied joy whose race is just begun.

The pale purple even
  Melts around thy flight;
Like a star of heaven,
  In the broad daylight
Thou art unseen, but yet I hear thy shrill
    delight.

Keen as are the arrows
  Of that silver sphere
Whose intense lamp narrows
  In the white dawn clear,
Until we hardly see, we feel, that it is there.

All the earth and air
  With thy voice is loud,
As when night is bare,
  From one lonely cloud
The moon rains out her beams, and heaven
    is overflowed.

What thou art we know not;
  What is most like thee?
From rainbow-clouds there flow not
  Drops so bright to see
As from thy presence showers a rain of mel-
    ody :—

Like a poet hidden
  In the light of thought,
Singing hymns unbidden,

Till the world is wrought
To sympathy with hopes and fears it heeded
  not :

Like a high-born maiden
 In a palace tower,
Soothing her love-laden
 Soul in secret hour
With music sweet as love which overflows
  her bower :

Like a glow-worm golden
 In a dell of dew,
Scattering unbeholden
 Its aerial hue
Among the flowers and grass which screen
  it from the view :

Like a rose embowered
 In its own green leaves,
By warm winds deflowered,
 Till the scent it gives
Makes faint with too much sweet these heavy-
  winged thieves.

Sound of vernal showers
 On the twinkling grass,
Rain-awakened flowers,—
 All that ever was,
Joyous and clear and fresh,—thy music doth
  surpass.

Teach us, sprite or bird,
 What sweet thoughts are thine :
I have never heard
 Praise of love sublime

That panted forth a flood of rapture so divine.

Chorus hymeneal
    Or triumphal chaunt,
Matched with thine, would be all
    But an empty vaunt—
A thing wherein we feel there is some hidden
    want.

What objects are the fountains
    Of thy happy strain?
What fields, or waves, or mountains?
    What shapes of sky or plain?
What love of thine own kind? What igno
    rance of pain?

With thy clear keen joyance
    Languor cannot be:
Shadow of annoyance
    Never came near thee:
Thou lovest, but ne'er knew love's had satiety.

Waking or asleep,
    Thou of death must deem
Things more true and deep
    Than we mortals dream,
Or how could thy notes flow in such a crystal
    stream?

We look before and after,
    And pine for what is not:
Our sincerest laughter
    With some pain is fraught;
Our sweetest songs are those that tell of
    saddest thought.

Yet, if we could scorn
    Hate and pride and fear,
If we were things born
    Not to shed a tear,
I know not how thy joy we ever should come
    near.

Better than all measures
    Of delightful sound,
Better than all treasures
    That in books are found,
Thy skill to poet were, thou scorner of the
    ground!

Teach me half the gladness
    That thy brain must know;
Such harmonious madness
    From my lips would flow
The world should listen then as I am listen-
    ing now.

                              Shelley.

———

A child had blown a bubble fair
That floated in the sunny air:
A hundred rainbows danced and swung
Upon its surface, as it hung
In films of changing color rolled,
Crimson, and amethyst, and gold,
With faintest streaks of azure sheen,
And curdling rivulets of green.
" If so the surface shines, " cried he,
" What marvel must the centre be! "
He caught it — on his empty hands
A drop of turbid water stands!   Sill.

EIGHTH STEP IN RENDERING.
SLIDES OF THE VOICE.

In the Slides of the Voice lies the music of speech. The slides make the tune to which a thing is said. This tune discloses unconsciously, the most subtle, innermost thought and feeling. The slides, tune or running commentary on the words is a language in itself the nearest to music, which is the universal language. The slides are often more significant and expressive than the words themselves.

This music of speech not only reveals thought and feeling, but clothes the language with beauty and makes it attractive. Slide is to speech what ornamentation is to architecture. By it beauty is added to utility. The decoration in architecture is found in arches, window tracery, parapet and pinnacles overlaid with elaborate carvings etc.

All that is attractive and beautiful in any art is the product of thought. This is particularly so in the music of speech. Through thought and feeling only, may the voice attain attractive, musical elements.

A piece of common cloth may be enriched and made attractive with elaborate embroidery or used as a canvas for a costly work of art. The value of the cloth is increased by the amount of thought put into it: so may a common, every-day voice become beautiful and attract-

ive by enriching the mind and heart. Try to get out of a study all there is in it. Beautiful slides in the voice do not come by chance but from inherent beauty of spirit and a full appreciation of the matter given. Learn to come sympathetically in touch with the great minds of literature, get their thoughts. Do not go out of self to do this but add others to self, then the music will come, not enforced, but true. Make all persuasive rather than argumentative. Persuasion is more effective than argument. Argument is often a challenge to a quarrel and to strike back. Persuasion leaves the mind free from antagonism, ready to follow on in the thought.

HAMLET'S INSTRUCTION TO THE PLAYERS.

Speak the speech, I pray you, as I pronounced it to you,— trippingly on the tongue : but if you mouth it, as many of our players do, I had as lief the town-crier spake my lines. Nor do not saw the air too much with your hand thus, but use all gently ; for in the very torrent, tempest, and, as I may say, whirlwind of your passion, you must acquire and beget a temperance that may give it smoothness. Oh ! it offends me to the soul, to hear a robustious, periwig-pated fellow tear a passion to tatters,— to very rags,— to split the ears of the groundlings ; who, for the most part, are capable of nothing but inexplicable dumb show and noise. I would have such a fellow whipped for o'erdoing Termagant : it out-herods Herod. Pray you avoid it.

Be not too tame neither, but let your own discretion be
your tutor. Suit the action to the word; the word to the
action; with this special observance — that you o'erstep not
the modesty of nature; for anything so overdone is from
the purpose of playing; whose end, both at the first and
now, was, and is, to hold, as 't were, the mirror up to nature;— to show virtue her own feature; scorn her own image; and the very age and body of the time, his form and
pressure. Now this, overdone or come tardy off, though
it make the unskillful laugh, cannot but make the judicious
grieve; the censure of which one, must, in your allowance,
o'erweigh a whole theater of others.

Oh! there be players, that I have seen play, and heard
others praise, and that highly, not to speak it profanely,
that, neither having the accent of Christians, nor the gait of
Christian, pagan, or man, have so strutted and bellowed,
that I have thought that some of nature's journeymen had
made men, and not made them well,— they imitated humanity so abominably!

" Hamlet. "   Shakespeare.

PORTIA'S PLEA FOR MERCY.

The quality of mercy is not strain'd
It droppeth, as the gentle rain from heaven,
Upon the place beneath : it is twice bless'd,
It blesseth him that gives, and him that takes:
' Tis mightiest in the mightiest; it becomes
The throned monarch better than his crown :
His scepter shows the force of temporal power,
The attribute to awe and majesty,
Wherein doth sit the dread and fear of kings.
But mercy is above his sceptered sway,

It is enthroned in the hearts of kings,
It is an attribute to God himself;
And earthly power doth then show likest God's
When mercy seasons justice.   Therefore, Jew,
Though justice be thy plea, consider this,—
That in the course of justice, none of us
Should see salvation; we do pray for mercy;
And that same prayer doth teach us all to render
The deeds of mercy.   I have spoke thus much
To mitigate the justice of thy plea;
Which if thou follow, this strict court of Venice
Must needs give sentence 'gainst the merchant there.

" MERCHANT OF VENICE. "   SHAKESPEARE.

POLONIUS' ADVICE TO LAERTES.

Farewell.   My blessing with you:
And these few precepts in thy memory
Look thou character.   Give thy thoughts no tongue,
Nor any unproportioned thought his act.
Be thou familiar, but by no means vulgar.
The friends thou hast, and their adoption tried,
Grapple them to thy soul with hooks of steel;
But do not dull thy palm with entertainment
Of each new-hatch'd, unfledg'd comrade.   Beware
Of entrance to a quarrel; but, being in,
Bear it, that the opposer may beware of thee.
Give every man thine ear, but few thy voice:
Take each man's censure, but reserve thy judgment.
Costly thy habit as thy purse can buy,
But not express'd in fancy; rich, not gaudy:
For the apparel oft proclaims the man:
And they in France, of the best rank and station,
Are most select and generous, chief in that.

Neither a borrower, nor a lender be :
For loan oft loses both itself and friend ;
And borrowing dulls the edge of husbandry.
This above all,— to thine own self be true ;
And it must follow, as the night the day,
Thou canst not then be false to any man.
" HAMLET. "   SHAKESPEARE.

THANATOPSIS.

To him who in the love of Nature holds
Communion with her visible forms, she speaks
A various language ; for his gayer hours
She has a voice of gladness, and a smile
And eloquence of beauty ; and she glides
Into his darker musings, with a mild
And healing sympathy, that steals away
Their sharpness, ere he is aware.

When thoughts
Of the last bitter hour come like a blight
Over thy spirit, and sad images
Of the stern agony, and shroud, and pall,
And breathless darkness, and the narrow house,
Make thee to shudder, and grow sick at heart, —
Go forth, under the open sky, and list
To Nature's teachings, while from all around —
Earth and her waters, and the depths of air —
Comes a still voice :—

Yet a few days, and thee
The all–beholding sun shall see no more
In all his course ; nor yet in the cold ground,
Where thy pale form is laid with many tears,

Nor in the embrace of ocean, shall exist
Thy image. Earth that nourished thee, shall claim
Thy growth, to be resolved to earth again,
And, lost each human trace, surrendering up
Thine individual being, shalt thou go
To mix forever with the elements,—
To be a brother to the insensible rock,
And to the sluggish clod, which the rude swain
Turns with his share, and treads upon.   The oak
Shall send his roots abroad, and pierce thy mold.

   Yet not to thine eternal resting-place
Shalt thou retire alone — nor couldst thou wish
Couch more magnificent.   Thou shalt lie down
With patriarchs of the infant world—with kings,
The powerful of the earth— the wise, the good,
Fair forms, and hoary seers, of ages past,
All in one mighty sepulcher.   The hills
Rock-ribbed, and ancient as the sun,— the vales
Stretching in pensive quietness between;
The venerable woods— rivers that move
In majesty, and the complaining brooks
That make the meadows green; and, poured round
       all,
Old ocean's gray and melancholy waste,—
Are but the solemn decorations all
Of the great tomb of man.

          The golden sun,
The planets, all the infinite host of heaven,
Are shining on the sad abodes of death,
Through the still lapse of ages.   All that tread
The globe, are but a handful to the tribes
That slumber in its bosom.   Take the wings
 Of morning, and the Barcan desert pierce,

Or lose thyself in the continuous woods
Where rolls the Oregon, and hears no sound
Save his own dashings — yet the dead are there;
And millions in those solitudes, since first
The flight of years began, have laid them down
In their last sleep— the dead there reign alone.

So shalt thou rest,— and what if thou withdraw
Unheeded by the living— and no friend
Take note of thy departure?   All that breathe
Will share thy destiny.   The gay will laugh
When thou art gone, the solemn brood of care
Plod on, and each one, as before, will chase
His favorite phantom; yet all these shall leave
Their mirth and their employments, and shall come
And make their bed with thee.

As the long train
Of ages glide away, the sons of men,
The youth in life's green spring, and he who goes
In the full strength of years, matron, and maid,
And the sweet babe, and the gray-headed man—
Shall one by one be gathered to thy side,
By those who, in their turn, shall follow them.

So live, that, when thy summons comes to join
The innumerable caravan, that moves
To that mysterious realm, where each shall take
His chamber in the silent halls of death,
Thou go not, like the quarry-slave, at night,
Scourged to his dungeon, but, sustained and soothed
By an unfaltering trust, approach thy grave,
Like one who wraps the drapery of his couch
About him, and lies down to pleasant dreams.

WILLIAM CULLEN BRYANT.

NINTH STEP IN RENDERING.
VITAL SLIDE.

Thought gives a slide in the voice, but feeling makes it Vital. Emotional speech prolongs the vowel. Emotional language requires longer slides than mental or didactic speech. The last named would be but inflection as compared with the Vital Slide or the slide colored with emotion.

Thought gives inflection to the consonant: feeling swells out or makes a slide on the emphatic vowel.

Long Vital Slide is marked in expressions of Surprise, Exclamation, Emphatic Interrogation, Supplication and other strong emotions.

WOLSEY TO CROMWELL.

Cromwell, I did not think to shed a tear,
In all my miseries; but thou hast forced me,
Out of thy honest truth, to play the woman.
And — when I am forgotten, as I shall be,
And sleep in dull cold marble, where no mention
Of me more must be heard of,— say, I taught thee;
Say, Wolsey — that once trod the ways of glory,
And sounded all the depths and shoals of honor —
Found thee a way, out of his wreck, to rise in;
A sure and safe one, though thy master missed it.
Mark but my fall, and that that ruined me,

Cromwell, I charge thee, fling away ambition:
By that sin fell the angels: how can man, then,
The image of his Maker hope to win by 't?
Love thyself last; cherish those hearts that hate thee;
Corruption wins not more than honesty:
Still in thy right hand carry gentle peace,
To silence envious tongues.   Be just, and fear not.
Let all the ends thou aim'st at be thy country's,
Thy God's and truth's; then if thou fall'st, O Crom-
     well,
Thou fall'st a blessed martyr!   Serve the king;
And—— Prithee, lead me in:
There take an inventory of all I have,
To the last penny; 'tis the king's; my robe,
And my integrity to Heaven, is all
I dare now call mine own.   O Cromwell, Cromwell,
Had I but served my God with half the zeal
I served my king, he would not in mine age
Have left me naked to mine enemies.

" KING HENRY VIII. "   SHAKESPEARE.

PRINCE ARTHUR.

Hubert.   Heat me those irons hot; and look thou
    stand
Within the arras.   When I strike my foot
Upon the bosom of the ground, rush forth
And bind the boy which you shall find wi' me
Fast to the chair; be heedful; hence, and watch.

    1st. Execu.   I hope your warrant will bear out
       the deed.

    Hub.   Uncleanly scruples!   fear not you; look
      to 't.

Young lad come forth ; I have to say with you.

   Arthur. Good-morrow, Hubert.

   Hub. Good-morrow little prince.

   Arth. As little prince as may be.

You are sad.

   Hub. Indeed, I have been merrier.

   Arth.   Mercy on me !

Methinks nobody should be sad but I.

Yet I remember when I was in France,

Young gentlemen would be sad as night

Ouly for wantonness. By my christendom,

So 1 were out of prison, and kept sheep,

I should be as merry as the day is long ;

And so T would be here, but that I doubt

My uncle practises more harm to me.

He is afraid of me, and I of him.

Is it my fault that I was Jeffrey's son ?

No, indeed, it's not ; and I would to heaven

I were your son, so you would love me, Hubert.

   Hub. (Aside.) If 1 talk to him, with his inno-
          cent prate,

He will awake my mercy, which lies dead ;

Therefore I will be sudden and despatch.

   Arth. Are you sick, Hubert ? You look pale
          to-day ;

In sooth, I would you were a little sick,

That I might sit all night and watch with you.

I warrant I love you more than you do me.

   Hub. (Aside.) His words do take possession
          of my bosom.

Read here, young Arthur.

How now, foolish rheum ?

Turning dispiteous torture out of door !

1 must be brief, lest resolution drop

Out at mine eyes in tender womanish tears.
Can you not read it? Is it not fair writ?

Arth.   Too fairly, Hubert, for so foul effect.
Must you with hot irons burn out both mine eyes?

Hub.   Young boy, I must.

Arth.   And will you?

Hub.   And I will!

Arth.   Have you the heart? When your head
        did but ache,
I knit my handkerchief about your brows,
The best I had, a princess wrought it me,
And I did never ask it you again;
And with my hand at midnight held your head,
And, like the watchful minutes to the hour,
Still and anon cheered up the heavy time
Saying, What lack you? and Where lies your grief?
Or, What good love may I perform for you?
Many a poor man's son would have lain still,
And ne'er have spoke a loving word to you;
But you, at your sick service, had a prince.
Nay, you may think my love was crafty love,
And call it cunning; do, an' if you will,
If heaven be pleased that you must use me ill
Why, then, you must. Will you put out mine eyes?
These eyes that never did, nor never shall
So much as frown on you?

Hub.   I have sworn to do it;
And with hot irons must I burn them out.

Arth.   Ah, none but in this iron age would do it!
The iron of itself, tho' heat red-hot,
Approaching near these eyes, would drink my tears
And quench his fiery indignation,
Even in the matter of mine innocence;
Nay, after that, consume away in rust,

But for containing fire to harm mine eyes.
Are you more stubborn hard than hammer'd
　　　　iron?
An' if an angel should have come to me,
And told me Hubert should put out mine eyes,
I would not have believed no tongue but Hubert's!
　Hub.　Come forth!
Do as I bid you.
　　Arth.　Oh, save me, Hubert, save me!　my eyes
　　　　are out
Even with the fierce looks of these bloody men.
　Hub.　Give me the iron, I say, and bind him here.
　　Arth.　Alas, why need you be so boisterous rough?
I will not struggle, I will stand stone still.
For heaven's sake, Hubert, let me not be bound.
Nay hear me Hubert, drive these men away
And I will sit as quiet as a lamb;
I will not stir, nor wince, nor speak a word,
Nor look upon the iron angerly;
Thrust but these men away, and I'll forgive you
Whatever torment you do put me to.
　Hub.　Go stand within; let me alone with him.
　1st. Execu.　I am best pleased to be from such
　　　　a deed.
　Arth.　Alas,I then have chid away my friend,
He hath a stern look, but a gentle heart;
Let him come back, that his compassion may give
　　　　life to yours.
　Hub.　Come, boy, prepare yourself!
　Arth.　Is there no remedy?
　Hub.　None, but to lose your eyes.
　Arth.　Oh, heaven, that there were but a mote in
　　　　yours;
A grain, a dust, a gnat, a wandering hair,

Any annoyance in that precious sense!
Then, feeling what small things are boisterous there,
Your vile intent must needs seem horrible.

 Hub. Is this your promise? Go to, hold your
   tongue.

 Arth. Hubert, the utterance of a brace of tongues
Must needs want pleading for a pair of eyes.
Let me not hold my tongue, let me not, Hubert;
Or Hubert, if you will, cut out my tongue,
So I may keep mine eyes. O spare mine eyes:
Though to no use, but still to look on you.
Lo, by my troth, the instrument is cold, and would
   not harm me.

 Hub. I can heat it, boy.

 Arth. No, in good sooth; the fire is dead wi' grief,
Being create for comfort, to be used
In undeserved extremes; see else yourself.
There is no malice in this burning coal;
The breath of heaven hath blown his spirit out,
And strewed repentant ashes on his head.

 Hub. But with my breath I can revive it, boy.

 Arth. An' if you do you will but make it blush
And glow with shame of your proceedings, Hubert,
All things that you should use to do me wrong,
Deny their office; only you do lack
That mercy which fierce fire and iron extends.

 Hub Well, see to live. I will not touch thine eyes
For all the treasure that thine uncle owes:
Yet am I sworn, and did purpose, boy   .
With this same very iron to burn them out.

 Arth. O! now you look like Hubert;
All this while, you were disguised.

 Hub.   Peace! no more, adieu!
Your uncle must not know but you are dead.

I'll fill these dogged spies with false reports.
And, pretty child sleep doubtless and secure,
That Hubert, for the wealth of all the world, will
    not offend thee.
    Arth.   O heaven!   I thank you, Hubert!
    Hub.   Peace: no more: go closely in with me.
Much danger do I undergo for thee.
   " KING JOHN. "   SHAKESPEARE.

RIP VAN WINKLE IN THE MOUNTAINS.

From " RIP VAN WINKLE as played by JOSEPH JEFFERSON. "
Permission by DODD, MEAD & COMPANY, NEW YORK.

Schneider! Schneider! What's the matter with
Schneider? Something must have scared that dog. There
he goes head over heels down the hill. Well, here I am
again — another night in the mountains! Heigho! these
old trees begin to know me, I reckon.

How are you, old fellows? Well, I like the trees, they
keep me from the wind and the rain, and they never blow
me up; and when I lay me down on the broad of my back,
they seem to bow their heads to me, an' say: Go to sleep,
Rip, go to sleep.

My, what a flash that was! Old Hendrick Hudson 's
lighting his pipe in the mountains to-night; now, we 'll hear
him roll the big balls along.

Well, — no — Schneider! No; whatever it is it's on
two legs. Why, what a funny thing is that a coming up
the hill? I thought nobody but me ever come nigh this
place.

(Enter dwarf.) Sit down, and make yourself comfortable. What? What 's the matter? Ain't ye goin' to
speak to a feller? I don't want to speak to you, then. Who
you think you was, that I want to speak to you, any more

than you want to speak to me; you hear what I say?

Donner an' Blitzen! What for a man is das? I have been walking over these mountains ever since I was a boy, an' I never saw a queer-looking codger like that before. He must be an old sea-snake, I reckon.

Well, why don't you say so, den? You mean you would like me to help you up with that keg?

Well sir, I don't do it.

No; there's no good you speakin' like that. I never seed you before, did I?

I don't want to see you again, needer. What have you got in that keg, schnapps?

I don't believe you.

Well, I'll help you. Go 'long pick up my gun, there and I'll follow you mit that keg on my shoulder. I'll follow you, old broadchops.

I say, old gentleman, I never was so high up in the mountains before. Look down into the valley there; it seems more as a mile. I— (Goblins appear one after another.)

You're another feller!

You're that other chap's brother?

You're another brother?

You're his old gran'father?

Donner and Blitzen! here's the whole family; I'm a dead man to a certainty.

My, my, I suppose they're speakin' about me!

No good shootin' at 'em; family's too big for one gun.

My, my, I don't like that kind of people at all! No, sir! I don't like any sech kind. I like that old gran'father worse than any of them.

How you was, old gentleman? I didn't mean to intrude on you, did I? What?

I'll tell you how it was; I met one of your gran'children, I don't know which is the one —

They 're all so much alike.   Well—

That's the same kind of a one. Any way this one he axed me to help him up the mountain mit dat keg.

Well, he was an old feller, an' I thought 1 would help him.

Was I right to help him? I say, was I right to help him?

If he was here, he would yust tell you the same thing—

I did n't want to come here, anyhow; no, sir, I didn't want to come to any such kind of a place.   .   .   .   .

You want me to drink mit you?

Well, I swore off drinkin'; but as this is the first time I see you, I won't count this one—

You drink mit me?   We drink mit one another?

What's the matter mit you, old gentleman, anyhow? You go and make so mit your head every time; was you deaf?

Oh, nein.   If you was deaf you wouldn't hear what I was sayin'.   Was you dumb?

So? You was dumb?

Has all of your family the same complaint?

All the boys dumb, hey? All the boys dumb.

Have you got any girls?

Don't you?   Such a big family, and all boys?

That's a pity; my that's a pity. Oh, my, if you had some dumb girls, what wives they would make—

Well, old gentleman, here's your good health, and all your family— may they live long and prosper.

What for licker is that!

Give me another one!

Oh, my, my head was so light, and now, it's heavy as lead!

Are you goin' to leave me, boys?   Are you goin' to leave me all alone?   Don't leave me; don't go away.

I will drink your good health. and your family's—

(Goblins vanish, Rip falls back heavily, in his long sleep.)

JOSEPH JEFFERSON.

TENTH STEP IN RENDERING.
SLIDE IN VOLUME.

Volume of Voice shows poetic fervor, the sublime, the reverential, that which the soul chooses as contrasted with that which it rejects. Slide in Volume comes from soul force that is positive and impels, rather than from that which is negative, or from a mental force that instructs and directs, or from physical force that sustains.

Beautiful expression with true musical slides is governed by the amount and variety of thought and feeling living in the mind and heart at the time of utterance.

The pathetic should be made so by the soul, rather than mental pathetic which is, in other words, " whine. " The pathetic requires, not a semitone, but a noble effort for control, a struggle with the breath. Slides of any kind " put on " have a false ring of insincerity which cannot be concealed. Such slides furnish another illustration of the principle : " weakness takes a strong attitude. "

So live, that when the mighty caravan,
Which halts one night–time in the vale of death,
Shall strike its white tents for the morning march ;
Thou shalt mount onward to the eternal hills,
Thy foot unwearied and thy strength renewed,
Like the strong eagle for the upward flight.

" *A Vision of Immortality.* "   BRYANT,

LANDING OF COLUMBUS.

The sails were furl'd; with many a melting close,
Solemn and slow the evening anthem rose,—
Rose to the Virgin.   'Twas the hour of day
When setting suns o'er summer seas display
A path of glory, opening in the west
To golden climes and islands of the blest;
And human voices on the silent air
Went o'er the waves in songs of gladness there!
Chosen of men!   'Twas thine at noon of night
First from the prow to hail the glimmering light?
(Emblem of Truth divine, whose secret ray
Enters the soul and makes the darkness day!)
" Pedro! Rodrigo! there methought it shone!
There—in the west! and now, alas, 'tis gone!—
'Twas all a dream! we gaze and gaze in vain!
But mark and speak not, there it comes again!
It moves!— what form unseen, what being there
With torch-like lustre fires the murky air?
His instincts, passions, say, how like our own!
Oh, when will day reveal a world unknown? "
Long on the deep the mists of morning lay;
Then rose, revealing as they rolled away
Half-circling hills, whose everlasting woods
Sweep with their sable skirts the shadowy floods:
And say, when all, to holy transport given,
Embraced and wept as at the gates of heaven,—
When one and all of us, repentant, ran,
And, on our faces, bless'd the wondrous man,—
Say, was I then deceived, or from the skies
Burst on my ear seraphic harmonies?
" Glory to God! " unnumber'd voices sung,—
" Glory to God! " the vales and mountains rung,

Voices that hail'd creation's primal morn.
And to the shepherds sung a Saviour born.
Slowly, bareheaded, through the surf we bore
The sacred cross, and kneeling kiss'd the shore.

ROGERS.

THE AMERICAN FLAG.

When Freedom, from her mountain height
   Unfurled her standard to the air,
She tore the azure robe of night,
   And set the stars of glory there!
She mingled with its gorgeous dyes
The milky baldric of the skies,
And striped its pure celestial white
With streakings of the morning light,
Then, from his mansion in the sun,
She called her eagle bearer down,
And gave into his mighty hand
The symbol of her chosen land!

Majestic monarch of the cloud!
   Who rear'st aloft thy regal form,
To hear the tempest-trumpings loud,
And see the lightning lances driven,
   When strive the warriors of the storm,
And rolls the thunder-drum of heaven,—
Child of the sun! to thee 'tis given
   To guard the banner of the free,
To hover in the sulphur smoke,
To ward away the battle stroke,
    And bid its blendings shine afar,
    Like rainbows on the cloud of war,
     The harbingers of victory!

Flag of the brave! thy folds shall fly,
The sign of hope and triumph high!
When speaks the signal–trumpet tone,
And the long line comes gleaming on,
Ere yet the life–blood, warm and wet,
Has dimmed the glistening bayonet,
Each soldier's eye shall brightly turn
To where thy sky-born glories burn,
And as his springing steps advance,
Catch war and vengeance from the glance.
And when the cannon–mouthings loud
Heave in wild wreaths the battle shroud,
And gory sabres rise and fall
Like shoots of flame on midnight's pall,
Then shall thy meteor glances glow,
   And cowering foes shall shrink beneath
Each gallant arm that strikes below
   That lovely messenger of death.

Flag of the seas! on ocean wave
Thy stars shall glitter o'er the brave;
When death, careering on the gale,
Sweeps darkly round the bellied sail,
And frighted waves rush wildly back
Before the broadside's reeling rack,
Each dying wanderer of the sea
Shall look at once to heaven and thee,
And smile to see thy splendors fly
In triumph o'er his closing eye.

Flag of the free heart's hope and home
   By angel hands to valor given,
Thy stars have lit the welkin dome,
   And all thy hues were born in heaven!
Forever float that standard sheet,

Where breathes the foe but falls before us
With Freedom's soil beneath our feet,
And Freedom's banner streaming o'er us!
                    JOSEPH RODMAN DRAKE.

BATTLE HYMN OF THE REPUBLIC.

Mine eyes have seen the glory of the coming of the Lord:
He is trampling out the vintage where the grapes of wrath
          are stored;
He hath loosed the fateful lightning of his terrible swift
          sword:
          His truth is marching on.

I have seen Him in the watch-fires of a hundred circling
          camps;
They have builded Him an altar in the evening dews and
          damps;
I can read His righteous sentence by the dim and flaring
          lamps.
          His day is marching on.

I have read a fiery gospel writ in burnished rows of steel:
" As ye deal with my contemners, so with you my grace
          shall deal;
Let the Hero born of woman, crush the serpent with his heel,
          Since God is marching on. "

He hath sounded forth the trumpet that shall never call
          retreat;
He is sifting out the hearts of men before his judgment-seat:
Oh! be swift, my soul, to answer him! Be jubilant, my feet!
          Our God is marching on.

In the beauty of the lilies Christ was born across the sea,
With a glory in his bosom that transfigures you and me:
As he died to make men holy, let us die to make men free,
  While God is marching on.

       JULIA WARD HOWE.

ERIN'S FLAG.

Unroll Erin's flag! fling its folds to the breeze!
Let it float o'er the land, let it wave o'er the seas;
Lift it out of the dust — let it wave as of yore,
When its chiefs with their clans stood around it and
  swore
That never, no, never, while God gave them life,
And they had an arm and a sword for the strife,
That never, no, never, that banner would yield,
As long as the heart of a Celt was its shield ;—
While the hand of a Celt had a weapon to wield,
And his last drop of blood was unshed on the field.

Lift it up! wave it high!—'tis as bright as of old;
Not a stain on its green, not a blot on its gold,
Though the woes and the wrongs of three hundred years
Have drenched Erin's sunburst with blood and with
  tears;
Though the clouds of oppression enshroud it in gloom,
And around it the thunders of tyranny boom,
Look aloft! look aloft! lo! the cloud's drifting by,
There is a gleam through the gloom, there is a light in
  the sky.
'Tis the sunburst resplendent, far-flashing on high;
Erin's dark night is waning, her day-dawn is nigh.

THE ART OF RENDERING

Lift it up! lift it up! the old banner of green;
The blood of its sons has but brightened its sheen.
What though the tyrant has trampled it down,
Are its folds not emblazoned with deeds of renown?
What though for ages it droops in the dust,
Shall it droop thus forever? no! no! God is just!

Take it up! take it up from the tyrant's foul tread,
Lest he tear the green flag, we will snatch its last shred.
And beneath it we'll bleed as our forefathers bled,
And we'll vow by the dust in the graves of our dead,
And we'll swear by the blood that the Briton has shed,
And we'll vow by the wrecks which through Erin he
       spread,
And we'll swear by the thousands who famished, unfed
Died down in the ditches — wild howling for bread;
And we'll vow by our heroes, whose spirits have fled,
And we'll swear by the bones in each coffinless bed.
That we'll battle the Briton through danger and dread;
That we'll cling to the cause which we glory to wed
Till the gleam of our steel and the shock of our lead
Shall prove to the foe that we meant what we said —
That we'll lift up the green, and we'll tear down the red.

Lift up the green flag! oh! it wants to go home,
Full long has its lot been to wander and roam;
It has followed the fate of its sons o'er the world,
But its folds, like their hopes, are not faded or furled;
Like a weary-winged bird, to the east and the west
It has flitted and fled, but it never shall rest,
Till pluming its pinions it sweeps o'er the main,
And speeds to the shore of its old home again,
Where its fetterless folds o'er each mountain and plain
Shall wave with a glory that never shall wane.

Take it up! take it up! bear it back from afar!
That banner must blaze 'mid the lightnings of war;
Lay your hands on its folds, lift your eyes to the sky,
And swear that you'll bear it triumphant or die;
And shout to the clans scattered far o'er the earth,
To join in the march to the land of their birth;
And wherever the exiles, 'neath heaven's broad dome,
Have been fated to suffer, to sorrow, and roam,
They'll bound on the sea, and away o'er the foam
They'll march to the music of " Home sweet home. "

FATHER RYAN.

A PROCESSIONAL HYMN.

The earth is the Lord's, and the fullness thereof; the world, and they that dwell therein. For he hath founded it upon the seas, and established it upon the floods.

" Who shall ascend into the hill of the Lord? or who shall stand in his holy place? "

" He that hath clean hands, and a pure heart; who hath not lifted up his soul unto vanity, nor sworn deceitfully. He shall receive the blessing from the Lord, and righteousness from the God of his salvation. "

This is the generation of them that seek him, that seek thy face, O Jacob.

" Lift up your heads, O ye gates; and be ye lift up, ye everlasting doors; and the King of glory shall come in. "

" Who is this King of glory? " " The Lord strong and mighty, the Lord mighty in battle. Lift up your heads, O ye gates: even lift them up, ye everlasting doors; and the King of glory shall come in. " " Who is this King of glory? " " The Lord of hosts, he is the King of glory. "

PSALM XXIV.

ELEVENTH STEP IN RENDERING.
PAUSE.

Pause is a loophole of silence through which a whole thought may shine out. Such points are not always marked by punctuation, but are indications of thought, and are points for suggestive expression.

In the silent places — the pauses — the mind gathers itself to present a new impulse of thought. In pause is shown the honest action of the mind.

The most common and deplorable fault of the inexperienced who attempt to speak in public is inability to give thought with the words. As a result the hurried pauses are of a uniform length, making such tiresome monotony and unnatural flow of words as to be most embarrassing to the speaker himself, to say nothing of the discomfort of the listener. " Parroting " may be left off and the true keynote of speech found in natural pauses.

The voice of the speaker as well as the ear of the listener requires a temporary period of rest. We must have before we can give. There must also be a mind to take before we can give. It is a fine art to be able to know when the listener has received a thought and is ready for the next. This may be gained in the pauses. Pauses vary in length to suit the importance of thought, short with superficial thought; long with heavy thought.

Where ideas are presented rapidly, the mind of the listener soon becomes weary and refuses to follow. It has been found by careful scientific tests that the mind is able to give attention only for a few seconds at a time. The mind attends in pulses and, as the normal wave of attention lasts only a few seconds, if the mind is compelled to attend longer at a single pulse the effort of listening is exhausting and unpleasant. Because of this, short sentences (not so short as to be choppy) are more satisfying. Thoughts which develop and present new aspects with interesting mental pictures, having natural pulses of rest, hold the attention of the listener and are an advantage to the speaker.

Pause may be skillfully used before words telling what is to follow. Think of pauses as loopholes through which you may show the whole idea before the words are said. Such suggestive pauses may be made most eloquent, giving in suitable places gesture or pantomimic action to reveal, without words, the contents of the mind. It is gratifying to the listener to read this suggestive language. It is sometimes startling to precipitate an abrupt change or turn of the thought without a moment's warning. A suggestion of an abrupt change should be shown in the pause.

Says Delsarte:— Silence is the father of speech, and must justify it. Every word which does not proceed from silence and find its vindication in silence, is a spurious word without claim or title to our regard. Origin is the stamp by which we recognize the intrinsic value of things. Let us, then, seek in silence the sufficient reason of speech, and remember that the more enlightened the mind is, the more concise is the speech that proceeds from it. Let us assume, then, that this conciseness keeps pace with the elevation of the mind, and that when the mind arrives at the perception of the true light, finding no words that can portray the glories open to its view, it keeps silent and admires. It is through silence that the mind rises to perfection, for silence is the speech of God.

A CHILD'S DREAM OF A STAR.

There was once a child, and he strolled about a good deal, and thought of a number of things. He had a sister who was a child too, and his constant companion.
They wondered at the beauty of the flowers; they wondered at the height and blueness of the sky; they wondered at the depth of the water; they wondered at the goodness and power of God, who made the lovely world.

They used to say to one another sometimes: Supposing all the children on the earth were to die, would the flowers and the water and the sky be sorry? They believed they would be sorry. For, said they, the buds are the children of the flowers, and the little playful streams that gambol down the hillsides are the children of the water, and the smallest bright specks playing at hide-and-seek in the sky all night must surely be the children of the stars; and they would all be grieved to see their playmates, the children of men, no more.

There was one clear-shining star that used to come out in the sky before the rest, near the church-spire, above the graves. It was larger and more beautiful, they thought, than all the others, and every night they watched for it, standing hand-in-hand at a window.
Whoever saw it first cried out: " I see the star. "
And after that, they cried out both together, knowing so well when it would rise, and where. So they grew to be such friends with it that, before lying down in their bed, they always looked out once again to bid it good-night; and when they were turning round, to sleep they used to say: " God bless the star! "

But while she was still very young — O, very young!— the sister drooped, and came to be so weak that she could no longer stand in the window at night, and then the child looked sadly out by himself, and when he saw the star, turned round and said to the patient, pale face on the bed, " I see the star! " and then a smile would come upon the face, and a weak little voice used to say: " God bless my brother and the star! "

And so the time came, all too soon, when the child looked out all alone, and when there was no face on the bed, and when there was a grave among the graves not there before, and when the star made long rays down toward him as he saw it through his tears.

Now, these rays were so bright, and they seemed to make such a shining way from earth to heaven, that when the child went to his solitary bed he dreamed about the star; and dreamed that, lying where he was, he saw a train of people taken up that sparkling road by angels; and the star, opening, showed him a great world of light, where many more such angels waited to receive them.

All these angels, who were waiting, turned their beaming eyes upon the people who were carried up into the star; and some came out from the long rows in which they stood, and fell upon the people's necks, and kissed them tenderly, and went away with them down avenues of light, and were so happy in their company that, lying in his bed, he wept for joy.

But there were many angels who did not go with them, and among them one he knew. The patient face that once had lain upon the bed was glorified and radiant, but his heart found out his sister among all the host.

His sister's angel lingered near the entrance of the star, and said to the leader among those who had brought the people thither:

" Is my brother come? "

And he said: " No! "

She was turning hopefully away, when the child stretched out his arms, and cried: " O, sister, I am here! take me! " And she turned her beaming eyes upon him— and it was night; and the star was shining into the room, making long rays down toward him as he saw it through his tears.

From that hour forth, the child looked out upon the star as the home he was to go to when his time should come; and he thought that he did not belong to the earth alone, but to the star too, because of his sister's angel gone before.

There was a baby born to be a brother to the child, and while he was so little that he never yet had spoken a word, he stretched out his tiny form on his bed, and died.

Again the child dreamed of the opened star, and of the company of angels, and the train of people, and the rows of angels, with their beaming eyes all turned upon those people's faces.

Said his sister's angel to the leader:

" Is my brother come? "

And he said: " Not that one, but another! "

As the child beheld his brother's angel in her arms, he cried: " O, my sister, I am here! take me! " And she turned and smiled upon him— and the star was shining.

He grew to be a young man, and was busy at his books, when an old servant came to him and said:

" Thy mother is no more. I bring her blessing on her darling son. "

Again at night he saw the star, and all that former company. Said his sister's angel to the leader: " Is my broth er come? "

And he said: " Thy mother! "

A mighty cry of joy went forth through all the star, because the mother was reunited to her two children. And he stretched out his arms and cried: " O, mother, sister, and brother, I am here! Take me! " And they answered him: " Not yet! "— and the star was shining.

He grew to be a man, whose hair was turning gray, and he was sitting in his chair by the fireside, heavy with grief, and with his face bedewed with tears, when the star opened once again.

Said his sister's angel to the leader: " Is my brother come? "

And he said: " Nay, but his maiden daughter ! "

And the man who had been the child saw his daughter, newly lost to him, a celestial creature among those three, and he said: " My daughter's head is on my sister's bosom, and her arm is around my mother's neck, and at her feet is the baby of old time, and I can bear the parting from her. God be praised. "

And the star was shining.

Thus the child came to be an old man, and his once smooth face was wrinkled, and his steps were slow and feeble, and his back was bent. And one night as he lay upon his bed, his children standing around, he cried, as he cried so long ago: " I see the star! "

They whispered one to another: " He is dying. "

And he said : " I am. My age is falling from me like a garment, and I move toward the star as a child. And O, my Father, now I thank thee that it has so often opened to receive those dear ones who await me ! "

And the star was shining: and it shines upon his grave.

CHARLES DICKENS.

ODE TO THE PASSIONS.

When Music, heavenly maid, was young,
While yet in early Greece she sung,
The Passions oft, to hear her shell,
Throng'd around her magic cell,—
Exulting, trembling, raging, fainting,
Possessed beyond the Muse's painting;
By turns, they felt the glowing mind
Disturbed, delighted, raised, refined :
Till once, 'tis said, when all were fired,
Filled with fury, rapt, inspired,
From the supporting myrtles round,
They snatched her instruments of sound;
And, as they oft had heard apart
Sweet lessons of her tuneful art,
Each — for Madness ruled the hour —
Would prove his own expressive power.

First, Fear, his hand, its skill to try,
    Amid the chords bewildered laid;
And back recoiled, he knew not why,
    E'en at the sound himself had made.—

Next Anger rushed — his eyes on fire,
    In lightnings owned his secret stings;
With one rude clash he struck the lyre,
    And swept, with hurried hand, the strings.

With woeful measures, wan Despair —
    Low, sullen sounds his grief beguiled;
A solemn, strange, and mingled air;
    'Twas sad by fits — by starts, 'twas wild.

But thou, O Hope ! with eyes so fair —
    What was thy delighted measure?

Still it whispered promised pleasure,
And bade the lovely scenes at distance hail;
  Still would her touch the strain prolong;
And from the rocks, the woods, the vale,
  She called on Echo still through all her song;
    And where her sweetest theme she chose,
A soft responsive voice was heard at every close;
  And Hope, enchanted, smiled, and waved
      her golden hair.

And longer had she sung, but with a frown
  Revenge impatient rose.
He threw his blood-stained sword in thunder
      down,
  And with a withering look,
  The war-denouncing trumpet took,
And blew a blast so loud and dread,
Were ne'er prophetic sounds so full of woe;
  And ever and anon, he beat
  The doubling drum with furious heat,
And though, sometimes, each dreary pause be-
      tween,
  Dejected Pity, at his side,
  Her soul-subduing voice applied;
Yet still he kept his wild, unaltered mien,
While each strained ball of sight seemed burst-
      ing from his head.

Thy numbers, Jealousy, to nought were fixed—
  Sad proof of thy distressful state:
Of differing themes the veering song was mixed;
And now it courted Love; now, raving, called
      on Hate.—
With eyes upraised, as one inspired,
  Pale Melancholy, sat retired,

And, from her wild, sequestered seat,
   In notes by distance made more sweet,
Poured through the mellow horn her pensive soul;
   And dashing soft from rocks around,
   Bubbling runnels joined the sound;
Thro' glades and glooms the mingled measure stole,
Or o'er some haunted stream with fond delay,
   Round a holy calm diffusing,
   Love of peace, and lonely musing,
In hollow murmurs died away.

But Oh! how altered was its sprightlier tone,
   When Cheerfulness, a nymph of healthiest hue,
   Her bow across her shoulder flung,
Her buskins gemmed with morning dew,
   Blew an inspiring air, that dale and thicket rung
The hunter's call, to Faun and Dryad known.
The oak-crowned sisters and their chaste-eyed queen
   Satyrs and sylvan boys were seen,
Peeping from forth their alleys green;
Brown exercise rejoiced to hear,
And Sport leaped up and seized his beechen spear.

Last came Joy's ecstatic trial;
   He, with viny crown advancing,
First to the lively pipe his hand addressed;
But soon he saw the brisk awakening viol,
   Whose sweet entrancing voice he loved the best.
They would have thought, who heard the strain,
They saw in Tempe's vale her native maids,
   Amid the festal-sounding shades,
To some unwearied minstrel dancing,
   While, as his flying fingers kissed the strings,
Love framed with Mirth a gay fantastic round,
   Loose were her tresses seen her zone unbound;

And he amid his frolic play,
As if he would the charming air repay,
Shook thousand odors from his dewy wings.

WILLIAM COLLINS.

A DAGGER OF THE MIND.

Is this a dagger which I see before me, the handle
Toward my hand?   Come, let me clutch thee.
I have thee not, and yet I see thee still.
Art thou not, fatal vision, sensible
To feeling as to sight? or art thou but
A dagger of the mind, a false creation,
Proceeding from a heat—oppressed brain?
I see thee yet, in form as palpable
As this which now I draw.
Thou marshall'st me the way that I was going;
And such an instrument I was to use.
Mine eyes are made the fools o' the other senses,
Or else worth all the rest; I see thee still,
And on thy blade and dudgeon gouts of blood,
Which was not so before.   There's no such thing:
It is the bloody business which informs
Thus to mine eyes.   Now o'er the one half-world
Nature seems dead, and wicked dreams abuse
The curtain'd sleep; witchcraft celebrates
Pale Hecate's offerings, and wither'd murder,
Alarum'd by his sentinel, the wolf,
Whose howl's his watch, thus with his stealthy pace,
With Tarquin's ravishing strides, towards his design
Moves like a ghost.   Thou sure and firm-set earth,
Hear not my steps, which way they walk, for fear
Thy very stones prate of my whereabout.   .   .   .
I go, and it is done; the bell invites me.

" MACBETH. "   SHAKESPEARE.

TWELFTH STEP IN RENDERING.
RELATION OF VALUES.

Relation of Values in speech may be likened to a pair of balances or scales. That which is being weighed receives more attention than the weights.

Under Relation of Values may be included what is commonly known as Comparisons of various kinds:—

Antithesis—the placing of opposites together.

Simile—declares one thing to be like another.

Metaphor—an implied comparison.

Ideas, Positive balanced with Negative; Heavy with Light; Limited with Limitless: that which we Choose with what we Reject; ideas of Comparison may be expressed or implied in a word alone or told in a sentence, a paragraph, or may be a longer expression.

Positive ideas should be made heavy and negative light. In debate make your own arguments weighty, your opponent's arguments light— ignored as if of little worth. It is not best to attack the opponent's arguments. Treat as unworthy of attack: colorless.

" Giving as good as is sent " defeats its own purpose.

In dealing with questions of morals, make Light weightier than darkness ; Beauty, Goodness, Truth of more weight than ugliness, deformity and error. In life as well as expression make Positives Heavy and Negatives Light. Love weighs more than hate ; Good than evil ; Light than darkness ; Life than death.

In the book of Proverbs are examples of Antithesis:—
" Better is a dry morsel, and quietness therewith, than an house full of sacrifices with strife. . . .

Whoso mocketh the poor reproacheth his Maker: and he that is glad at calamities shall not be unpunished. "

> Earth gets its price for what Earth gives us;
>   The beggar is taxed for a corner to die in,
> The priest hath his fee who comes and shrives us,
>   We bargain for the graves we lie in.
> At the devil's booth all things are sold,
> Each ounce of dross costs its ounce of gold ;
>   For a cap and bells our lives we pay,
> Bubbles we buy with a whole soul's tasking ;
>   'Tis heaven alone that is given away,
> 'Tis only God may be had for the asking.
> No price is set on the lavish summer
> June may be had by the poorest comer.

" *Vision of Sir Launfal.* " *Lowell.*

Suppose that you are the best part of England ; that you who have become the slaves ought to have been the masters, and that those who are the masters ought to have been the slaves ! If it is a noble and whole–hearted England whose bidding you are bound to do, it is well ; but if you are your-selves the best of her heart, and the England you have left be but a half-hearted England, how say you of your obedience ? You were too proud to become shop-keepers ; are you satisfied then to become the servants of shop-keep-ers ? You were too proud to become merchants or farmers; will you have merchants or farmers for your field-marshals ? You imagine yourselves to be the army of England : how, if you should find yourselves at last only the police of her manufacturing towns, and the beadles of her little Bethels ?

" *Address at Royal Military Academy.* " *Ruskin.*

In rendering the Simile, hold up the idea that is being likened to another or to several others with greater prominence than anything else with which it is likened or compared. It is a fault to reverse this order and allow the mind to be so taken with the elaborate notions used in the comparison as to lose sight of the prime idea. This chief idea, as it is put in the balances and weighed with one idea after another, should be held in the mind throughout the entire process, even if a paragraph long, as of more value than anything, or all things with which it is compared.

> They came, and Eudora stood robed and crowned,
> The bride of the morn, with her train around.
> *Jewels* flashed out from her braided hair,
> Like starry dews midst the roses there;
> Pearls on her bosom quivering shone,
> Heaved by her heart through its golden zone;
> But a *brow*, as those gems of the ocean pale,
> Gleamed from beneath her transparent veil;
> Changeful and faint was her fair *cheek's* hue,
> Tho' clear as a flower which the light looks through.

" *Bride of the Greek Isle.* " *Mrs. Hemans.*

The tent was unlooped; I pulled up the spear that obstructed, and under 1 stooped. . . I groped my way on.

" Here is David, thy servant ! " And no voice replied. At the first I saw naught but the blackness; but soon I descried a something more black than the blackness—the vast, the upright main prop which sustains the pavilion: and slow into sight grew a figure against it, gigantic and blackest of all. Then a sunbeam, that burst through the tent-roof, showed *Saul*. He stood as erect as that tent-prop, both arms stretched out wide on the great cross-support in the centre, that goes to each side; he relaxed not a muscle but hung there as, caught in his pangs and waiting his

change, the king serpent all heavily hangs, far away from his
kind, in the pine, till deliverance come with the spring-
time,— so agonized Saul, drear and stark, blind and dumb.
" *Saul.* "   *Robert Browning.*

> There is sweet *music* here that softer falls
> Than petals from blown roses on the grass,
> Or night-dews on still waters between walls
> Of shadowy granite, in a gleaming pass;
> *Music* that gentlier on the spirit lies,
> Than tir'd eyelids upon tir'd eyes.

" *The Lotos-Eaters.*"   *Tennyson.*

In metaphor hold the thought all through the compar
ison on the real idea thus contrasted:—

The Lord is my shepherd; I shall not want. He maketh
me to lie down in green pastures: he leadeth me beside the
still waters. He restoreth my soul: he leadeth me in the
paths of righteousness for his name's sake. Yea, though I
walk through the valley of the shadow of death, I will fear
no evil: for thou art with me; thy rod and thy staff they
comfort me.

Thou preparest a table before me in the presence of mine
enemies: thou anointest my head with oil; my cup runneth
over. Surely Goodness and Mercy shall follow me all the
days of my life: and I will dwell in the house of the *Lord*
forever.— " *A Song of Trust.* " *Twenty-third Psalm.*

> I, writing thus, am still what men call young;
> I have not so far left the coasts of life
> To travel inland, that I cannot hear
> That murmur of the water infinite
> Which unweaned babies smile at in their sleep,
> When wondered at for smiling.— *Mrs. Browning.*

All that I know
  Of a certain star
Is, it can throw
  (Like the angled spar)
Now a dart of red,
  Now a dart of blue ;
Till my friends have said
  They would fain see, too,
My star that dartles the red and the blue !
  Then it stops like a bird ; like a flower,
      hangs furled :
  They must solace themselves with the
      Saturn above it.
What matter to me if their star is a world ?
  Mine has opened its soul to me ; therefore
      I love it.

" *My Star.* "   *Robert Browning.*

Make positive ideas heavier than negative ideas.—

" Your words have been stout against me, " saith the
Lord. "Yet ye say, ' What have we spoken so much against
thee ? '   Ye have said, ' It is vain to serve God : and what
profit is it that we have kept his ordinance, and that we have
walked mournfully before the Lord of hosts?   And now
we call the proud happy ; yea, they that work wickedness
are set up ; yea, they that tempt God are even delivered. ' "

Then they that feared the Lord spake often one to
another : and the Lord hearkened, and heard it, and a book
of remembrance was written before him for them that
feared the Lord, and that thought upon his name.

" And they shall be mine, " saith the Lord of hosts,
" in that day when I make up my jewels ; and I will spare
them, as a man spareth his own son that serveth him.
Then shall ye return, and discern between the righteous

and the wicked, between him that serveth God and him
that serveth him not. ''   *Malachi.*

> Reflected in the lake, I love
>   To see the stars of evening glow,
> So tranquil in the heavens above,
>   So restless in the wave below.
> Thus heavenly hope is all serene,
>   But earthly hope, how bright soe'er,
> Still fluctuates o'er this changing scene,
>   As false and fleeting as 'tis fair.   *Heber.*

In the tempest of life, when the wave and the gale
Are around and above, if thy footing should fail—
If thine eyes should grow dim, and thy caution depart—
Look aloft, and be firm, and be fearless of heart.

If the friend who embraced in prosperity's glow,
With a smile for each joy and a tear for each woe,
Should betray thee when sorrows, like clouds, are arrayed,
Look aloft to the friendship which never shall fade.

Should the visions which hope spreads in light to thine eye,
Like the tints of the rainbow, but brighten to fly,
Then turn, and, through tears of repentant regret,
Look aloft to the sun that is never to set.

Should they who are nearest and dearest thy heart—
Thy friends and companions—in sorrow depart,
Look aloft from the darkness and dust of the tomb,
To that soil where '' affection is ever in bloom. ''

And oh, when Death comes in his terrors, to cast
His fears on the future, his pall on the past,
In that moment of darkness, with hope in thy heart,
And a smile in thine eye, *Look aloft*, and depart.
'' *Look Aloft.* ''   *J. Lawrence.*

SELF-DEPENDENCE.

Weary of myself, and sick of asking
What I am, and what I ought to be,
At this vessel's prow I stand, which bears me
Forward, forward, o'er the starlit sea.

And a look of passionate desire
O'er the sea and to the stars I send;
" Ye who from my childhood up have calm'd me,
Calm me, ah, compose me to the end!

Ah, once more," I cried " ye stars, ye waters,
On my heart your mighty charm renew;
Still, still let me, as I gaze upon you,
Feel my soul becoming vast like you! "

From the intense, clear, star-sown vault of heaven,
Over the lit sea's unquiet way,
In the rustling night air came the answer,—
" Wouldst thou be as these are? Live as they.

Unaffrighted by the silence round them,
Undistracted by the sights they see,
These demand not that the things without them
Yield them love, amusement, sympathy.

And with joy the stars perform their shining,
And the sea its long moon-silver'd roll;
For self-poised they live, nor pine with noting
All the fever of some differing soul.

Bounded by themselves, and unregardful
In what state God's other works may be,
In their own tasks all their powers pouring,
These attain the mighty life you see. "

O air-born voice! long since, severely clear,
A cry like thine in mine own heart I hear;
" Resolve to be thyself; and know that he
Who finds himself loses his misery! "

MATTHEW ARNOLD.

PURE, COLD WATER.

There, there is the liquor which God, the Eternal, brews for all his children.   Not in the simmering still, over smoky fires, choked with poisonous gases, surrounded with the stench of sickening odors and corruptions, doth your Father in heaven prepare the precious essence of life— pure, cold water; but in the green glade and grassy dell, where the red deer wanders, and the child loves to play, there God brews it: and down, low down in the deepest valleys, where the fountain murmurs and the rills sing; and high upon the mountain tops, where the naked granite glitters like gold in the sun, where the storm-cloud broods and the thunder-storms crash; and far out on the wide, wild sea, where the hurricane howls music, and the big waves roll the chorus, sweeping the march of God — there He brews it, that beverage of life — health-giving water.

And everywhere it is a thing of life and beauty—gleaming in the dew-drop; singing in the summer rain; shining in the ice-gem, till the trees all seem turned to living jewels; spreading a golden veil over the setting sun, or a white gauze around the midnight moon; sporting in the cataract; folding its bright snow-curtains softly about the wintery world; and weaving the many-colored bow, that seraph's zone of the sky — whose warp is the raindrop of the earth, whose woof is the sunbeam of heaven, all checked over with the celestial flowers, by the mystic hand of refraction.

Still always it is beautiful, that blessed life-water! No poison bubbles on its brink ; its foam brings not madness and murder ; no blood stains its limpid glass ; pale widows and starving orphans weep not burning tears in its depths ; no drunkard's shrieking ghost, from the grave, curses it in the words of eternal despair! Speak out, my friends : would you exchange it for the demon's drink, alcohol? A shout like the roar of the tempest, answered, " No ! "

JOHN B. GOUGH.

CIVIC RIGHTS FOR THE JEWS.

My honorable friend has appealed to us as Christians. Let me, then, ask him how he understands that great commandment which *comprises* the law and the prophets. Can we be said to do unto others as we would that they should do unto us, if we inflict on them even the smallest pain ? As Christians, surely we are bound to consider, first, whether, by excluding the Jews from all public trust we give them pain ; and, secondly, whether it be necessary to give them that pain in order to avert some greater evil. That by excluding them from public trust, we inflict pain on them, my honorable friend will not dispute. As a Christian, therefore, he is bound to relieve them from pain, unless he can show, what I am sure he has not yet shown, that it is necessary to the general good that they should continue to suffer.

" But where, " he says, " are you to stop, if once you admit into the House of Commons people who deny the authority of the Gospels? Will you let in a Mussulman? Will you let in a Parsee? Will you let in a Hindoo, who worships a lump of stone with seven heads? " I will answer my honorable friend's question by another. Where does he mean to stop. Is he ready to roast unbelievers at slow fires? If not let him tell us why ; and I will engage to prove that his reason is just as decisive against the intolerance which he thinks a duty as against the intolerance which he thinks a crime. Once admit that we are bound to inflict pain on a man because he is not of our religion, and where are you to stop? Why stop at the point fixed by my honorable friend rather than at the point fixed by the honorable member for Oldham (Cobbett,) who would make the Jews incapable of holding land?

And why stop at the point fixed by the honorable member for Oldham rather than at the point which would have been fixed by a Spanish inquisitor of the sixteenth century?

When once you enter on a course of persecution, I defy you to find any reason for making a halt till you have reached the extreme point. When my honorable friend tells us that he will allow the Jews to possess property to any amount, but that he will not allow them to possess the smallest political power, he holds contradictory language. Property is power. . . . .

"But, " says my honorable friend, " it has been prophesied that the Jews are to be wanderers on the face of the earth, and that they are not to mix on terms of equality with the people of the countries in which they sojourn. "

Now, sir, I am confident that I can demonstrate that this is not the sense of any prophecy which is part of Holy Writ. For it is an undoubted fact, that in the United States of America Jewish citizens do possess all the privileges possessed by Christian citizens. Therefore, if the prophecies mean that the Jews never shall, during their wanderings, be admitted by other nations to equal participation of political rights, the prophecies are false. But the prophecies are certainly not false. Therefore their meaning cannot be that which is attributed to them by my honorable friend. . . . .

Nobody knows better than my honorable friend, the member for the University of Oxford, that there is nothing in their national character which unfits them for the highest duties of citizens. He knows, that in the infancy of civilization, when our island was as savage as New Guinea, when letters and arts were still unknown to Athens, when scarcely a thatched hut stood on what was after the site of Rome, this contemned people had their fenced cities and cedar palaces, their splendid temple, their fleets of merchant ships, their schools of sacred learning, their great statesmen and soldiers, their natural philosophers, their historians, and their poets. What nation ever contended more manfully against overwhelming odds for its independence and religion? What nation ever, in its last agonies, gave such signal proofs of what may be accomplished by a brave despair? And if, in the course of many centuries, the oppressed descendants of warriors and sages have degenerated from the qualities of their fathers, if, while excluded from the blessings of law, and bowed down under the yoke of slavery, they have contracted some of the vices of outlaws and of slaves, shall we consider this as matter of reproach to thém? Shall we not rather consider it as matter of shame and remorse to ourselves? Let us do justice to them. Let us open to them the door of the House of Commons. Let us open to them every career in which ability and energy can be displayed. Till we have done this, let us not presume to say that there is no genius among the countrymen of Isaiah, no heroism among the descendants of the Maccabees.

Lord Macaulay.

There is a decisive instant in all matters; and if you look languidly, you are sure to miss it. Nature seems always, somehow, trying to make you miss it. " I will see that through, " you must say, " without turning my head; " or you won't see the trick of it at all. — *Ruskin.*

THIRTEENTH STEP IN RENDERING.
VOLUME OF VOICE.

Volume of Voice comes from volume of thought and feeling. It has to do with noble emotions : sublimity, reverence, adoration, grandeur, poetic fervor, patriotic sentiment, when uttered with a deep under-current of feeling. Unlike the Conversational and the Dramatic Styles which deal with the commonplace, Volume of Voice is used in exalted, dignified expressions, therefore is used in the Oratorical Style.

Oratory comes from "orare," (to speak in a pleading manner.) The emotional element makes it truly eloquent. "Oratory is the flowering, the culminating of all the graces of expression, the flowering of the virtues. Oratory may be compared to the discoursing of grand music, to an organ with a thousand stops, moving the profoundest of human emotions." Oratory requires a knowledge of expression of body and the arts of voice, gesture, and mastery of the same, beside, a soul well stored with burning thoughts and feelings.

The expression must be simplicity itself, suggesting and awakening thought and feeling in the subtlest, simplest manner, concealing all effort. Oratory requires concentrated energy and skill such as is used by the singer who renders grand and noble music with few but dignified outward movements. " The highest art is to conceal art. "

It has been said of Orators :— Cicero,—a conflagration. Demosthenes,— a hurricane. Saint Paul,— a god of eloquence. Clay,—fiery, magnetic. Spurgeon,— voice fine, magnetic. Webster,— while perspiration ran down his face; his body was in comparative quietude— his eyes burned, yet repose seemed the normal condition.

Lacardaire,— voice at first feeble — clear, massive, susceptible of force and passion, grew more fervent, deepened and strengthened to a wonderful degree. He began simply, suddenly took a turn like lightning ; he was seized and the listener carried with him. Not learning by heart, it was a soul that broke forth like a tide through the walls of flesh, and cast itself reckless and desperate into the soul of another ; this is greater than speech. Eloquence is the soul which takes the place of our own. Extemporaneous speech takes the head from the shoulders.

STUDY FOR VOLUME OF VOICE.

We may have wondered why the charming *gift*, as it is called, of Oratory is so rare that only two or three real and truly great Orators appear in a generation. Something may be wrong. The seed-for producing this choice species may be planted wrong-side-out. We do know that when the average student — they with graduating orations not excepted— attempts to render the Oratorical style, he stiffens his muscles and assumes a swollen appearance which can be compared to nothing in all the field of nature and art but a turkey gobbler on parade. He declaims in a loud, strained voice, destitute of that which charms.
Nor is the student alone deluded into the " wrong-side-out" style. It is much to be regretted that finished scholars thus abuse their mother tongue. The man of holy orders too often voices the sacred message in a most unholy way. We

are all familiar with what is known as the " ministerial
tone. "   (They who employ such tones, as a natural result
are often afflicted with "clergyman's sore throat. ")
It so happens our best examples are poor guides to imitate.

The best guide must come from within yourself.

In the practical drill for Volume of Voice, much depends
on getting the right start.   The point of difference between
the right way and the wrong way is apparently so small
at the start, one may easily miss the right way.   Here, as in
the other studies, let the mind not only lead but let it com-
pel the voice.   Make no effort to use a large voice.   Only
as the sublime ideas possess the soul causing it to respond,
will the voice respond and expand naturally.   Volume can
not be " put on " without positive injury.

Let us illustrate somewhat the mental side of our work
for volume, using for our study " The Ocean, " by Byron,
which follows.   First go through it contrasting the ordinary,
commonplace ideas with the grand, sublime ideas ; the limited with the limitless.   The " drop of rain, "   " snowy
flake, " etc. limited.   Send the mind out in an effort to take
in the " glorious mirror where the Almighty's form glasses
(reflects) itself. "   Try to see the limitless ideas reflected
in this boundless mirror.   Then the mind must reach out
still beyond the vast deep to the unknowable, " the image
of eternity, " " the throne of the Invisible. "   Make vast
and limitless all that refers in any way to the Ocean,— the
pronouns and all.   Concentrate the mind many times on
the pictures before attempting to read it aloud, then read
ideas instead of words, letting the voice respond naturally.
As the mental grows in ability to expand and respond will
the voice expand and grow in volume.   Do not force the
voice ; let the mind lead ; be content to take time to grow;
repeat, repeat, repeat the concentration of the mind on the
sublime pictures then respond honestly as you are impressed.

Volume of Voice may be cultivated in another way in connection with the foregoing study. Impersonate, in the private study, some great, dignified character, orator or states-man with some grave or noble feeling dominant. For ex-ample: with costume, manner and voice play Brutus in the orchard scene in " Julius Cæsar. " Try to comprehend the dignity and majesty of his noble character and the deep emotions ruling him as he contemplates, for the good of Rome, the assassination of Cæsar. Let the mental concep-tion of the character dominate the voice.

The student may gain a point of advantage in practice for Volume of Voice by getting first the pitch, as in singing. For low pitch say— " awe, awe, awe, " prolong, feel the vibration in the chest by placing the hand there. Get the pitch very gently. Do not force the voice.

By making use of only the two studies named— " The Ocean " and " Brutus in the Orchard " — as a drill exercise, voices have been wonderfully improved. This drill must always be more of a mental than a vocal gymnastic. Ever aim for INTENSITY RATHER THAN LOUDNESS for herein lies the secret of success. This order reversed defeats either the novice or the sage.

After the student is once sure that he has made the right start training the voice for volume, while he should contin-ue the drill on the first studies, he may take up new studies. Look for the sublime in nature, ideas of the Deity, abstract, limitless ideas of Patriotism, Love, as in I Corinthians XIII, Judgment, Conviction of Sin, Sense of Duty, etc. Expres-sions of ignoble passion is never allowed in Oratory.

As Oratory is the highest form of human expression, the student can well afford to pay the price of earnest effort.

Grand, sublime thought and feeling given out with a deep mellow voice and with intensity behind it has power to ennoble. Deep voice moves like the deep toned organ.

THE OCEAN.

Roll on, thou deep and dark blue Ocean — roll !
Ten thousand fleets sweep over thee in vain ;
Man marks the earth with ruin — his control
Stops with the shore ; upon the watery plain
The wrecks are all thy deed, nor doth remain
A shadow of man's ravage, save his own,
When, for a moment, like a drop of rain ,
He sinks into thy depths with bubbling groan,
Without a grave, unknelled, uncoffined, and unknown.

The armaments which thunderstrike the walls
Of rock–built cities, bidding nations quake,
And monarchs tremble in their capitals ;
The oak leviathans, whose huge ribs make
Their clay creator the vain title take
Of lord of thee, and arbiter of war :
These are thy toys, and, as the snowy flake,
They melt into thy yeast of waves, which mar
Alike the Armada's pride, or spoils of Trafalgar.

Thy shores are empires, changed in all save thee —
Assyria, Greece, Rome, Carthage,— what are they ?
Thy waters wasted them while they were free,
And many a tyrant since ; their shores obey
The stranger, slave, or savage ; their decay
Has dried up realms to deserts : not so thou ;
Unchangeable, save to thy wild waves' play —
Time writes no wrinkle on thine azure brow —
Such as creation's dawn beheld, thou rollest now.

Thou glorious mirror, where the Almighty's form
Glasses itself in tempests ; in all time,
Calm or convulsed — in breeze, or gale, or storm,

Icing the pole, or in the torrid clime
Dark–heaving;—boundless, endless and sublime—
The image of Eternity—the throne
Of the Invisible; even from out thy slime
The monsters of the deep are made; each zone
Obeys thee: thou goest forth, dread, fathomless, alone.

And I have loved thee, Ocean! and my joy
Of youthful sport was on thy breast to be
Borne, like thy bubbles, onward: from a boy
I wantoned with thy breakers—they to me
Were a delight; and if thy freshening sea
Made them a terror, 'twas a pleasing fear;
For I was, as it were, a child of thee,
And trusted to thy billows far and near,
And laid my hand upon thy mane—as I do here.

LORD BYRON.

BRUTUS IN THE ORCHARD.

It must be by his death: and, for my part,
I know no personal cause to spurn at him,
But for the general.   He would be crowned:—
How that might change his nature, there's the
          question:
It is the bright day that brings forth the adder,
And that craves wary walking.   Crown him?—that;
And then, I grant, we put a sting in him,
That at his will he may do danger with.
The abuse of greatness is, when it disjoins
Remorse from power: and, to speak truth of Cæsar,
I have not known when his affections swayed
More than his reason.   But 'tis a common proof,

That lowliness is young ambition's ladder,
Whereto the climber-upward turns his face;
But when he once attains the upmost round,
He then unto the ladder turns his back,
Looks in the clouds, scorning the base degrees,
By which he did ascend.   So Cæsar may:
Then, lest he may, prevent.   And, since the quarrel
Will bear no colour for the thing he is,
Fashion it thus: that what he is, augmented,
Would run to these and these extremities:
And therefore think him as a serpent's egg,
Which, hatched, would as his kind grow mischievous;
And kill him in the shell.   .   .   .   .
    The exhalations whizzing in the air
Give so much light that I may read by them.
                    (Opens letter, and reads.)
' Brutus, thou sleep'st: awake, and see thyself.
Shall Rome, &c. —Speak, strike, redress! '
' Brutus, thou sleep'st: awake! '—
Such instigations have been often dropped
Where I have took them up.
' Shall Rome, &c. '   Thus must I piece it out :
Shall Rome stand under one man's awe?   What,
       Rome?
My ancestors did from the streets of Rome
The Tarquin drive, when he was called a king.
' Speak, strike, redress!' — Am I entreated
To speak, and strike?   O Rome, I make thee promise,
If the redress will follow, thou receiv'st
Thy full petition at the hand of Brutus.   .   .   .
    Between the acting of a dreadful thing
And the first motion, all the interim is
Like a phantasma or a hideous dream.

" Julius Cæsar. "   Shakespeare.

VOICES OF THE SEA.

The sea with all its moods has a perpetual charm for the traveler. It speaks to him of God and man. Its depths, its breadths, its fullness, its waves are constantly saying, " The sea is His, and He made it. " In its changing moods are reflected all the experiences of mankind. Peace is reflected in its calm, trouble in its storms, joy in its coruscation, and life in its movement.

There is the voice of affliction. The Psalmist was passing through deep trouble when he sang, " All thy waves and thy billows are gone over me. " It suggests the picture of a storm at sea when the mightiest ship is tossed like a cockle shell upon the billows, and washed from bow to stern by the waves. It speaks of consecutive troubles like wave following wave, and billow following billow. " Misfortunes come not single spies ,but in battalions. " When the storm lashes the sea into fury and lifts the waters into dangerous heights it would seem as if calm could never again be restored, and that everything in the path of the waves must perish. It is then that the sea spells trouble and furnishes an unparalleled picture of affliction. Behind the hand of God is the heart of God: therefore the Psalmist sings, " The Lord will command his loving kindness in the daytime, and in the night his song shall be with me. " When the voice of the sea of trouble is answered by the voice of hope and faith and praise, there is victory for the soul even when temporarily overwhelmed by affliction.

There is the voice of unrest. It was the prophet Isaiah who said : " The wicked are like the troubled sea, when it cannot rest, whose waters cast up mire and dirt. There is no peace, saith my God, to the wicked. " The restlessness of the sea is one of the features which impresses the traveler. It is never still. Either the wind, the sun, or the currents keep it constantly in motion. It is the prey of every outside and inside influence. The winds toss it about with ease, the tides draw it around the world, the currents divert its waters where they will. So it is with the wicked. They have no peace, because peace is the result of balance, poise, power, and there can be none of these in the life of the wicked, since they are out of center, out of harmony with God.

There is the voice of pardon. It was another prophet who said, " Thou wilt cast all their sins into the depths of the sea. " This is a beautiful picture of the forgiveness of sins. It speaks of the fullness and the finality of forgiveness.

There is the voice of resurrection. In the apocalyptic vision of John he saw the sea giving up the dead and heard the voice of resurrection. We cannot look at the sea without beholding the grave of unnumbered multitudes who have died at sea. No slab marks their last resting place, no casket holds their remains, no flowers decorate their graves. Their bodies lie in the deep cathedral caverns of the sea and the subterranean voices of the ocean chant their requiem. But the day is coming when the sea shall give up the dead that are in it. And so the sea speaks of resurrection.

There is the voice of consummation. It was the seer of Patmos who also anticipated the time when there shall be no more sea. The new earth is to have no sea. In this glorious consummation there is to be no salt sea separating friends, and no salt tears, for God shall wipe away all tears from their eyes, and death shall be no more : neither shall there be mourning, nor crying, nor pain any more. The first things are passed away.

These are the voices of the sea. May you hear the voice of God in them and, hearing, may you be saved and comforted. REV. JOHN A. EARL, D. D.

CHRISTIAN EDUCATION.

When a youth, I read of the Alps and their majestic splen·dor until it became a passion to see their star-pricking peaks. At last my ambition was gratified. Arriving in Lausanne and gazing southward over Lake Geneva, I saw the wonderful, far-famed glories of the "White Giants." Beyond the lower mountains were the higher, in successive crystal galleries as if they were the stairs to the Gate of Pearl. They exceeded in grandeur my wildest dreams, and my imagination transformed them into all manner of crea-tions; they were immense candles which some tall angel lit every morning with the first ray of light, and in the evening they blazed with the last flames of day; they were stupendous pillars supporting the walls of the City of Gold; they were Titanic Colossi lifting their shoulders through the clouds to support the sky lest it fall. I hastened to ap-proach them, to walk in the valleys where trailed their white robes and worship in the vestibule of their splendor. I confess, however, to a disappointment; distance had given them an enchantment; for their crystalline heights hid the sun and cast a shadow on all beneath. They sent down over their uncouth and ragged sides rivers of ice, cold as the stream of death, the terrible avalanche, grinding, crushing, and destroying every vestige of life and beauty it touched; its path is the highway of destruction, and its presence the blight of winter.

Far more attractive to me was the placid river meander·ing through the valleys and meadows, quickening the life of trees and the beauty of flowers, distilling health, joy and manifold blessings whither-so-ever it flowed. I could almost forgive my fellowman for kneeling in affectionate devotion and worshiping the river.

There is an education that dares the vision and inspires

the wonderment of the common people; it beckons the student to tread its dizzy heights and " become as Gods; " but its throne is the icy brain, there is no life in its light, nor sympathy in its radiance. Its influence blights the bloom of hope and faith in the soul; it chills the atmosphere where spiritual emotions and aspirations germ and grow and they shrivel; it nurtures no moral virtues and fosters no spiritual graces. It is a glare that blinds the soul so it can no longer " see God ", for that is the blessedness of the " pure in heart; " and the heart has not been helped to the measure of stirring one pulse-beat to " make for righteousness. " This is not the learning and education that develops the student into " a perfect man unto the measure of the stature of the fullness of Christ. " The education that will accomplish this result is the need of the age; the schools and colleges that furnish such education meet the burning need of the Kingdom of God among men, for *it* seems to flow from beneath the throne of God, freighted with the riches of Paradise.

" EDUCATION. "   REV. H. O. ROWLANDS, D. D.

GOD.

The following poem is a translation from the Russian. It has been translated into Japanese by the Emperor, and is hung up, embroidered with gold, in the temple of Jeddo. It has also been translated into the Chinese and Tartar languages, written on rich silk, and suspended in the Imperial palace at Pekin.

O thou eternal One! whose presence bright
All space doth occupy, all motion guide;
Unchanged through time's all-devastating flight;
Thou only God! There is no God beside!
Being above all beings! Three-in-one!

Whom none can comprehend, and none explore;
Who fill'st existence with Thyself alone;
Embracing all—supporting—ruling o'er—
Being whom we call God—and know no more!
   In its sublime research, philosophy
May measure out the ocean deep— may count
The sands or the sun's rays—but God! for Thee
There is no weight nor measure;—none can mount
Up to Thy mysteries. Reason's brightest spark,
Though kindled by Thy light, in vain would try
To trace Thy counsels, infinite and dark;
And thought is lost ere thought can soar so high—
E'en like past moments in eternity.
   Thou from primeval nothingness didst call,
First chaos, then existence;—Lord! on Thee
Eternity had its foundation;—all
Sprung forth from Thee;—of light, joy, harmony,
Sole origin;— all life, all beauty, Thine.
Thy word created all, and doth create;
Thy splendor fills all space with rays divine;
Thou art, and wert, and shalt be! Glorious,
Light-giving, life-sustaining, Potentate!
   Thy chains the unmeasured universe surround;
Upheld by Thee, by Thee inspired with breath!
Thou the beginning with the end hast bound,
And beautifully mingled life and death!
As sparks mount upward from the fiery blaze,
So suns are born, so worlds spring forth from Thee,
And as the spangles in the sunny rays
Shine around the silver snow, the pageantry
Of heaven's bright army glitters in Thy praise.
   A million torches lighted by Thy hand
Wander unwearied through the blue abyss;
They own Thy power, accomplish Thy command,

All gay with life, all eloquent with bliss.
What shall we call them? Pyres of crystal light —
A glorious company of golden streams—
Lamps of celestial ether burning bright—
Suns lighting systems with their joyful beams?
But thou to these art as the noon to night.

    Yes! as a drop of water in the sea,
All this magnificence in Thee is lost ;—
What are ten thousand worlds compared to Thee?
And what am I then? Heaven's unnumbered host,
Though multiplied by myriads, and arrayed
In all the glory of sublimest thought,
Is but an atom in the balance weighed
Against Thy greatness,—is a cipher brought
Against infinity! What am I then? Naught!
Naught! But the effluence of Thy light divine,
Pervading worlds, hath reached my bosom too ;
Yes, in my spirit doth Thy spirit shine,
As shines the sunbeam in a drop of dew.

    Naught! but I live, and on hope's pinions fly
Eager toward Thy presence; for in Thee
I live, and breathe, and dwell; aspiring high
Even to the throne of Thy divinity.
I am, O God! and surely Thou must be!
Thou art! directing, guiding all, Thou art!
Direct my understanding then to Thee ;
Control my spirit, guide my wandering heart;
Though but an atom midst immensity,
Still I am something, fashioned by Thy hand!
I hold a middle rank, 'twixt heaven and earth,
On the last verge of mortal being stand,
Close to the realm where angels have their birth,
Just on the boundaries of the spirit land!
The chain of being is complete in me;

In me is matter's last gradation lost,
And the next step is spirit—Deity !
I can command the lightning and am dust!
A monarch, and a slave; a worm, a god !
Whence came I here, and how ? so marvelously
Constructed and conceived?   Unknown ! this clod
Lives surely through some higher energy ;
For from itself alone it could not be!
Creator, yes !   Thy wisdom and Thy word
Created me !   Thou source of life and good !
Thou spirit of my spirit, and my Lord !
Thy light, Thy love, in the bright plenitude,
Filled me with an immortal soul, to spring
Over the abyss of death, and bade it wear
The garments of eternal day, and wing
Its heavenly flight beyond the little sphere,
Even to its source—to Thee—its author there.

Oh thoughts ineffable !   Oh visions blest !
Though worthless our conception all of Thee,
Yet shall Thy shadowed image fill our breast,
And waft its homage to Thy Deity.
God ! thus alone my lonely thoughts can soar ;
Thus seek Thy presence—Being wise and good,
Midst Thy vast works admire, obey, adore ;
And, when the tongue is eloquent no more,
The soul shall speak in tears of gratitude.

DERZHAVIN.

PATMOS.

It was well on in the afternoon of a spring day that our
steamer slowly passed the Isle of Patmos.   We were on our
way northward to Smyrna, and thence on to Constantinople.
As if to add special appropriateness to the occasion, with us
too, it was "the Lord's Day. "   The quiet of a Sabbath hush

rested on the company of voyagers who had just bidden farewell to the sacred sceues of the Holy Land. It was a perfect day. Not a cloud rested on the peaceful sky that brooded over us, nor was there the ripple of a wave on the indescribable blue of that wondrous sea. Were it not for the throb and jar of the machinery, we might almost have supposed that the ship was at a standstill.

Seated under the awning, with our Bibles open, the book of Revelation was read while the eye passed constantly from the printed page westward to the rocky shore where the things " which are written in this book " had taken place. It was an experience never to be forgotten. Immediately we had passed the island, the sun, like a great ball of fire, gradually approached its setting. A sunset at sea is always impressive, and that evening we observed it with peculiar interest, scarcely daring to breathe. At last the rim touched the waters, and instantly the whole Aegean blazed forth into shimmering pathways of golden splendor extending from our ship outward to the furthest edge of the distant horizon. Yes, we saw it! " the sea of glass mingled with fire."

Patmos is not a large island? It extends only some ten miles from north to south, but so deeply indented are its shores that the coast-line is thirty-seven miles in length. Its shape has been curiously compared to " a horse's head and neck, the nose pointing eastward. " It is of volcanic origin. The island gathers into three main mountain masses of brown rock, bare, jagged, desolate, its highest summit attaining a height of about 950 feet. Its pagan insignificance is indicated by the fact that it is referred to only thrice in classical literature, and then receives but the barest mention. As if unknown to the world even at the time of the Apocalypse, John speaks of it as " the isle called Patmos. "

But greatness does not depend upon the bulk. Once in our world's history the curtains parted from before that

" lone rocky isle of the sea, " and disclosed the last white-haired survivor of the Apostolic band walking along its heights with his glorified Lord, and then slowly the curtains closed again. It was enough. We would not part with this one vision for half the history of the world. No island on our planet after this can ever begin to compare with it for interest. Down to the end of time it will occupy a leading place in immortal story, and the heart of the world will ever beat faster because of the unveiling of the unseen that was there revealed.

" PATMOS LETTERS. "   DR. JOHN L. CAMPBELL.

PEACE ON EARTH.

The Christian Church has no greater message to utter in the councils of nations, with all the emphasis and moral authority within her power, than the words of Jesus to Peter " Put up again thy sword into its place, " and making her way through forts and fortifications, over ramparts and battlements, brushing aside guns and bayonets, reach the people of these Christian lands, and stir them in the name of the Lord with the challenge " Let us have peace. "

Just think of some of the evils and horrors of war, evils and horrors that the civilized world ought to remember, instead of being absorbed with the glittering glories of war. Think of the desolation of the ravaged battle-zones, the paralysis of industry and commerce, and the reckless destruction of property that travel with contending armies. Think of the suffering and sacrifice, not only of those fighting at the front, but of those martyrs of the home left behind. Think of the savage passions aroused in the hearts of the victors, and the hatred and vindictiveness born and nursed in the hearts of the vanquished. Think of the cost

in men and money, in what President David Starr Jordan
affirms is the best and bravest of a country's manhood, and
in the millions of money the rest of the nation must toil
and slave to provide, taking the bread from the mouth
of the children to satisfy the ferocity of the dogs of war;
and think, consider, realize that all this and much, Oh!
much more, is the tribute paid by Christian nations to barbarism, paid for the most part to avoidable, unnecessary, unjustifiable, intolerable barbarism. Think, I say, and induce
others to think of the cruel cost of war, war that after all
cannot settle moral issues, for arbitrament of war only decides who is strong, not who is wrong, war only establishes
the dominance of might, not of right. Without going into
the harrowing recital of the awful cost in shattered bodies,
and broken hearts, and shadowed homes, and weakened
and burdened states, think of the crushing cost in money,
think of the wealth of the rich and the blood of the poor,
yea, the very blood of the multitudes that must needs be
poured out to sustain, but never to satisfy, the barbarism of
militarism. Think what it means to the social and eco-
nomic life of the people that seventy-two (72) per cent. of
our governmental expenditures is for war, war in its prepa-
rations and war in its results.

And what for? We don't want to fight anybody, and
nobody wants to fight us. We were never invaded in the
time of our weakness, and we are surely not likely to be in
these times of our might, and as for our Island Possessions,
there is very little danger of anybody stealing them over-
night.

Do you realize that every one of our foreign wars was
fought on our initiative, and that not one would be able to
justify itself to-day before a court of moral conscience, not
one? The war of 1812 with England was unnecessary and
fruitless; that of 1846 with Mexico was fruitful, but un-

just and unjustifiable, and that of 1898 with Spain was altruistic, but jingoish, unnecessary, and never would have broken out but that the explosion of the ill-fated " Maine " let loose the passions of our people, and tore the reins out of the hands of reason and justice.

War belongs to animalism, not to humanism ; to barbarism, not to civilization, most positively not to Christian civilization ; to the brutal reign of might, not to the gracious reign of right; to the night of the past, not to the day of the coming age. Washington said " My first wish is to see this plague of mankind banished from the earth. " Jefferson declared " I abhor war, and view it as the greatest scourge of mankind. " Grim old Sherman, who ought to know, said " The glory of war is all moonshine. war is hell, " and General Grant, our conquering glory-crowned soldier, uttered this conviction, " There never was a time when, in my opinion, some way could not have been found of preventing the drawing of the sword. "

Surely, surely, surely, disciples of Jesus Christ, followers of the Prince of Peace should show the world a more excellent way, and teach the nations to lay aside the crimes of war, and learn together the graces of brotherhood.

" In time of peace prepare for war " is a relic of paganism, and belongs to by-gone ages when every foreigner was an enemy and every stranger a foe. Wisdom and common sense should laugh such an adage to scorn in these enlightened days. In the time of peace prepare to perpetuate peace. But to be forever thinking of war and talking of war and writing of war and planning for war and preparing for war is a preposterous way of insuring peace. Nay, let us think of peace and talk of peace and write of peace and plan for peace and prepare for peace, then we shall have peace.

A hundred years ago we entered into agreement with one of the mightiest nations of earth, with a border line extend

ing four thousand miles along the entire length of our northern frontier, not to build a single fort on either side, nor
float a single warship on the great lakes, and for a century
these two countries, the United States of America and the
Dominion of Canada, with the whole of the British Empire
behind her, have lived in undisturbed peace, with an un-
protected frontier reaching clear across the widest stretch
of the continent. Do you think that this story of a century of bloodless and peaceful history could have been
written, if in times of peace the great Republic and the
mighty Empire had been preparing for war, if each had been
vying with the other to see who could raise the most formi-
dable fortifications, and build the most destructive floating
fortresses, and had looked at each other through the glistening bore of frowning guns threateningly pointed at each
other? No, not without a miracle that no one has a right
to expect from God, and any ground at all to hope for from
men. Here is a concrete example of complete disarm-
ament tested by the experience of a hundred years, and
what we have done with England in Canada, why may we
not do, in large measure, with England elsewhere, and with
other nations everywhere. The Church of the Prince of
Peace, speaking the language of love and justice, stands
forth in the Parliament of the Nations, and declares that
there is a better way to establish honorable and prosperous
peace than by killing and slaughtering our fellowmen, and
that there are better defences than armies and navies, battlements and battleships, for " Unto us a child is born . .
the government shall be upon his shoulder : and his name
shall be called . . . Prince of Peace. " " He shall
judge between nations, and they shall beat their swords into plowshares and their spears into pruning hooks ; nation
shall not lift up sword against nation, neither shall they
learn war any more. " REV. SAMUEL J. SKEVINGTON.

FOURTEENTH STEP IN RENDERING.
LYRIC.

Lyric Poetry is the poetry of self-expression: love, hatred, anger, grief, and other emotions are its distinctive subjects. Lyrics are both sacred and secular: Psalms and Hymns are sacred lyrics. Unity of this style requires that the poem be limited to the expression of a single emotion coloring the whole poem. The meter should be suggested by the subject.

An Ode is a lyric where exalted feeling is expressed. It is the " voice of poetry in frenzy. " Odes may also be either sacred or secular. One of the finest Odes is Wordsworth's " Imitations of Immortality. "

An Elegy is a lyric with melancholy feeling. Gray's Elegy; " In Memoriam, " Tennyson; " Thyrsis, " Matthew Arnold.

A Sonnet is a little song, (poet's ecstasy) is a lyric of fourteen lines. The Sonnet expresses a single sentiment.

All forms of Lyric Poetry are subjective, dealing with feelings rather than that which is objective or what appeals to the outer senses. As this style is subjective, the action of the whole being is concentric. In meditative selections the body folds up as to arms and limbs, the eye looks into the heights or the depths, in a " brown study. " An attitude of the body in harmony with the feeling intensifies and helps true expression.

In this step, even as in Forming Pictures, find the unity which will be one central feeling, often intense : aim to bring out this one feeling running throughout. For example : the twenty-third Psalm is a song of trust ; the eighth Psalm is a profound study and contemplation of nature compared with man, adoring wonder; " Nightfall " has for its center the " memory of other days. "

Ones personality and the fervor of feeling manifested in rendering the Lyric Style is of far greater importance than the incidents mentioned in the poems. Sonnets are also personal and are rendered as directed for Lyrics.

Many of our Hymns and Sacred Songs are Lyrics and should be so rendered as to bring out the feeling under the lines. As a rule hymns are rendered thoughtlessly, in a monotonous " ministerial tone," thus marring and ruining the beauty of the sweetest and most personal of all the songs of our language.

In rendering the following subjective studies, while the action is concentric and somewhat stilled, aim not to have it the stillness of death but the stillness of life, intensity. This stillness of life may be likened to a buzz saw in such rapid motion that it seems positive repose ; or to a spirited horse held in check ; or to a deep stream flowing silently. The shallow stream broken up into ripples makes noise.

To render the profound, sacred, personal feelings of the Lyric in a noisy declamatory style is closely akin to profanity. Here, as in no other style, there should be appreciation and intensity for it is " from an abundance of life comes sweetness. "

NIGHTFALL.

Alone I stand,
On either hand
In gathering gloom stretch sea and land;
Beneath my feet,
With ceaseless beat,
The waters murmur low and sweet.

Slow falls the night:
The tender light
Of stars grows brighter and more bright,
The lingering ray
Of dying day
Sinks deeper down and fades away.

Now fast, now slow,
The south winds blow,
And softly whisper, breathing low;
With gentle grace
They kiss my face,
Or fold me in their cool embrace.

Where one pale star,
O'er waters far,
Droops down to touch the harbor bar,
A faint light gleams,
A light that seems
To grow and grow till nature teems

With mellow haze;
And to my gaze
Comes proudly rising, with its rays
No longer dim,
The moon; its rim
In splendor gilds the billowy brim.

I watch it gain
The heavenly plain ;
Behind it trails a starry train—
While low and sweet
The wavelets beat
Their murmuring music at my feet.

Fair night of June !
Yon silver moon
Gleams pale and still.   The tender tune,
Faint–floating, plays,
In moonlit lays,
A melody of other days.

'Tis sacred ground ;
A peace profound
Comes o'er my soul.   I hear no sound,
Save at my feet
The ceaseless beat
Of waters murmuring low and sweet.

W. W. Ellsworth.

LONGING FOR HOME.

A song of a boat :—
There was once a boat on a billow :
Lightly she rocked to her port remote,
And the foam was white in her wake like snow,
And her frail mast bowed when the breeze would blow,
And bent like a wand of willow.

I shaded my eyes one day when a boat
Went curtseying over the billow,
I marked her course till a dancing mote

She faded out on the moonlit foam,
And I stayed behind in the dear loved home ;
   And my thoughts all day were about the boat
   And my dreams upon the pillow.

I pray you hear my song of a boat,
     For it is but short :—
My boat, you shall find none fairer afloat,
     In river or port.
Long I looked out for the lad she bore,
     On the open desolate sea,
And I think he sailed to the heavenly shore,
     For he came not back to me —
            Ah me !

     A song of a nest :—
   There was once a nest in a hollow:
Down in the mosses and knot-grass pressed,
  Soft and warm, and full to the brim —
  Vetches leaned over it purple and dim,
    With buttercup buds to follow.

I pray you hear my song of a nest,
     For it is not long :—
You shall never light, in a summer quest
     The bushes among —
Shall never light on a prouder sitter,
     A fairer nestful, nor ever know
A softer sound than their tender twitter,
     That wind-like did come and go.

  I had a nestful once of my own,
     Ah happy, happy I !
Right dearly I loved them : but when they were grown
     They spread out their wings to fly —

O, one after one they flew away
  Far up to the heavenly blue,
To the better country, the upper day,
  And — I wish I was going too.

I pray you, what is the nest to me,
  My empty nest?
And what is the shore where I stood to see
  My boat sail down to the west?
Can I call that home where I anchor yet,
  Though my good man has sailed?
Can I call that home where my nest was set,
  Now all its hope hath failed?
Nay, but the port where my sailor went,
  And the land where my nestlings be:
There is the home where my thoughts are sent,
  The only home for me—
        Ah me!

 " Songs of Seven. "   Jean Ingelow.

SONG OF THE MYSTIC.

I walk down the Valley of Silence—
  Down the dim, voiceless valley— alone!
And I hear not the fall of a footstep
  Around me, save God's and my own ;
And the hush of my heart is as holy
  As hovers where angels have flown !

Long ago was I weary of voices
  Whose music my heart could not win;
Long ago was I weary of noises
  That fretted my soul with their din ;

Long ago was I weary of places
    Where I met but the human— and sin.

I walked in the world with the worldly;
    I craved what the world never gave;
And I said: " In the world each Ideal,
    That shines like a star on life's wave,
Is wrecked on the shores of the Real,
    And sleeps like a dream in a grave. "

And still did I pine for the Perfect,
    And still found the False with the True;
I sought 'mid the Human for Heaven,
    But caught a mere glimpse of its Blue;
And I wept when the clouds of the Mortal
    Veiled even that glimpse from my view.

And I toiled on, heart-tired of the Human;
    And I moaned 'mid the mazes of men;
Till I knelt, long ago, at an altar
    And I heard a voice call me—since then
I walk down the Valley of Silence
    That lies far beyond mortal ken.

Do you ask what I found in the Valley?
    'Tis my Trysting Place with the Divine
And I fell at the feet of the Holy,
    And above me a voice said: " Be mine. "
And there arose from the depths of my spirit
    An echo— " My heart shall be thine. "

Do you ask how I live in the Valley?
    I weep—and I dream—and I pray.
But my tears are as sweet as the dewdrops
    That fall on the roses in May;
And my prayer like a perfume from Censers,
    Ascendeth to God night and day.

In the hush of the Valley of Silence
  I dream all the songs that I sing;
And the music floats down the dim Valley,
  Till each finds a word for a wing,
That to hearts, like the Dove of the Deluge,
  A message of Peace they may bring.

But far on the deep there are billows
  That never shall break on the beach;
And I have heard songs in the Silence,
  That never shall float into speech;
And I have had dreams in the Valley,
  Too lofty for language to reach.

And I have seen thoughts in the Valley—
  Ah! me, how my spirit was stirred!
And they wear holy veils on their faces,
  Their footsteps can scarcely be heard,
They pass through the Valley like Virgins,
  Too pure for the touch of a word!

Do you ask me the place of the Valley,
  Ye hearts that are harrowed by Care?
It lieth afar between mountains,
  And God and His angels are there;
And one is the dark mount of Sorrow,
  And one the bright mountain of Prayer!

                        Father Ryan.

O may I join the Choir Invisible
Of those immortal dead who live again
In minds made better by their presence. . . .
Feed pure love, beget the smiles that have no cruelty,
Be the sweet presence of a good diffused. . . .
So shall I join the Choir Invisible
Whose music is the gladness of the world.— *Eliot.*

THE CHAMBERED NAUTILUS.

This is the ship of pearl, which, poets feign,
    Sails the unshadowed main,—
    The venturous bark that flings
On the sweet summer wind its purpled wings
In gulfs enchanted, where the siren sings,
    And coral reefs lie bare,
Where the cold sea-maids rise to sun their streaming
      hair.

Its web of living gauze no more unfurl:
    Wrecked is the ship of pearl!
    And every chambered cell,
Where its dim dreaming life was wont to dwell,
As the frail tenant shaped his growing shell,
    Before thee lies revealed—
Its irised ceiling rent, its sunless crypt unsealed!

Year after year beheld the silent toil
    That spread his lustrous coil;
    Still, as the spiral grew,
He left the past year's dwelling for the new,
Stole with soft step its shining archway through,
    Built up its idle door,
Stretched in his last-found home, and knew the old
      no more.

Thanks for the heavenly message brought by thee,
    Child of the wandering sea,
    Cast from her lap, forlorn!
From thy dead lips a clearer note is born
Than ever Triton blew from wreathed horn!
    While on mine ear it rings,
Through the deep caves of thought I hear a voice
      that sings:

" *Build thee more stately mansions, O my soul,*
　As the swift seasons roll !
　Leave thy low-vaulted past !
Let each new temple, nobler than the last,
Shut thee from heaven, with a dome more vast,
　Till thou at length art free,
Leaving thine outgrown shell by life's unresting
　　sea ! "

O. W. HOLMES.

A CRY FROM THE WILDERNESS.

O God, thou art my God; early will I seek thee: my
soul thirsteth for thee, my flesh longeth for thee in a dry
and thirsty land, where no water is; to see thy power and
thy glory, so as I have seen thee in the sanctuary. Because
thy lovingkindness is better than life, my lips shall praise
thee. Thus will I bless thee while I live: I will lift up my
hands in thy name. My soul shall be satisfied as with
marrow and fatness; and my mouth shall praise thee with
joyful lips: when I remember thee upon my bed, and meditate on thee in the night watches. Because thou hast been
my help, therefore in the shadow of thy wings will I
rejoice. My soul followeth hard after thee: thy right
hand upholdeth me. But those that seek my soul, to destroy it, shall go into the lower parts of the earth. They
shall fall by the sword: they shall be a portion for foxes.
But the king shall rejoice in God; every one that sweareth
by him shall glory: but the mouth of them that speak lies
shall be stopped.

PSALMS LXIII.

THE LOST CHORD.

Seated one day at the organ,
   I was weary and ill at ease,
And my fingers wandered idly
   Over the noisy keys.

I know not what I was playing,
   Or what I was dreaming then ;
But, I struck one chord of music,
   Like the sound of a great Amen.

It flooded the crimson twilight,
   Like the close of an Angel's Psalm,
And it lay on my fevered spirit
   With a touch of infinite calm.

It quieted pain and sorrow,
   Like love overcoming strife ;
It seemed the harmonious echo
   From our discordant life.

It linked all perplexed meanings
   Into one of perfect peace,
And trembled away into silence
   As though it were loath to cease.

I have sought, but I seek it vainly
   That one lost chord divine
That came from the soul of the organ
   And entered into mine.

It may be that Death's bright angel
   Will speak in that chord again :
It may be that only in Heaven
   I shall hear that grand Amen.

                   ADELAIDE A. PROCTER.

And slowly answered Arthur from the barge:
" The old order changeth, yielding place to new,
And God fulfils himself in many ways,
Lest one good custom should corrupt the world.
Comfort thyself : what comfort is in me ?
1 have lived my life, and that which I have done
May He within himself make pure! but thou,
If thou shouldst never see my face again,
Pray for my soul.   More things are wrought by prayer
Than this world dreams of.   Wherefore, let thy voice
Rise like a fountain for me night and day.
For what are men better than sheep or goats
That nourish a blind life within the brain,
If, knowing God, they lift not hands of prayer
Both for themselves and those who call them friend ?
For so the whole round earth is every way
Bound by gold chains about the feet of God.
But now farewell.   I am going a long way
With these thou seest— if indeed I go—
(For all my mind is clouded with a doubt)
To the island-valley of Avilion ;
Where falls not hail, or rain, or any snow,
Nor ever wind blows loudly ; but it lies
Deep-meadow'd, happy, fair with orchard-lawns
And bowery hollows crown'd with summer sea,
Where I will heal me of my grievous wound. "
So said he, and the barge with oar and sail
Moved from the brink like some full-breasted swan
That, fluting a wild carol ere her death,
Ruffles her pure cold plume, and takes the flood
With swarthy webs.   Long stood Sir Bedivere
Revolving many memories, till the hull
Look'd one black dot against the verge of dawn,
And on the mere the wailing died away.

" MORTE D'ARTHUR. "   TENNYSON.

THE DAY IS DONE.

The day is done, and the darkness
  Falls from the wings of Night,
As a feather is wafted downward
  From an eagle in his flight.

I see the lights of the village
  Gleam through the rain and the mist,
And a feeling of sadness comes o'er me
  That my soul cannot resist:

A feeling of sadness and longing,
  That is not akin to pain,
And resembles sorrow only
  As the mist resembles the rain.

Come, read to me some poem,
  Some simple and heartfelt lay,
That shall soothe this restless feeling,
  And banish the thoughts of day.

Not from the grand old masters,
  Not from the bards sublime,
Whose distant footsteps echo
  Through the corridors of Time.

For, like strains of martial music,
  Their mighty thoughts suggest
Life's endless toil and endeavor;
  And to-night I long for rest.

Read from some humbler poet,
  Whose songs gushed from his heart,
As showers from the clouds of summer,
  Or tears from the eyelids start;

Who, through long days of labor,
  And nights devoid of ease,

Still heard in his soul the music
  Of wonderful melodies.

Such songs have power to quiet
  The restless pulse of care,
And come like the benediction
  That follows after prayer.

Then read from the treasured volume
  The poem of thy choice,
And lend to the rhyme of the poet
  The beauty of thy voice.

And the night shall be filled with music
  And the cares, that infest the day,
Shall fold their tents, like the Arabs,
  And as silently steal away.

LONGFELLOW.

ALLAH.

Allah gives light in darkness,
  Allah gives rest in pain,
Cheeks that are white with weeping
  Allah paints red again.

The flowers and the blossoms wither,
  Years vanish with flying fleet;
But my heart will live on forever,
  That here in sadness beat.

Gladly to Allah's dwelling
  Yonder would I take flight;
There will the darkness vanish.
  There will my eyes have sight.

LONGFELLOW.

SONG OF LOVE AND DEATH.

Sweet is true love tho' given in vain, in vain ;
And sweet is death who puts an end to pain :
I know not which is sweeter, no, not I.

Love, art thou sweet ? then bitter death must be :
Love, thou art bitter ; sweet is death to me.
O Love, if death be sweeter, let me die.

Sweet love, that seems not made to fade away,
Sweet death, that seems to make us loveless clay,
I know not which is sweeter, no, not I.

I fain would follow love, if that could be ;
I needs must follow death, who calls for me ;
Call and I follow, I follow ! let me die.

" ELAINE. " TENNYSON.

CROSSING THE BAR.

Sunset and evening star
 And one clear call for me !
And may there be no moaning of the bar
 When I put out to sea.

But such a tide as moving seems asleep,
 Too full for sound and foam
When that which drew from out the boundless deep
 Turns again home.

Twilight and evening bell
 And after that the dark ;
And may there be no sadness of farewell
 When I embark ;

For though from out our bourne of time and place
 The flood may bear me far,
I hope to see my Pilot face to face
 When I have crost the bar. TENNYSON.

ABIDE WITH ME.

Abide with me!   Fast falls the eventide,
The darkness deepens—Lord, with me abide!
When other helpers fail, and comforts flee,
Help of the helpless, oh, abide with me!

Swift to its close ebbs out life's little day;
Earth's joys grow dim, its glories pass away;
Change and decay in all around I see;
O Thou, who changest not, abide with me!

I need Thy presence every passing hour,
What but Thy grace can foil the tempter's power?
Who, like Thyself, my guide and stay can be?
Through cloud and sunshine, oh, abide with me!

Not a brief glance I long, a passing word;
But as Thou dwell'st with Thy disciples, Lord,
Familiar, condescending, patient, free,
Come, not to sojourn, but abide with me!

Hold Thou Thy cross before my closing eyes;
Shine through the gloom, and point me to the skies;
Heaven's morning breaks, and earth's vain shadows
        flee!
In life, in death, O Lord, abide with me!

LYTE.

LEAD KINDLY LIGHT.

Lead, kindly light! amid th' encircling gloom,
        Lead Thou me on;
The night is dark, and 1 am far from home,
        Lead Thou me on;
Keep Thou my feet; I do not ask to see
The distant scene; one step enough for me.

I was not ever thus, nor prayed that Thou
    Shouldst lead me on;
I loved to choose and see my path; but now
    Lead Thou me on;
I loved the garish day, and spite of fears,
  Pride ruled my will.   Remember not past years.

So long Thy power has blest me, sure it still
    Will lead me on
O'er moor and fen, o'er crag and torrent till
    The night is gone:
And with the morn those angel-faces smile
Which I have loved long since, and lost awhile.
CARDINAL NEWMAN.

STILL, STILL WITH THEE.

Still, still with Thee—when purple morning breaketh,
  When the bird waketh, and the shadows flee;
Fairer than morning, lovelier than the daylight.
  Dawns the sweet consciousness, I am with Thee!

Alone with Thee—amid the mystic shadows,
  The solemn hush of nature newly born;
Alone with Thee in breathless adoration
  In the calm dew and freshness of the morn.

When sinks the soul subdued by toil, to slumber,
  Its closing eye looks up to Thee in prayer;
Sweet the repose beneath thy wings o'ershading
  But sweeter still to wake and find Thee there.

So shall it be at last in that bright morning.
  When the soul waketh, and life's shadows flee,
Oh, in that hour, fairer than daylight dawning,
  Shall rise the glorious thought—I am with Thee.
HARRIET BEECHER STOWE.

FIFTEENTH STEP IN RENDERING.
SOLILOQUY.

Soliloquy comes from " solus " alone, and " loqui"
to speak. It therefore means " to speak alone."
Soliloquy is a talking to one's self or with one's self.
It is a discourse uttered in solitude.

In this style, the real innermost self is revealed.
Here is the greatest freedom possible of mental action
and expression. The person talks with self as if self
were another person, asks question and answers them.
Long pauses are made for deliberation. Freedom of
movement,—standing, sitting, walking with the hands
behind the back etc., with unlimited expression of
whatever feeling is dominant, is allowed.

HAMLET'S SOLILOQUY.

To be, or not to be,— that is the question :—
Whether 'tis nobler in the mind to suffer
The slings and arrows of outrageous fortune,
Or to take arms against a sea of troubles,
And by opposing end them.— To die;— to sleep;—
No more;— and, by a sleep, to say we end
The heart-ache, and the thousand natural shocks
That flesh is heir to,— 't is a consummation
Devoutly to be wished.

　　　　To die ;— to sleep ;—
To sleep ! perchance to dream ;— Ay, there's the rub ;

For in that sleep of death what dreams may come,
When we have shuffled off this mortal coil,
Must give us pause.   There's the respect
That makes calamity of so long life:
For who would bear the whips and scorns of time,
The oppressor's wrong, the proud man's contumely,
The pangs of despised love, the law's delay,
The insolence of office, and the spurns
That patient merit of the unworthy takes,
When he himself might his quietus make
With a bare bodkin?

                 Who would fardels bear,
To grunt and sweat under a weary life;
But that the dread of something after death,——
The undiscovered country from whose bourn
No traveler returns,—puzzles the will,
And makes us rather bear those ills we have,
Than fly to others that we know not of?
Thus conscience does make cowards of us all;
And thus the native hue of resolution
Is sicklied o'er with the pale cast of thought;
And enterprises of great pith and moment,
With this regard, their currents turn awry,
And lose the name of action.

" HAMLET. "   SHAKESPEARE.

KING OF DENMARK. REMORSE.

O, my offence is rank, it smells to heaven;
It hath the primal eldest curse upon 't,
A brother's murder. Pray can I not,
Though inclination be as sharp as will:
My stronger guilt defeats my strong intent;
And, like a man to double business bound,

I stand in pause where I shall first begin,
And both neglect.   What if this cursed hand
Were thicker than itself with brother's blood,
Is there not rain enough in the sweet heavens
To wash it white as snow? Whereto serves mercy
But to confront the visage of offence?
And what's in prayer but this twofold force,
To be forestalled ere we come to fall,
Or pardon'd being down?   Then I'll look up;
My fault is past.   But, O, what form of prayer
Can serve my turn? ' Forgive me my foul murder? '
That cannot be ; since I am still possess'd
Of those effects for which I did the murder,—
My crown, mine own ambition, and my queen.
May one be pardon'd and retain the offence ?
In the corrupted currents of this world
Offence's gilded hand may shove by justice,
And oft 'tis seen the wicked prize itself
Buys out the law : but 'tis not so above;
There is no shuffling, there the action lies
In his true nature; and we ourselves compell'd,
Even to the teeth and forehead of our faults,
To give in evidence.   What then?   What rests?
Try what repentance can : what can it not ?
Yet what can it when one cannot repent?
   O wretched state ! O bosom black as death !
O limed soul, that, struggling to be free,
Art more engaged ! Help, angels ! Make assay.
Bow, stubborn knees ; and, heart with strings of
       steel,
Be soft as sinews of the new-born babe!
All may be well.

" HAMLET. "   SHAKESPEARE.

WHAT MY LOVER SAID.

By the merest chance, in the twilight gloom,
   In the orchard path he met me;
In the tall wet grass, with its faint perfume,
And I tried to pass but he made no room—
   Oh, I tried, but he would not let me.
So I stood and blushed till the grass grew red,
   With my face bent down above it;
While he took my hand as he whispering said—
How the clover lifted each pink, sweet head
To listen to all that my lover said;
   Oh, the clover in bloom—how I love it!

In the high wet grass went the path to hide;
   And the low wet leaves hung over;
But I could not pass on either side,
For I found myself when I vainly tried
   In the arms of my steadfast lover.
And he held me there and he raised my head,
   While closed the path before me:
And he looked down into my eyes and said—
How the leaves bent down from the boughs overhead
To listen to all that my lover said—
   Oh, the leaves hanging lightly o'er me!

Had he moved aside but a little way
   I could surely then have passed him;
And he knew I never could wish to stay,
And would not have heard what he had to say
   Could I only aside have cast him.
It was almost dark, and the moments sped,
   And the searching night wind found us,
But he drew me nearer and softly said—
How the pure sweet wind grew still instead

To listen to all that my lover said;
   Oh, the whispering wind around us!

I am sure he knew when he held me fast,
   That I must be all unwilling,
For I tried to go, and I would have passed,
As the night was come with its dew, at last,
   And the sky with its stars was filling.
But he clasped me close when I would have fled,
   And he made me hear his story,
And his soul came out from his lips and said—
How the stars crept out when the white moon led,
To listen to all that my lover said,
   Oh, the moon and the stars in glory!

I know that the grass and the leaves will not tell;
   And I'm sure that the wind, precious rover,
Will carry my secret so safely and well
   That no being shall ever discover
One word of the many that rapidly fell
   From the eager lips of my lover;
   And the moon and the stars that looked over
Shall never reveal what a fairy–like spell
They wove round about us that night in the dell,
   In the path through the dew–laden clover;
Nor echo the whispers that made my heart swell,
   As they fell from the lips of my lover.

HOMER GREENE.

ALONE.

I miss you, my darling, my darling,
   The embers burn low on the hearth;
And still is the stir of the household,
   And hushed is the voice of its mirth;

The rain plashes fast on the terrace,
The winds past the lattices moan;
The midnight chimes out from the minster,
    And I am alone.

I want you, my darling, my darling;
  I am tired with care and with fret;
I would nestle in silence beside you,
  And all but your presence forget,
In the hush of the happiness given,
To those who through trusting have grown
To the fullness of love in contentment,
    But I am alone.

I call you, my darling, my darling;
  My voice echoes back on my heart;
I stretch my arms to you in longing,
  And lo! they fall empty, apart.
I whisper the sweet words you taught me,
The words that we only have known,
Till the blank of the dumb air is bitter,
    For I am alone.

I need you, my darling, my darling;
  With its yearning my very heart aches;
The load that divides us weighs harder;
  I shrink from the jar that it makes.
Old sorrows rise up to beset me;
Old doubts make my spirit their own.
Oh, come through the darkness and save me,
    For I am alone.

ROBERT J. BURDETTE.

SIXTEENTH STEP IN RENDERING.

MONOLOGUE.

Monologue is a Dramatic composition for a single performer. A Monologue is a play where only one character appears. The speech and action may imply or suggest other actors.

The speech and action should be governed by the principles of Dramatic Art. The Monologue may be given with scenery and costume, or without : the speaker may suggest both ; he may use descriptive language.

QUEEN VASHTI'S LAMENT.

Is this all the love that he bore me, my husband, to publish
      my face
To the nobles of Media and Persia, whose hearts are be-
      sotted and base?
Did he think me a slave, me, Vashti, the Beautiful, me,
      Queen of queens,
To summon me thus for a show to the midst of his baccha-
      nal scenes?

I stand like an image of brass, I, Vashti, in the sight of
      such men !
No, sooner, a thousand times sooner, the mouth of the
      lioness' den.
Did he love me, or is he, too, though the King, but a
      brute like the rest !
But ever before, ... toward me he showed honor
      and grace ;

He was King, I was Queen, and those nobles, he made them
        remember their place,
But now all is changed ; I am vile, they are honored, they
        push me aside,
A butt for Memucan and Shethar and Meres, gone mad in
        their pride !

Shall I faint, shall I pine, shall I sicken and die for the loss
        of his love?
Not I ; I am queen of myself, though the stars fall from
        heaven above.
The stars ! ha ! the torment is there, for my light is put out
        by a star,
That has dazzled the eyes of the King and his court and
        his captains of war.

He was lonely, they say, and he looked like a ghost, as he
        sat at his wine,
On the couch, where, of yore, by his side, his Beautiful
        used to recline ;
But the King is a slave to his pride; to his oath and the laws
        of the Medes,
And he cannot call Vashti again, though his poor heart is
        wounded and bleeds.

So they sought through the land for a wife, while the King
        thought of me all the while——
I can see him, this moment, with eyes that are lost for the
        loss of a smile,
Gazing dreamily on while each maiden is temptingly
        passed in review,
While the love in his heart is awake with the thought of a
        face that he knew !
Then she came, when his heart was grown weary with loving
        the dream of the past !

She is fair— I could curse her for that, if I thought that
    this passion would last !
But, e'en if it last, all the love is for me, and, through good
    and through ill,
The King will remember his Vashti, will think of his Beau-
    tiful still.

What is it?   Oft as I lie awake and my pillow is wet with
    tears
There comes— it came to me just now— a flash, then dis-
    appears ;
A flash of thought that makes this life a re-enacted scene,
That makes me dream what was will be, and what is now,
    has been.

And I, when age on age has rolled, shall sit on the royal
    throne,
And the King shall love his Vashti, his Beautiful, his own,
And for the joy of what has been and what again will be,
I'll try to bear this awful weight of lonely misery !
The star ! Queen Esther ! blazing light that burns into my
    soul !
The star ! the star ! Oh ! flickering light of life beyond
    control !
O King ! remember Vashti, thy Beautiful, thy own,
Who loved thee and will love thee still, when Esther's light
    has flown !

JOHN READE.

A TALE.

What a pretty tale you told me
    Once upon a time—
Said you found it somewhere (scold me!)
    Was it prose or was it rhyme,

Greek, or Latin?   Greek, you said,
While your shoulder propped my head.

Anyhow there's no forgetting
    This much if no more,
That a poet (pray, no petting !)
    Yes, a bard, sir, famed of yore,
Went where such like used to go,
Singing for a prize, you know.

Well, he had to sing, nor merely
    Sing but play the lyre ;
Playing was important clearly
Quite as singing ; I desire,
Sir, you keep the fact in mind
For a purpose that's behind.

There stood he, while deep attention
    Held the judges round,
—Judges able, I should mention,
    To detect the slightest sound
Sung or played amiss : such ears
Had old judges, it appears !

None the less he sang out boldly,
    Played in time and tune,
Till the judges, weighing coldly
    Each note's worth, seemed, late or soon,
Sure to smile " In vain one tries
Picking faults out : take the prize   "

When, a mischief ! Were they seven
    Strings the lyre possessed ?
Oh, and afterwards eleven ,
    Thank you !   Well, sir,— who had guessed
Such ill luck in store ? — it happed
One of those same seven strings snapped.

All was lost, then! No! a cricket
　(What " cicada? " Pooh!)
—Some mad thing that left its thicket
　For mere love of music—flew
With its little heart on fire,
Lighted on the crippled lyre.

So that when (Ah joy!) our singer
　For his truant string
Feels with disconcerted finger,
　What does cricket else but fling
Fiery heart forth, sound the note
Wanted by the throbbing throat?

Ay, and ever to the ending,
　Cricket chirps at need,
Executes the hand's intending,
　Promptly, perfectly,—indeed
Saves the singer from defeat
With her chirrup low and sweet.

Till, at ending, all the judges
　Cry with one assent
" Take the prize—a prize who grudges
　Such a voice and instrument?
Why. we took your lyre for harp,
So it shrilled us forth F sharp! "

Did the conquerer spurn the creature,
　Once its service done?
That's no such uncommon feature
　In the case when Music's son
Finds his Lotte's power too spent
For aiding soul-development.

No! This other, on returning
　Homeward, prize in hand,

Satisfied his bosom's yearning;
 (Sir, I hope you understand !)
—Said " Some record there must be
Of this cricket's help to me ! "

So, he made himself a statue :
 Marble stood, life-size ;
On the lyre, he pointed at you,
 Perched his partner in the prize ;
Never more apart you found
Her, he throned, from him, she crowned.

That's the tale : its application ?
 Somebody I know
Hopes one day for reputation
 Through his poetry that's—Oh,
All so learned and so wise,
And deserving of a prize !

If he gains one, will some ticket,
 When his statue's built,
Tell the gazer " 'Twas a cricket
 Helped my crippled lyre, whose lilt
Sweet and low, when strength usurped
Softness' place i' the scale, she chirped ?

 For as victory was nighest,
  While I sang and played,—
With my lyre at lowest, highest,
  Right alike,—one string that made
' Love ' sound soft was snapt in twain,
Never to be heard again,—

Had not a kind cricket fluttered,
 Perched upon the place
Vacant left, and duly uttered
 ' Love, Love, Love, ' whene'er the bass

Asked the treble to atone
For its somewhat sombre drone. "

But you don't know music!   Wherefore
   Keep on casting pearls
To a—poet ?   All I care for
   Is—to tell him that a girl's
" Love " comes aptly in when gruff
Grows his singing.   There, enough !
ROBERT BROWNING.

THE WAGES OF SIN.

Say, old pard, you see that dwellin' in that yonder clump
     of trees
Tumblin' down and lookin' awkward like a sinner on his
     knees?
See them vines a hangin' faithful to the house and cistern
     shed
Like the soul that keeps a clingin' to the hopes it knows is
     dead ?
Well, I'm not a cryin' baby, whinin' round and sheddin'
     tears,
For I've lived on disappointment now for more than thirty
     years.
I have lived a life as wicked as the devil's oldest son,
And I've spent no time repentin' for the deviltry I've done.
And I'm known in all these diggins as the toughest of the
     crew,
And I don't talk tender hearted to a livin' soul but you.
Them that's never felt a wound, pard, is the ones that laughs
     at scars,
And the man that's got his freedom sneers at them behind
     the bars.

Oh, it sets my heart a throbbin' when I look on that old
        place,
Where my hopes was crushed and trampled by a devil!
        See that face !
See him, pard ! He's in the doorway ! See that mad glare
        in his eye !
See him scowl and stare around him ! Hear him swear that
        she shall die !
See, he's got a bloody dagger !— He has killed her !—
        She is dead !
O, my God, may heaven's curses rain upon his murderous
        head !
Pard, don't catch an' hold me that way—· I'm not mad !
        He's often there
In that dark deserted doorway scowlin' on me with a stare
That would drive me mad forever, if I didn't chance to
        know
That the devil got his spirit more than thirty years ago.

Yes, I'm all right now—— The story ?- Certainly. Its
        thirty years
Since I looked on that old dwellin' without fightin' back
        my tears.
If an angel ventured from the pearly gates above
An' deluged an earthly household with a flood of light and
        love
That's the house that entertained her ; that's the home her
        presence blessed.
And (for I was pure and young then) I was her most
        welcome guest.
Love her ? Pard, a mortal bosom never harbored love like
        mine
For a mortal—she was mortal— but to me she was divine.
All my thoughts an' all my bein', all my hopes to her was
        wed—

But I changed from man to devil when I found my hopes
    was dead.
It was this way, pard, she loved me as I loved her an'
    in me
Hoped to find a soul-companion for all time that was to be.

You have read of man's creation—of the garden full of
    flowers—
How he lived in such contentment there among its walks
    and bowers;
But the sweetest flowers were withered, crushed and blighted,
    one and all
When the poison of the serpent left his trail upon them all.
She an' I was in our Eden all alone, when there arose
One whose heart and mind was fashioned somethin' like
    mine, I suppose,
For he loved her, pard, and wooed her with an eloquence
    and skill
That if she had been more fickle, might have changed her
    girlish will,
But she flew to me for refuge and declined to hear him
    more,
Though he offered her position, jewels, wealth and gold
    galore.

Pard, I've noticed love ain't always hangin' round where
    diamonds shine,
Love don't always look for jewels— Love ain't mortal—
    it's divine.
Oh, he loved her with a madness worthy of a better man,
And he wooed her with a fervor that to desperation ran.
Pard, the blackest, maddest monster that the bounds of hell
    has crossed,
Is a proud and jealous lover, when he finds his suit is lost.

Yes, 'twas in that very doorway one still evenin' when the
    moon
Just had kissed the bright horizon— " Good bye, I will be
    back soon. " ——
And its first bright rays was fallin' on her fairy form and
    face,
And my sweetheart stood there splendid in her ever match-
    less grace,
When he fondly looked upon her, caught her lily hand and
    said ;
" Kate, if that man ever claims you, it will be when you
    are dead ! "
Then she raised her raven lashes just in time to see him
    start
Brandishin' a gleamin' dagger— and he stabbed her to
    the heart !
Stabbed my darlin' ! Yes, he stabbed her ! Stabbed her
    with his wicked blade,
And her heart blood leaped and sputtered through the cru-
    el wound he made.
Pard, they say some imperfection in our guidin' star of
    Fate,
While it fetches what we long for, often brings it up too
    late ;
But for me I'm always waitin'— surely that was never said
For a man who waits forever on a hope he knows is dead.

When I saw 'em lay my darlin' in the cold and clammy
    ground
I knew my heart was buried underneath that cruel mound ;
I was wild with grief and anger and I kneeled above her
    breast,
And I gave eternal freedom to the devil I possessed——
Swore by all the holy angels by her spirit and her God,

That the devil who had killed her should not live upon the
  sod

Of the earth that now possessed her, and that I would never
  rest

Till this hand that I had pledged her, sunk a dagger in his
  breast !

Pard, I killed him ! This same dagger cut him and his
  soul apart !

Seven times this keen blade quivered joyously in his false
  heart !

Oh, I danced in wildest triumph as he writhed upon the
  ground

And his hateful blood came pourin' from each madly gapin'
  wound !

There I left him, cold and lifeless with his eyes and mouth
  aghast

And I knowed he had his wages for his services at last !

He was dead, I know he was, pard, for I saw him stiff and
  cold,

And I know that he was gathered safe into the devil's fold.

But somehow, his corpse or spirit, something like he was
  in life

Seems to go wherever I go, brandishin' that bloody knife !

And I guess he'll pay me up, pard, when at last I'm gathered in,

For the Book says Death's the wages that the devil pays
  for sin.

BOOTH LOWREY.

SUBJECTIVE POEMS.

IT IS NOT TOO LATE.

" And is it too late?
No, for time is a fiction and limits no fate.
Thought alone is eternal.   Time thralls it in vain
For the thought that springs upward and yearns to re-
gain
The pure source of spirit, there is no too late.
                                        Owen Meredith.

The day will come when the faithful hand
  Shall grasp its reward long sought;
The day will come when the heart's demand
  In some way shall be wrought.
The day will come when the soul that yearns
  And throbs with a sad unrest
Shall find release and shall rest in peace—
  The guest of a tranquil breast.

The day will come when the cheerless ray
  That pales at the careworn heart
Shall shine forth bright as the glad noonday
  And darkness and clouds depart.
The day will come when the soul that *waits*
  And *braves* as the seasons roll
Shall bask in the sunshine pure and sweet
  Of its heaven appointed goal.

Oh, the days are dark when the soul is sad
  The flowers bloom and fade
The sickening rays of the sun seem chill
  As a damp and darkening shade.

But I hear a voice on the evening breeze
  That comes from the far–off home.
And bids me wait for the hand of fate
  And whispers, " *The day will come.* "

BOOTH LOWREY.

YOU CAME.

The days went by with monotonous tread,
Each like the day that was spent and dead;
And my heart beat on to a dull sad rhyme,
Like muffled bells that had lost their chime.

Until one day, like a sunbeam bright,
You came, and chased away my night:
And I forgot that life was sad
And all the world grew young and glad.

A laugh came rippling down the years;
A rainbow gleamed through all my tears;
And the notes of a sweet and tender strain
Were borne to me on the wings of Pain.

The truth you brought, I needed so:
The heart's choice flowers from sorrows grow.
May you be blessed through life, the same
As you blessed my life, the day you came.

ELIZABETH PURSER.

SOUL SYMPATHY.

In my waking, in my sleeping
  Shadows come upon me creeping
Till these eyes grow dim with weeping,
  See the light of life no more.

For my spirit's mute appealing
  There's a calmness o'er me stealing,
And a light from Heaven revealing
  Truths that I have known before.

Am I waking?   Am I dreaming?
  Is it real?   Is it seeming?
Heaven's light upon me streaming,
  Still the shadows round me roll!
Then 'tis true that I must borrow
  Some dear fellow-mortal's sorrow
Thro' the night, but soon the morrow
  Will awake that other soul.

Will awake her to new beauty,
  Will arouse her to her duty
And bestow on her the booty
  Of the conquerer,— by and by.
Then this soul in rapture singing,
  Will awake glad echoes ringing
In mine, while we soar on clinging
  To a hope that cannot die.

HARRIET MABRY.

SUNLIGHT AND SHADOW.

The hardest thing you had to do
Thro' all these passing years,
And yet the noblest thing you did
Was to smile thro' all your tears.

Tho' darkest night–clouds 'round you hung,
Your soul was rack'd by fears,
By far the bravest thing you did
Was to smile through all your tears.

Thro' deepest grief alone you went,
The world had clos'd its ears,
God knows the grandest thing you did,
Was to smile thro' all your tears.

BERTRAND E. RIGGS.

YOUTH MEMORIES.

I remember oft and sadly,
  The days of my young years,
When in my wild and roving thoughts
  I knew no earthly fears ;
When blithely gay I ran to meet
  Each face I could then see ;
And loving, trusting, to each one,
  So thought each one to me.

I remember, oh, how often,
  The scenes of my merry home,
When but a little laughing lad,
  In all my boyish bloom,
When I with brother, sister, both
  So joyous passed the day,
And scarce a thought of trouble came,
  But all was blithe and gay.

I remember sister's kindness,
  Sister Emma's loving smile,
As in our little mischief sports
  We laughed away the while.
Her ringing laugh, her sparkling eye,
  Her sisterly embrace,
These from my fitful memory
  No cares can e'er efface.

I remember, but too sadly,
　At last when I was grown,
And out upon the wide, wide world
　I wandered forth alone;
I saw the tear steal from her eye,
　With grief her bosom swell,
The trembling hand she gave to me,
　The kiss, the last farewell.

Time has placed us far apart,
　And many scenes have passed.
But oft I think of sister's kiss,
　The gentlest and the last.
That dearest sister, ever kind,
　I nevermore may see;
Yet in my dreamy fitful thoughts
　She ever smiles on me.

And now amid my worldly cares,
　I fondly think of home,
Content and innocent as I lived there,
　And ne'er had thought to roam.
'Tis true, the time once haply was
　When all was love and Heaven,
I'd fellowshipped no wilful wrong,
　To nought of sin was given.

But now I'm older, and perhaps
　Wiser, yet wisely wild.
But still I'm farther off from Heaven,
　Than when I was a child.
Then I ne'er saw my destiny,
　In the flood light of our age,
By the vigils of my past life,
　Writ out on Nature's page.

Older, wiser, though am I,
　More learned in deeds of wrong,
I often long for ignorance
　The same I had when young.
Youth learned through age is wisest far
　Of all the worldly wise.
But age yet leaves its leprous mark,
　Youth's innocence defies.

Heaven, I trust, will bear me up
　Through all my wayward ways
For sake of hopes I entertain
　Of youth in coming days,
As slowly now I plod along.
　The *past* lights up my way,
The *present* bids me early grasp
　The *future* better day.

　　　　　ALBA HONYWELL.

Me wherever my life is lived.　O to be self-balanced
for contingencies!

O to confront night, storms, hunger, ridicule, accidents,
rebuffs, as the trees and animals do!

O the orator's joys! To inflate the chest—to roll the thunder of the voice out from the ribs and throat.　To make the
people rage, weep, hate, desire, with yourself.　To lead
America—to quell America with a great tongue.

O the joy of a manly selfhood! To walk with erect carriage, a step springy and elastic!　To look with calm gaze or
with flashing eye! To speak with a full and sonorous voice
out of a broad chest! To confront with your personality all
the other personalities of the earth!　O to have my life
henceforth my poem of joys!　　　WALT WHITMAN.

ADDITIONAL STUDIES IN RENDERING.

ANIMATION.

The Chariot Race. *Wallace.* Fenno's Favorites, No. 6.
Darius Green and His Flying Machine. *J. T. Trowbridge.*
A Song of Victory. *Exodus XV.*
Doom of Claudius and Cynthia. *Thompson.* Fav. No. 1.
Mary's Night Ride. *George W. Cable.* Fav. No. 7.

CONVERSATIONAL.

Mrs. Caudle. *Douglas Jerrold.*
The Land of Shining Gold. *George R. Simms.* Fav. No. 7.
The Kingdom of Heaven. *Matthew XIII.*
Aunty Doleful's Visit. *M. K. Dallas.* Fenno's Elocution.
Laughing in Meeting. *H. B. Stowe.* Fenno's Elocution.

NARRATIVE STYLE.

The Tea-Kettle and the Cricket. *Dickens.* Fav. No. 9.
The Fiddling Parson. *Davy Crocket.* Fav. No. 10.
Battle of Quebec. *Bancroft.*
A Day at Niagara. *Mark Twain.* Fenno's Elocution.

DESCRIPTIVE STYLE.

Storming the Ice Palace. *W. H. H. Murray.* Fav. No. 2.
Sunrise on the Mississippi. *Mark Twain.* Fav. No. 1.
Winter in Louisville. *Frank H. Fenno.* Fav. No. 2.
The Garden. *Pope.*
" Peace, Be Still. " Fav. No. 2.

FORMING PICTURES.

One Niche the Highest. *Elihu Burrett.* Fav. No. 7.
Elsie's Child. *Julia C. Dorr.* Fav. No. 1.
Shamus O'Brien. *Samuel Lover.* Fenno's Elocution.
" God Knows. " *Benjamin F. Taylor.* Fav. No 5

VITAL, ANIMATED PICTURES.

Burning of Chicago. *Carleton.* Fenno's Elocution.
Pharaoh's Army Crossing the Red Sea. *Exodus XIV.*
Sennacherib's Army. *Lord Byron.*
An Arctic Aurora. Fav. No. 2.

IDEAL PICTURES.

The Culprit Fay. *J. Rodman Drake.* Fav. No. 2.
Ballad of Babie Bell. *Thomas Bailey Aldrich.*
The Rainbow. Fenno's Elocution.
Robert of Lincoln. *William Cullen Bryant.*

SLIDES OF THE VOICE.

The Pen and the Tongue. *H. W. Beecher.* Fav. No. 9.
Benefits of Wisdom. *Proverbs IV.*
The Hour of Prayer. *Victor Hugo.*
Shylock to Antonio. *Shakespeare.*

VITAL SLIDE.

The Great Bell Roland. *Tilton.* Fenno's Elocution.
The Fate of Virginia. *Macaulay.*
Forging the Anchor. *Samuel Ferguson.* Fav. No. 10.

SLIDE IN VOLUME.

The Bells. *Edgar Allan Poe.* Fenno's Elocution.
The Vineyard of the Lord. *Isaiah V, IX, X : 4.*
The Happy Warrior. Wordsworth.
O Captain! My Captain. *Walt Whitman.*

PAUSE.

All in Each. *Ralph Waldo Emerson.* Fav. No. 9.
The Hymn on the Nativity. *Milton.*
Aux Italiens. *Owen Meredith.* Fav. No. 10.

RELATION OF VALUES.

Virtues vs. Vices. *Proverbs.*
Whiskey—its Poetry and Prose. Fav No. 5.
The Character of Charles I. *Macaulay.*

VOLUME OF VOICE

Paul Before Agrippa. *Acts XXVI.*
The Black Horse and His Rider. *Sheppard.* Fav. No. 3.
Heroes of the Land of Penn. *George Lippard.* Fav. No. 2.
The Unknown Speaker. Fav. No. 5.
A Camp Meeting in Texas. *John B. Gough.* Fav. No. 9.
God's First Temples. *William Cullen Bryant.* Fav. No. 5.

LYRIC.

Sunrise. *Sidney Lanier.*
Gradatim. *J. G. Holland.*
Love Song and Reply. Prometheus Unbound. *Shelley.*
Lamentation. *Jean Ingelow.*
Regret. *Jean Ingelow.*
The Tides. *Longfellow.*
'Tis the Last Rose of Summer. *Moore.*

SOLILOQUY.

Anthony over the Body of Cæsar. *Shakespeare.*
A Dagger of the Mind. Macbeth. *Shakespeare.* P. 233.
The Cardinal's Soliloquy. *E. Bulwer Lytton.*
Job Curses the Day of his Birth. *Job. III.*

MONOLOGUE.

A Man After Her Own Heart. *Edwin Drew.* Fav. No. 5.
The Hat. *Coquelin.* Fav. No. 6.
My Last Duchess. *Robert Browning.*
A Forgiveness. *Robert Browning.*

FENNO'S
SCIENCE OF SPEECH

A Condensed and comprehensive treatise on the culture of Body,
Mind and Voice, to be used in connection
with

THE ART OF RENDERING

Comprising

Chart of Elocution, Laws of Voice and Action, Articulation, Charts
and Illustrations. Designed to be used as a text-book
in the class-room, and for private study as well as
by readers and speakers generally

By FRANK H. FENNO, A.M., F.S.Sc.

Teacher, Lecturer, and Author of "Fenno's Elocution," "Lectures
on Elocution," etc. Compiler of "Fenno's Favorites"

Revised and Enlarged by

MRS. FRANK H. FENNO, B. O.

THE MENTAL METHOD.
I. Theory. III. Scientific.
II. Practice. IV. Artistic.

In The Science of Speech, the result of the author's careful in-
vestigations during many years, the unchangeable Laws of Voice
and Action are developed step by step, formulated and taught. In
this Natural Scientific Method of Voice Culture, Gesture, Enunciation,
and Modulation, the principle is, "Not imitation, but strict con-
formity to the Laws of Speech, and these laws the only basis of
criticism."

Twelvemo, Cloth, 167 pages; Price, $1.25.

FENNO'S ELOCUTION

— OR —

How To Read and Speak

A COMPREHENSIVE AND SYSTEMATIC SERIES OF EXERCISES
FOR

Gesture, Calisthenics, and Cultivation of the Voice

A COLLECTION OF 150 LITERARY GEMS FOR READING AND
SPEAKING.

By FRANK H. FENNO, A.M., F.S.Sc.

IN FOUR PARTS:

I. Theoretical. III. Helps to Study.

II. Vocal Culture. IV. Readings and Recitals.

A WORK thoroughly adapted to the wants of both the student and the amateur reader. It covers every essential point in Articulation, Modulation and Gesture. The chapter on "Vocal Culture" carefully outlines, with exercises, an important feature to proper cultivation and development. "Helps to Study" show clearly the importance of care and accuracy, and assure a degree of perfection, to all who thoroughly master them, well worth striving for. The "Readings and Recitals" have been selected with the greatest care, and throughout show the work of an accomplished elocutionist.

12mo, Cloth, Extra, 414 pages; Price, $1.25.

FENNO'S FAVORITES

— FOR —

Reading and Speaking

— COMPILED BY —

FRANK H. FENNO, A.M., F.S.Sc.

TEN NUMBERS NOW READY.

Nos. 1, 2, 3, 5, 6, 7, 9 and 10

Contain 100 Choice Selections for Reading and Speaking.

Nos. 4 and 8

Contain 50 Choice Dialogues for Speaking and Acting, WITH DEF-INITE PARTICULARS AS TO COSTUMES, SCENES, ENTREES, ETC.

These selections have been edited with much care by Prof. Fenno, who is thoroughly acquainted with the various tastes and capacities of readers of all ages, and with the field of literature best suited to this purpose. The need of variety and general usefulness has been kept steadily in view. The pieces are all of a high character. A judicious variety of prose and poetry, of humor, pathos and tragedy. Those best adapted for elocutionary purposes have been chosen in each case. Many pieces are original, and appear for the first time in these volumes.

Each number is prefaced with a practical essay on some branch of elocution. The books are uniform in appearance. The type is large and clear, the paper good, and the size handy.

The merit of these books is proven by the favor with which they have been received. More than 200,000 copies have already been sold.

Substantially bound, 12mo, Paper 30 cts. each.

Each Number Complete in Itself.

FENNO'S FAVORITES, NO. 1.—PRINCIPLES OF GESTURE.

The Reaper's Dream.
Our Magna Charta.
The Ride of Death.
A Wood Carver's Romance.
William Brown of Oregon.
Interviewing Mrs. Young.
On the Concord Road
The Slave's Dream
Jimmy Brown's Steam-Chair.
Unknown.
Fatherless Joe.
Scene at Niagara Falls.
"Don't Feel too Big."
Columbia Crumb
The Leap of Roushan Beg.
Greatest Walk on Record.
Beasie's Christmas Dream.
The World We Live in.
Our Welcome.
The Well-Digger
The Blind Preacher.
Larrie O'Dee.
Found Dead.
The Jiners.
The Mount of the Holy Cross.
A Pathetic Old Man.
The Fireman's Prayer.
Life.
Lookout Mountain.
The Emancipation of Man.
Samson.
Waste Not, Want Not
The Old Sergeant.

Wapshot's Woes.
The Palace o' the King.
In the Mining Town.
Yacob Wegenheiserangenfeldte Setting a Hen.
The Jackdaw of Rheims.
The Maiden's Prayer.
Boabyschell's Confession.
Erin's Flag.
Trouble in the Choir.
Brother Watkins.
After the Sale.
Asking the Guv'nor.
Father Roach.
Baggage Master Brick's Lunch-Can.
The Lightning-Rod Dispenser.
An Original Love Story.
The Doom of Claudius and Cynthia.
Elsie's Child.
Kentucky Philosophy
A Thanksgiving Dinner.
The Honest Deacon.
The Two Mills.
Glad Tidings.
The Fate of Sergeant Thin.
The Two Ideals.
Night on Shiloh.
The German Family on the Cars.
Glideroy.
The Child's Dream
Mind Shildren.
Cheerfulness.
Building the Years.
Rhymes for House-Cleaning Times.

The Engine.
S'posin'.
Jane Conquest.
The Lady or the Tiger.
Love on Skates.
A Baptist on Presbyter ans.
God's Beverage.
Hannah Jane.
The Palmetto and the Pine.
A Railway Matinée.
The Law of Death.
The Easter Altar-Cloth.
The Ballad of Hiram Hover.
On the Other Train.
The Old Fair Story.
The Ship on Fire.
My Madcap Darling.
The Tides are Rising.
The Minstrel's Curse.
Patient Mercy Jones
Sunrise on the Mississippi.
Try the Fun.
Searching for the Slain.
The Briefless Barrister.
Jet
A Negro's Account of the Prodigal Son.
Durandarte and Balerme.
The Dead Colonel in the Blue.
Paying Toll.
Annals of the Poor.
The Photograph Album.
The Martyrs of Sandomir
Uncle Moses and the Comet.
Building and Being.

FENNO'S FAVORITES, NO. 2.—HOW TO IMPERSONATE.

The Curriculum of Life.
A Visit to Jack Frost's Palace.
A Rhyme of the Navy.
She Wanted to Learn Elocution.
The Destruction of Pompeii.
Suffering and Hope
The Stern Parent.
A New Declaration.
The Golden Axe.
A Boy's Lecture on 'Knives.'
Stonewall Jackson's Death.
Was it Job that had Warts on Him.
On the Stairway.
Roland and Diana.
The Irish Schoolmaster.
A Picture of the Past.
Piano-Music.
Relation of the Mosquito to the Human Family.
"That's but Nat'ral"
Curfew Bells.
When the Clock Strikes XXI.
The Arctic Martyrs
The Lion's Ride.
Smelling by Telephone.
The Ten Virgins.
How Jake Found Him.
Hiawatha Johnson's Wooing.
How Uncle Henry Dyed His Hair.
Wendell Phillips.
"The Roll Bengol Tagger,"
The Pilgrim's Vision.
A Solemn Warning.

The Humble Servant Girl.
Our Ain Countrie.
The Pewee and the Wild Rose.
Mr. Grimshaw's Mistake.
The Recognition.
An Arctic Aurora.
A Welsh Classic.
Negro Worship in the South.
For a Warning.
Woman vs. Heroism.
Willie Wee's Grace.
Drinking a Tear.
Fat and Lean.
Winter in Louisville.
The Sioux Chief's Daughter.
The Sad-Eyed Stranger.
How we Tried to Whip the Teacher.
"Peace, be Still!"
Sunday Fishin'.
The Damsel of Peru.
The New Era.
The Insulted Pig.
The Great Commander.
The Circle of Death.
The After-Dinner Orator
The Storming of the Ice-Palace.
A Ballad of Capri.
Cho-che-Bang and Chi-chii-Boo.
A Musical Contest
Fridolin.
The Story of Don Vejes
Bachelor Brown.
The Christmas Prayer.
Uncle Skinflint's Christmas Gift.

The Culprit Fay.
Nancy.
The Story of Ingomar.
"One of the Little Ones"
The Old Reading Class
Off Barnegat.
The Going of Arthur.
The Tapestry Weavers.
Aunt Jemima's Courtship.
Heroes of the Land of Penn.
Dot Maid Mit Hazel Hair.
An Italian Legend.
Night Brings out the Stars.
The "Shiner" and the Waifs.
The Bobbin Ran Out.
The Bugle.
Entering In.
Diffidence.
Brother Gardner on Wickedness.
A Smart Boy.
Mansie Wanch's First and Last Play.
The Hermit of the Cave.
The First Sabbath.
New Year's Chimes
Little Elfie's Plea.
Our Choir.
A New Year Address.
The M-Man wich didn't drink W-W-W-Water.
The Baby is Dead.
The Unfinished Song.
The Maniac's Love
Man, His Proverbial Ill-Luck and Continual Foolishness.
Bettina Mazzi.
"Over the Range."

FENNO'S FAVORITES, NO. 3.—CULTURE OF THE VOICE.

A Hero of 1780.
God in the Sunrise.
Before the Wedding.
Neddie's Thanksgiving Visit.
Purpose in Life.
A Little Child.
The Tender Heart.
Big Ben Bolton.
The First Predicted Eclipse
Sixteen and Sixty.
The Ballad of Beffana.
Clerk Muggins.
A Life's Hymn.
In the Catacombs.
Went Out That Way.
Come Under My Plaidie.
The Prettiest Girl.
A Sly Old Rat.
Handsome Girl in a Crowded Car.
Death.
Old Amazin' Grace
The Cranes of Ibycus.
The Pretty Roller Skater
Reflections on the Needle.
The Hot Axle.
The Fountain of Youth.
Uncle Ned's Defence.
Arkansas Justice.
The Way it is Said
'Der Dog und der Lobster"
The Black Horse and His Rider.
The Last Hymn.
Fame.
Curly-Head

The Irish Picket.
How It Struck Jim.
Gaffer Gray.
Ethiopiomania.
Unto Death.
An Evening Idyl.
The Removal.
Bill Nye's Mine.
The Seventh Plague of Egypt.
When the Cows Come Home.
Love at the Seaside.
The Church Spider.
"Dem Codicils."
The Ancient Miner's Story.
An Irish School
A Fight with the Flood.
True Courage
A Single Hair.
By the Shore of the River.
How Kate Shelly Crossed the Bridge
Difficult Love-Making.
The Alpine Flower.
Keturah's Christmas.
Six Times an Orphan.
Five.
The Surveyor and the School Ma'am.
Miss M'Lindy's Courtship.
The Wandering Jew.
The Valentine.
A Donation Party.
The Supper of St. Gregory.
Minding the Hens.
Our Baby.

The School at Talladega.
The Friars' Christmas.
The Two Roads.
The Gladiator
Pat and the Frogs.
What a Woman Can Do.
The Neglected Pattern
Leadville Jim.
Parson Jinglejaw and the Sewing Circle
A Tussle with Immigrants.
An Eastern Story.
The Goat and the Swing.
Major Jones's Courtship.
The Lovers.
The Mountain Snow-Wraith.
Bossing a Bar'l in April.
The Golden Gate.
The Victim
What Drove Me into a Lunatic Asylum.
Dave Brigga.
Lasca.
Sam's Letter.
George Washington.
Spectacles.
The Quarrel.
The Arithmetic Lesson.
Brave Alta Wayne.
The Ship of Faith
The Boy and the Frog.
The Tragedy.
The First Day.
The Spinning-Wheel Song.
"Angels Bright and Fair."

FENNO'S FAVORITES, NO. 5.—READING—READING IN PUBLIC.

A Drop of Ink.
The Engineer's Story.
A Boy Again.
"Nearer to Thee."
The Victor of Marengo
Since Mickey Got Kilt in the War.
The Dark River.
The Drummer-Boy of Kent.
Sun Dust.
A Lesson to Lovers.
The Joys of Millionaires.
Elizabeth Zane.
Blood-Money.
Her Evidence.
The Puzzled Priest.
The Farmer's Club.
Courageous Johnny.
"Cut, Cut Pehind."
The Coliseum.
The Monk's Magnificat.
Mullins the Agnostic
The Flood and the Ark.
German Opera.
Italian Opera.
The Clown's Romance.
Death of Garfield.
The Glacier Bed
The Ballad of Cassandra Brown.
I'll be at Home Thanksgivin'.
God's First Temples
The Man and the Foxes.
Pompeii.
The Spinning-Wheel Song.
The Old Continentals
Sufferings of the Pilgrims.

A Rude Awakening.
"God Knows."
Geoffrey and Beatrice.
Scientific Jones.
My First Ax.
A Small Boy's Composition on Cats.
A Ballad of the North.
"Inasmuch"
Heard them Counted.
The Origin of Scandal.
Mrs. Noodle's Conundrum.
Looking Out for Number One.
No Kiss.
Mrs. Piper.
The Challenge.
The Veterans.
The Two Gates.
The Bell of Zanora.
A Man After Her Own Heart.
Shadows on the Curtain.
The Christening.
I Want! I Want!
The Unknown Speaker.
The Joshua of 1776
"I'll Report to God the Reason Why."
Josiah Allen at Saratoga.
Sunset Prophecy
The Deacon's Courtship
Whiskey—Its Poetry and Prose.
The Nine Suitors.
In Answer.
Penn's Monument
The Dutchman and the Raven.

Composition on the Ant-Eater.
Jim's Little Pra'r.
"Them Flurdy Hens"
The Loom of Life.
An Essay on Butter-Making.
An Idyl.
Miss Witchazel and Mr. Thistlepod.
Michael's Mallet.
The Man Who Would Not Sleep With His Brother.
Ginevra.
The King and the Child.
Giving Mrs. Scudder the Small-Pox
"Yes, I'm Guilty."
The Elf-Child.
Sambo's Dilemma.
The Pilot's Story.
For the Chief's Daughter.
Burdock's Music Box.
Rebel, or Loyalist.
A Little Peach.
Love Flying in at the Window.
The Whistler.
A Spool of Thread.
The Bell of Liberty.
Because
A Culprit.
Taking an Elevator.
The Boy's Complaint.
He Never Told a Lie.
"Ask Mamma"
Let Down the Bars.
The Catholic Psalm

FENNO'S FAVORITES, NO. 6.—SCHOOLROOM ELOCUTION—A FEW WORDS TO TEACHERS.

The Hat.
Miss Splicer Tries the Toboggan
Billy's Rose
David and Goliath.
My Guest.
Der Oak und Der Vine.
The Bride of Reichenstein.
A Sleigh-Ride.
The Aesthetic Cat-Tail.
The Lock of Hair.
Joe Ford the Fireman
The Chariot Race.
The Tartar who Caught a Tartar.
Tommy's Composition on Women.
Lincoln's Last Dream.
Rome Wasn't Built in a Day.
Waking the Dead.
Eve.
The Evils of War.
How Cyrus Laid the Cable.
Petah.
Sir William Napier and Little Joan.
Disadvantages of Moral Courage.
A Church Scene.
A Permanent Boarder.
Farmer Jonathan's Decision.
Tim
Dream of Pilate's Wife.
Aunt Nabby.
The Drunkard's Dream.
The Earth.
The Light on Deadman's Bar.

Pat and the Deacon.
James A. Garfield.
A Love Song.
Some Old Friends
The Modern Ravens.
Why Old Jasper Was Not Sent to the Penitentiary.
Kit Carson's Wife
The Chimes of Amsterdam
A Voice from the Poor-House.
Behind Time.
The Comet.
Paudeen O'Rafferty's Say-Voyage.
In School-Days.
"Please to Say Amen"
Mark Twain as a Farmer.
On the Frontier.
Murder Will Out.
Darby and Joan.
The Bible and Liberty.
The King's Daughters.
An Inquiring Friend.
A Christmas Ballad
The Cripple Boy's Story.
The Story of a Stowaway.
Josiah and the Mermaid.
The Rum Evil.
The Freckled Faced Girl
Eighteen and Eighty.
Our Craft is Small.
An Aesthetic Housekeeper.
Hatem Tol.
MacDonald's Charge at Wagram.
Petit Jean
A Rogue
The Moneyless Man

The Bashful Man's Story.
Has Charity Begun.
An August Idyl
The Round of Life
The Doctrine of Chance.
Ticket O'Leave.
Art Matters in Indiana.
Virginny.
Harry's Christmas
Rome and Carthage.
A Scene at Jericho.
Washington.
Grandpa and Bess.
Partnership.
One Glass too Much.
Burdette in Toledo.
"Remember the Sabbath Day."
Shacob's Lament.
In Liquor.
Jerusalem by Moonlight.
The Battle Above the Clouds.
The Irishman's Panorama.
Review of the Grand Army.
The Worm of the Still.
How Terry Saved His Bacon.
Caedmon.
Death-Bed of Benedict Arnold.
The Adventures of Miltiadae Peterkin Paul.
A Tarrytown Romance.
The Flying Dutchman
The Swell.
Flash—The Fireman's Story.
Fritz and His Betsy Fall Out.

FENNO'S FAVORITES, NO. 7.—THE MISSION OF SPEECH

Marcel.
The Swan Song.
The Sword of Gram
The Cow and the Bishop.
Indifference.
The Squire's Bargain
The Thanksgiving in Boston Harbor
As the Pigeon Flies
The Minuet.
Grandma's Angel.
Tommy Brown.
The Ladder of St Augustine.
The Old Actor's Story.
The Fading Leaf.
"Limpy Tim."
A Sleepy Little School
Andre and Hale
Echo and the Ferry
The Finding of the Cross.
A Second Trial.
One Niche the Highest.
The Good Reciter.
Baby in Church.
Aunt Jemina on the Woman Question.
An Incident of the War.
The Ride of Grandmother Lee
"No Saloons Up There."
The Battle of Bunker Hill.
Proof Positive.
Ancient and Modern Oratory.
Little Christel.
The Idiot Lad
A Battery in Hot Action.
One of the Heroes

Jimmy Brown's Sister's Wedding.
The Spanish Mother.
Address to Bartholdi's Statue.
The Scholar in Politics.
The Lady Judith's Vision.
The Old Woman's Railway Signal.
Count Zinzendorf.
The Book Agent Beats the Bandit.
In the Signal Box
Jean Valjean, the Convict.
Money Musk.
The King and the Cottage.
The Value of Punctuality
The Two Villages
Mary's Night Ride.
Perplexity.
A Yachtman's Speech.
The Sailing of King Olaf
Bill, the Engineer.
"Kiss Me, Mamma."
Zarah.
The Army of the Potomac.
A New Year's Deed.
Cavern Scene from "She"
A Girl Heroine.
"Wash Dolly up Like That."
What's an Anthem?
A Born Orator.
There is No Death.
The Land of Shining Gold.
A Tale of Long Ago.
A Public School Idyl.
The New South.
The Tear of Repentance.

How It Struck Jim.
Nellie's Victory.
The Telegram
Katrina's Visit to New York.
Mary Garvin.
Sir Rupert's Wife.
Lead the Way.
Something Great.
Farmer Stebbins at Ocean Grove.
Toussaint L'Overture.
The Preacher's Vacation.
We've Always Been Provided For.
Aunt Polly's "George Washington."
Lady Wentworth
A Lesson of Thankfulness
The McSwats Swear Off.
The Time to Hate.
The Substitute.
A Weak of Practice.
The Flag's Birthday.
A Russian Courtship.
La Fayette.
Garfield's Ride.
The Two Brothers.
The Ruling Passion.
The Drummer Boy of Mission Ridge.
The Pencil Tree.
The Fancy-Work Maiden.
The Lady Rohesia.
Gettysburg.
A Boy's Essay on Columbus.
Echo Dell.

FENNO'S FAVORITES, NO. 9.—A WORD TO PARENTS.

With Books
Elam Chase's Fiddle.
Napoleon.
The Little Western Man
He Danced at her Wedding.
The Story of the Cable.
The White Cross of Savoy.
The Daffodils.
Joe Bird, the Impostor.
When Grandpa was a Little Boy.
The Demon of the Fire.
A New Year's Address.
The Prayer-Gage.
Bach'ler Bill's Thanksgivin'.
The Violin's Voice.
Alec Yeaton's Son.
Her Excuse.
The Policeman's Story.
Dark-Eyed Mehetabel.
A Notable Tilt
"Let Your Women Keep Silence in the Churches"
What She Said and What She Did.
Extract from "Michael Strogoff"
A Dream of the Sea.
Indirection.
The Photograph Habit
"I wish I was a Grown-up."
Thanksgivin' Pumpkin Pies
A Child's Power.
The Sailor Boy's Dream.
Young America in Pinafore.
The Transition Woman, Or, Sailing by the Stars, Not by the Wake.

A Gettysburg Sketch.
Classical Music.
Rivermouth Rocks
A Thank-Ye-Ma'am.
The Cheerful Locksmith.
Unfinished Music.
The Bootblack.
No Room for Mother.
The Liberty Bell.
There's a Beautiful Land by the Spoiler Untrod.
Mrs. Blake's Visit to the White Mountains
In the Autumn Weather.
Herve Riel.
Take Your Hands out of Your Pockets.
The Little Martyr of Smyrna.
The Wail of an Anachronistic Survival.
Intemperance.
On the Shores of Tennessee.
The Gauger and the Sibyl.
Heroes.
Wakin' the Young 'Uns.
A Woman's Sentiment
The Engineer's Last Run.
The Agnostic by his Brother's Bier.
Selling the Baby.
Reuben James.
The Tea-Kettle and the Cricket.
Chimneys.
When this Old Flag was New.
The Bartholdi Statue.
Which Side Are You On?
Mother's Doughnuts.
Glimpses into Cloudland.

The Legend of the Two Kings.
Nott Shott.
All's Punishment.
Aunt Tabitha
The Pen and the Tongue
"There will be Briars where Berries Grow"
The Dream of Greatness.
Old Kitchen Reveries.
A Laughing Chorus
Women—A Girl's Essay.
Johnny's Pocket.
They Had no Poet and so They Died.
The Blind Sea.
In a Hundred Years.
A Lesson to Lovers.
Commerce.
The Soldier's Reprieve.
He Could Argyfy.
The Battle of Naseby
Grandma at the Masquerade.
Destruction of Pompeii.
Only a Tramp.
Bill Mason's Bride.
The Legend of Adiernfel.
Baby's Autograph
The Song of Monterey.
That Awful Ghost
All in Each.
A Ballad of Brave Women.
The Kitten of the Regiment.
The Old Clock on the Stair.
A Camp Meeting in Texas
Unseen Yet Seen.
Midsummer
The Pedagogue's Wooing.

FENNO'S FAVORITES, NO. 10.—ELOCUTION IN THE PULPIT.

The Debating Society.
A Dream of Song.
Two Passengers.
Dan Periton's Ride.
The Kaiser-Blume.
Making Hopkins' Last Moments Easy
La Petite Coquette.
The Kitchen Clock.
Dicky's Christmas.
Haunted Castles.
Flattering Grandma.
The End of All.
A Legend of Hesse.
Examined for a Registered Letter.
The Forging of the Anchor.
Lessons.
Saved by a Song.
The Dark Bridal.
Beggar Jim.
Tims.
Better Things.
Impediment Joe.
The Perpetuity of Nature.
The Bell of Atri.
The City Choir.
Home, Sweet Home.
The Old Minstrel.
The Rivulet.
Words.
The Meekest Man
The Women of Mumbles Head
The Devil's Wife.
Old Daddy Turner.
The Ballad of Breakneck
The Little Middle Daughter.

The Light from over the Range.
Embarkation of the Pilgrims
The Lost Chime.
"Dat ar Bill."
Aux Italiens.
Enchantment.
Only a Newsboy.
My First Love.
The Outcast's Return.
Beethoven's Moonlight Sonata.
The Lifeboat.
Engaged.
A Summer Lesson.
The Festal Day has Come.
The Love-Knot.
The Minister's Daughter.
Greatness of the Universe.
"Come Unto Me"
Which was the Richer?
The Volunteer Organist.
Like Mother Used to Make.
The Fiddling Parson.
The Engineer's Story.
Proof vs. Argument.
The Gray Champion.
Hide and Seek.
The Flag on Fort Sumter.
The Queen's Jewels
At the Loom.
The Month of Apple Blossoms.
What the Echo Said.
Arloa.
A Child's Dream of a Star.

In the Cross of Christ I Glory.
Disappointing.
Manhood.
Light on the Hill-Tops.
The Punkin Frost.
The New Pastor.
Back From the War.
St Nicholas.
Lost and Found.
Went into Hieroglyphics.
Eternal Justice.
The Dying Shoemaker.
A Day of Our Country
Trouble in the "Amen Corner."
Indignant Nellie.
All Hands Lie Down.
Monument Mountain.
To Seneca Lake
The World's First Wedding.
The Gleam in the House of Azab.
Only in Dreams
The Fate of European Kings.
A Turkish Tale
The Evergreen Mountains of Life.
Expression
The Trooper.
John Chinaman's Protest.
The Miseries of War
Song of Marion's Men.
Sockery Kadahcut's Kat.
Sword and Plough.
A Reminiscence of Andrew Jackson.